ALSO BY DAVID M. ROBERTSON

Denmark Vesey:
The Buried History of America's Largest Slave
Rebellion and the Man Who Led It

Booth

Sly and Able: A Political Biography of James F. Byrnes

A PASSIONATE PILGRIM

A PASSIONATE PILGRIM

A Biography of Bishop James A. Pike

David M. Robertson

ALFRED A. KNOPF

NEW YORK

2004

THIS IS A BORZOI BOOK
PUBLISHED BY ALFRED A. KNOPF

Copyright © 2004 by David M. Robertson

All rights reserved under International and Pan-American
Copyright Conventions. Published in the United States by
Alfred A. Knopf, a division of Random House, Inc., New York,
and simultaneously in Canada by Random House of Canada
Limited, Toronto. Distributed by Random House, Inc., New York.

www.aaknopf.com

Knopf, Borzoi Books, and the colophon are registered trademarks
of Random House, Inc.

Library of Congress Cataloging-in-Publication Data
Robertson, David, [date]
A passionate pilgrim : a biography of Bishop James A. Pike / David Robertson.
p.   cm.
ISBN 0-375-41187-9
1. Pike, James A. (James Albert), 1913–1969.   2. Episcopal Church—
Bishops—Biography.   I. Title.

BX5995.P54R63   2004
283'.092—dc22   2003065902
[B]

Manufactured in the United States of America
First Edition

For Brian and Jeannie

Jesus I know, and Paul I know, but who are you?

—query of a demon, ACTS 19:15

Contents

Acknowledgments

Writing a biography, as Harold Nicolson warned, "is the preoccupation and the solace, not of certainty, but of doubt." Perhaps trebly so, as not only must the writer keep faith that another person's life—even one so various and self-contradictory as James Pike's—can be apprehended in words, but also the publisher and the author's agent must hold faith against doubts that the author can, eventually, do the job. I wish to thank my wise editor at Knopf, Ash Green, and my fine literary agent, John Ware, for their faith that I can write well and profitably about others' lives.

Two disparate but equally literate and witty groups of people, those in the restaurant and bar trade in Cincinnati and those among the staff at that city's public library, also have encouraged and aided me. I wish particularly to thank Dan Aren, Andy Balterman, Jack Barrett, Georgeanne Bradford, Scott Brown, Steve Glazier, Christy Lerner, Luba Ostashevsky, and Bruce Sherwood for favors received. Archivists, fellow writers and journalists, and other professionals all have shared with me their memories or knowledge about Pike. They include Elizabeth Daniels, retired Vassar professor; Carolyn Davis of Syracuse University; Wayne Kempton, archivist of the Episcopal Diocese of New York; Michael Lampen, archivist of the Episcopal Diocese of California; Louise Loveall of the *Jerusalem Post*; Lucinda McDermont Piro, author of the play *Shatter the Vessel*; and Jocelyn Wilk of Columbia University.

Any errors of fact in this biography are to be assumed the responsibility of the author. Any divergence of opinion within this book from the accepted knowledge about Bishop Pike or his theologies is made in the spirit of William James, who believed that we inhabit a *multiverse* of truths, an assertion that certainly delighted Bishop Pike during his lifetime.

Cincinnati, Ohio
2003

A PASSIONATE PILGRIM

Introduction:
Journey into the Wilderness

[*ascending a mountain*]
BRAND: This is my destined road.
PEASANT: Ay, and who said so?
BRAND: God
    said so; the God I serve.
PEASANT: Man-of-God, you've got nerve.
    But just heed what I say!
    Though you're bishop or dean,
    Or some such holy man,
    you'll be dead before day.

       —HENRIK IBSEN, *Brand*,
       translated by Geoffrey Hill

The dry riverbed called Wadi Mashash by the Arabs belongs to an unforgiving landscape. Tracing roughly southeastward and constantly downward for about twenty miles through the Judean foothills, this boulder-strewn passage seems to offer a natural route to any traveler walking from the desert highlands to the lower Jordan Valley. But the clay path of the wadi is littered with shards of white limestone and sharp flint, making it difficult and painful for the traveler to keep a certain footing. Once entered, the wadi can prove dangerous to anyone trying to climb out of it. The sheer walls of either side of the old riverbed can rise hundreds of feet. Additionally, as it descends the mountains the wadi branches out into rocky, narrow labyrinths of innumerable dead ends, or into passages that may suddenly bring the traveler over unforeseen, and fatal, cliffs.

It is not advisable to venture into the Wadi Mashash on foot in any circumstances, if one has a choice. Daytime temperatures can soar as high as 130 degrees Fahrenheit even in early autumn, and the only shade available comes from overhanging rocks. These small areas of relief must also be shared with the traditional inhabitants of the desert, the scorpion and the serpent. The only other frequently seen signs of animal life are the small and intensely energetic clouds of black flies, immediately drawn to the sweat or the urine of the traveler. How these black flies subsist within the wadi when there are no human travelers is a mystery.

Many nations and religions have claimed sovereignty over the area around the Wadi Mashash, but few people have chosen to live there. An exception were the Essenes, Jews who established their religious community at Qumran near the Dead Sea more than two thousand years ago. All that is left of those people now is their empty stone buildings, their silent cemeteries, and their holy scrolls that were hidden away in caves. It was also into this wilderness that Jesus of Nazareth was said to have retreated alone, to pray and fast. It was here that Jesus was recorded for the only time throughout his ministry as meeting face-to-face with the Adversary, or Satan, who tempted the Nazarene to change stones into bread or demonstrate his miraculous powers by falling unharmed from a high elevation. Why this particular desert was chosen by Jesus as the place for his temptations and solitary prayers is not explained by the existing scriptures.

On the afternoon of September 7, 1969, members of the Israeli border police descended cautiously down the ravines of the Wadi Mashash. Each of them carried a loaded firearm at the ready. This wasteland west of the Dead Sea had been uneasily occupied by Israel since conquest over Jordan in the Six-Day War of 1967; although the stated mission of the police patrol on this afternoon was not to initiate any combat, the official policy of the Israeli military and civil authorities was for its members to display their weapons at all times when venturing into the occupied territory.

Their presence here had been required since a morning five days earlier, when a young American woman had staggered out of the wadi, limping in pain from a badly twisted ankle, her body severely dehydrated from exposure, covered with cuts and insect bites. She told an astonished group of passing Arab workmen that she had been walking in this medical condition for ten hours with no water or food. She begged them for help, to return with her to her husband, whom she had left resting in the desert. The Arabs were merciful, but, sensing trouble, carried the blond woman to Nahal Kallia and then departed.

There the Israeli authorities learned that she was Diane Kennedy Pike, and that her missing husband was the Episcopal bishop James A. Pike. His name was immediately recognizable to many even within the non-Christian quarters of Jerusalem. Bishop Pike was at that time perhaps the most infamous, as well as famous, Protestant religious figure in many of the world's capitals. The subject of a widely publicized heresy investigation by his fellow bishops, Pike had been both praised and damned throughout the decade by believers in such disparate capitals as Washington, Salisbury, and Rome.

The worldly reputation of James Pike, a former New Dealer who voluntarily had given up his law practice for a career in the Episcopal Church, was the result, in equal parts, of his social activism, his public embrace of psychic séances, his cheerful friendliness to nonbelievers, and his own sure instincts for self-publicity. All these qualities were expressed in his often quoted wit. "I didn't stop being a lawyer," Bishop Pike would joke to journalists, both before and after he was accused of Christian heresy, "I just changed clients."

To his friends, James Pike put observers in mind of a Renaissance Christian humanist, suddenly transported to the twentieth century. But after three marriages, public struggles with alcoholism and other addictions, and his open questioning of some basic Christian tenets, his religious enemies had to reach further back into history to find the maledictions they thought appropriate to Pike: heresiarch, apostate, sophist.

After the apparent resolution of the heresy charges against Pike in the United States, his wife explained, the couple had taken a celebratory trip to Israel to visit the Essene archaeological sites at Qumran. She and her husband had rented a Ford and driven into the desert. The two had not thought it necessary to be accompanied by a local guide, to obtain a topographic map, or to carry any liquids, other than two bottles of Coca-Cola. The Israeli authorities were sympathetic but horrified at the couple's apparent naïveté about the desert.

The Pikes had become lost, she said, and without any detailed map, had inadvertently driven onto the rocky bed of the wadi, where the car became stuck. Bishop Pike, who had a history of health ailments and at age fifty-six was more than two decades older than his wife, had been unable to keep pace with her as the two of them attempted to walk out of the desert. He had insisted that Diane Pike go on alone, and send back help and water to him as soon as she found her way out of the wilderness. Pike would follow her trail as best as he was able. That had been one day ago, she told the Israelis.

Now, nearly a week into scouring miles inside the wadi, on Sunday, September 7, the major in command of this district was convinced his police force was engaged in a search for a body rather than a survivor. Overhead flights by a military helicopter, the release of search dogs into the desert canyons, and even the promise of a cash bounty to nearby Bedouin tribesmen for the safe return of the lost American had produced no results on the whereabouts of Bishop James Pike. The search task of Major Enosh Givati also had not been improved by the arrival in Jerusalem of dozens of international journalists, clamoring for details; for them the disappearance of Pike was a major story. "Bishop Pike Missing in Dead Sea Desert" was headlined on newspapers throughout the English-speaking world. The potent symbolism of America's most controversial ecclesiastical figure being lost in the place where Jesus had once wandered was irresistible to news editors from London to New York City to San Francisco.

An additional souring of the moods of the military and border police officers as they directed the actions of three hundred searchers in 100-degree heat may have been caused by the widely printed speculations that week by many of the bishop's Christian enemies that he was not lost at all. "Pike'll turn up," one Episcopal bishop in the United States had announced cynically. "It's just another publicity stunt."

The searchers also had not been aided by the dreams or self-described "visions" of Diane Pike, who, along with her husband, was a firm believer in parapsychological phenomena. She initially had welcomed the arrival of delegations of other such believers in Israel following the publicity of Pike's disappearance, while she recovered in a Jerusalem hotel. She had thought their psychic "readings"—holding a small lead weight at the end of a string over a map of the wadi—might indicate in which ravine or box canyon her husband was concealed while he rested or recovered from injuries. She insistently conveyed the results of these readings to the Israeli searchers. Yet as the patrols went daily to those very areas and found no trace of Pike, and as the number of days increased during which he presumably was without water or food, the psychic predictions became increasingly pessimistic. Several of the psychic devotees now reported to her visions of James Pike's body lying on its side in a position of prayer.

The Israeli police officer in charge of this day's search party now spoke sharply to his men as they half-slid and half-walked down the steep sides into a previously unexplored area of the wadi. It always paid to be very careful in this place, and the officer did not assume that the dead body of an American bishop was necessarily worth the life of a young Israeli policeman. Earlier one of the searchers had broken his leg when leaving the wadi. Falls could easily happen from these high ravines of dry clay and stones, where the desert soil was of the light-brown color and friableness of stale biscuit.

An answering shout from a policeman who had advanced out of sight along the rocky bottom of the wadi floor indicated that either there had been another accident among the searchers or that something significant had been sighted. A pair of sunglasses and then a plastic contact lens case had been found, apparently arranged on the wadi floor to point in the direction a traveler had walked. The military radios crackled with hurried transmissions. The border policemen and some civilian searchers had sighted an unmoving figure, apparently either resting or stuck, underneath the shade of a large rock about halfway up the opposite side of the wadi. The other searchers gathered. The figure above them on the canyon wall did not respond to their shouts, either in English or Hebrew.

A pair of field glasses was trained on the clothing and the face of the unmoving body on the wall by a young policeman. Another radio message was transmitted. The clothing was identical to that described by his wife as being worn by Pike when they had become lost in the desert, and the reason for the body's immobility was now obvious. Bishop Pike was dead. His body had apparently fallen to this position about sixty feet from the top of the wadi at least several days earlier, and since then had been exposed to the desert heat and to the flies. The physical corruption of the bishop's swollen face and torso was advanced.

A military helicopter was dispatched to help the searchers extricate the body from its difficult location, and Diane Pike, who was present at the rear of the search party, was informed of his death and cautioned not to insist on viewing her husband's remains. An official news announcement was prepared for the journalists assembling in Jerusalem. Several of the mediums who had tended to Diane Pike at her Jerusalem hotel later noted that the bishop had been found just as they had predicted, lying on his side with his arms brought forward into a position of prayer—although whether this postmortem position was also the familiar "boxer" stance frequently seen by pathologists in bodies killed by sudden blunt trauma was not discussed.

The only mystery was what had compelled Bishop Pike to attempt the dangerous climb to the top of the wadi's wall, from which he had then fallen to his death. A *New York Times* reporter speculated that the bishop "was climbing a steep cliff, either to extricate himself from a box canyon or to get better vantage, when he slipped." The accident might have been survivable if there had been anything growing in this desert— a clump of grass, a sunburned bush, or a tree's ancient roots—which Pike could have grasped as he fell. But as chance or his fate would have it, nothing stopped him from accelerating for about sixty to seventy feet, until his broken body eventually came to rest beneath a rock. It was a fall not great, but sufficient.

The combination of notoriety and fame ascribed to Bishop James Pike in 1969 may now seem a religious anachronism to a culture increasingly observant of its own secularism. Pike wandered to his death in the Judean wilderness the same year as the first manned landing on the moon, the casual acceptance of adult nudity in popular motion pictures, and escalating casualties among U.S. troops in Vietnam. The death by misadventure of a bishop accused of heresy seemed misplaced as a major news story on the front pages headlining that year's other consequential events, as if the controversies occasioned by Pike—such as his frequent denials of the Virgin Birth, or his insistence that he talked with the spirits of the dead—belonged to the chronicles of an earlier century.

But the spiritual hopes and doubts of multitudes of modern Christian believers—and particularly would-be believers—have continued to be shaped into the twenty-first century by the strange life and temptations of Bishop Pike. The same decades that saw Pike's rise and fall within his church also witnessed the popular expression "God is dead" and the archaeological discoveries that revealed more about the historical Jesus than perhaps anything had since the original disciples walked the earth. Pike sought to reconcile the two, and this calling led him to investigate and support the claims of parapsychology, Pentecostal forms of worship and "speaking in tongues," the ordination of women as deacons, and an unapologetic political activism. Such beliefs and pursuits were anathema to the majority of Christians in the United States in the late 1950s and early 1960s. Consequently, to many orthodox believers of his generation, Pike was both a theological and a personal pariah. But the exponential growth of independent, charismatic churches into the twenty-first century, the widespread acceptance in non–Roman Catholic churches of female clergy, and the continuing longing expressed in American popular culture for mystic and gnostic expressions of Christianity make it possible to discern the continuing intellectual spirit of James Pike.

A reading of the news articles after his death reveals that Pike had an imaginative grasp of the spiritual and intellectual concerns carried by hundreds of thousands of people as they approached the third millennium since the birth of Jesus. The London *Times* characterized Pike as "a wild, tempestuous, and lonely spirit" who had attempted "revolutionizing establishmentarian Christianity." The *Washington Post* further described Pike in its obituary as a "wiry and diminutive man" of a frustrating "complexity and contradiction." The newspaper stated that in both the benevolence of his pastoral services and the excesses of his private life, Pike had projected to others an "almost haunted energy."

The *New York Times*, more familiarly, remembered that Bishop Pike, during his residency in the city as the chaplain of Columbia University and the dean of the Cathedral of St. John the Divine, had "a passion for martinis," an oblique reference to his long struggle with alcoholism; but the *Times* also noted Pike's pioneering attempts to ordain women in the Episcopal Church, his nonjudgmental welcoming of homosexuals to his communion, his organized resistance to his church's institutional racial segregation, and his following among university students and viewers of *The Dean Pike Show*.

But not all memories or obituaries of Pike were so benevolent, and not everyone believed that the demons that Pike said he experienced were only theological metaphors. A national leader of the Southern Baptist Convention publicly described Pike as "a prophet of the devil, a non-Christian attempting to destroy the Christian faith." Within his own Episcopal Church, an elderly minister in 1966 thanked God after hearing of the suicide of Pike's son that there was "one less Pike." Even the *New York Times*, in an otherwise praiseful obituary, wrote that Pike had angered the orthodox of all Christian communions by his jeering descriptions of such beliefs as the ascension of Jesus into heaven after the resurrection; such a vision, Pike had written, reminded him of an astronaut "who didn't come back."

The religious antipathies aroused by Pike both before and after his death cannot be dismissed simply as the result of clerical jealousies, intellectual small-mindedness, or sectarian hatreds—James Pike was a genuinely disturbing man. His personal shortcomings, known to both his enemies and his friends during his tenure as an Episcopal bishop, were but the surface tensions of an inner darkness and turmoil revealed after his death. There were the suicides, for example. An alarming number of people intimately connected to Pike attempted to take their lives during the years they were closest to him—his daughter, his son, and one of his extramarital lovers. Two of them, his son and his lover, succeeded. Pike certainly had a criminal complicity in the latter death. In a moment of what some might call existential honesty—or others might simply call human evil—he had taunted his lover after an argument one night to take her own life. He then handed her a full bottle of sedatives. When she became comatose later that evening, Pike delayed telephoning for medical help while he frantically moved her body out of his residence and into her own apartment and destroyed any evidence of his relationship with her. Yet, characteristically, Pike carried on his person afterward a note written by this woman implicating him in her death. He placed the note close to his skin, beneath his dark clerical suit for months, apparently either as a prudent way of hiding it or as an act of self-mortification.

There were other destructive impulses. Pike publicized his struggles with alcoholism throughout his life, in part because he had little choice; while serving as the Episcopal bishop of the diocese of California, there were persistent rumors that he had been detained on occasions by the San Francisco police for drunken driving or public intoxication. After his death there were candid discussions among his friends of his covert experiments with hallucinogenic drugs while he was on sabbatical leave at Cambridge University, his attempt to reach "the other side" of deceased personalities in a spiritual afterlife. There were also his compulsive adulteries and his three marriages, occasioned by the physical appeal he projected to both males and females.

Bishop James Pike was not always the morally superior figure his champions hoped he had become, but he was by no means the categorically evil man his enemies claimed he was. Like two other disturbing iconoclasts of his time, the psychiatrist R. D. Lang, who celebrated madness as holistic, and Herbert Marcuse, who equated philosophical belief with revolutionary action, Pike by his very excesses and vulnerability compels us to examine the limits of religious belief, or at least the limits of moral rebirth and human forgiveness. Inside the private darkness where Bishop Pike as an individual struggled with his self-destructiveness, his furtive sexual impulses, his own selfishness—in other words, inside his soul—was a man not tempted more frequently than anyone else, nor necessarily more fallible. He was simply more naked.

I

The Pious Boy from Hollywood

Hollywood High's first celebrity graduate of the new decade
was not a movie star, at least not in the conventional sense of the term.
James A. Pike, the controversial Episcopal bishop of California who became
the first American religious figure to break into national television,
received his diploma from Hollywood High with the summer class of 1930.

—JOHN BLUMENTHAL, *Hollywood High: The History of*
America's Most Famous Public School, 1988

James Albert Pike was born on February 14, 1913, in Oklahoma City, Oklahoma, but for much of the twentieth century he considered himself a Californian. As an adult, Pike had slight interest in the Kentucky origins of his parents or their early attempts at homesteading in Oklahoma. A correspondent once wrote him, shortly before he became the Episcopal bishop of California, asking whether he was related to the notable nineteenth-century military adventurer and frontiersman Zebulon Pike; the future bishop wrote back candidly replying that he did not know if he was a descendant of this pioneer, and it had never occurred to him to wonder whether he was related beyond his immediate family to *any* earlier Pikes. The twentieth-century James Pike understood his history as beginning in Los Angeles, California, a city where he was moved by his widowed mother when he was eight years old.

His mother, Pearl Agatha Pike, was a formidable woman. She had made her way across the country from Curdsville, Kentucky, becoming, successively, by age thirty-one, a farmwife, a mother, a widow, and a self-supporting single parent. She and Pike's father, also named James Albert, were third-generation Kentucky descendants of the pioneer families, surprisingly numerous, who in the late eighteenth century had carried their Roman Catholicism with them from the eastern seaboard to the Kentucky frontier. The area southwest of Louisville along the mountainous turnings of the Ohio River became known as the "Pike counties" due to the large numbers with that surname who settled there by the early 1800s. They built frontier churches named for early Roman saints, established academies to teach their children the catechism, and married into other families of the same faith, such as the Goodrums or the Wimsatts. Bishop Pike of California could have counted, had he been interested, at least one Roman Catholic priest and one nun among his ancestors before Pearl Agatha Wimsatt married James Albert Pike at St. Stephen's Church, in the diocese of Owensboro, Kentucky, in 1907.

Pearl Pike soon took financial and emotional control of their marriage. The same year as their wedding, they moved to Oklahoma to take advantage of the Homestead Act's offer of title to 160 acres to any settler willing to improve unclaimed western land. James Pike Sr., who had contracted tuberculosis, plainly was not meant to be a farmer. For the first planting season, as her husband struggled to clear their land of mesquite brush, Pearl supplied them with ready cash by teaching part-time and, occasionally, playing piano in theaters as accompaniment to silent films. Her husband's health was somewhat improved by a short recuperative visit to Arizona, and Pearl Pike persuaded the Oklahoma school where she taught to hire her husband as the principal—although in later years she was quick to add, "I told him what to do, of course."

James Pike soon became too consumptive to work the farm, and the couple moved to Oklahoma City, where Pearl obtained a job as a full-time teacher. In 1912, she learned that she was pregnant. Hers was a difficult pregnancy to carry to term, and, with her husband increasingly weakened, she asked her mother to come from Kentucky to act both as a comforter and as a midwife. She went into labor for a full day and much of the succeeding night; finally, after midnight, James Pike Jr. was born in the early morning hours of St. Valentine's Day, February 14, 1913. His father would survive him by only two years.

The future bishop was thereby fated by his birth and his father's subsequent death to be the sole male within a matriarchal family, its only child, and a cradle Catholic. His mother doted on him. Even in her old age she enjoyed telling visitors how her son had "started out a winner." When he was one year old, in Pearl Pike's retelling, "I entered him in the Better Babies contest at the state fair, and he received the first prize, the highest score out of four hundred babies; and when he was two years old he won it again."

After his father's death from tuberculosis in 1915, the future bishop's friends later remembered, "for all practical purposes, James had known no father." Pearl Pike reacted to her husband's death as she later reacted in her life to all such adversities: decisively, pragmatically, and unsentimentally. She rejected staying permanently in Oklahoma or returning back east to Kentucky. Although she had no relatives awaiting her in Los Angeles, the average yearly salary for a public schoolteacher in California was nearly twice the combined yearly salaries for teachers in Oklahoma and Kentucky; and Los Angeles was then widely advertised in the Midwest as overflowing "with medium-priced apartment houses." She and her son moved to the city in 1921.

California thus became for the young James Pike the locale of his boyhood and adolescent memories, but the family's relocation was also the source of his deepest social insecurities. From ages eight to ten, Pike attended five different schools and called six different addresses home, as his mother moved from one affordable rental location to another, including, briefly, an apartment on Sunset Boulevard. Eventually, his mother purchased a house a few blocks south of Hollywood and Vine.

There were also occasional male visitors at their new home. "I was rather young and not too bad to look at," Pearl Pike later recalled of her first widowhood in Hollywood, "and went with lots of men and had opportunities to marry." James Pike apparently both felt jealous for his mother's company and identified with her situation. By elementary school age, he had developed a habit of seeking out his mother before his bedtime and kneeling beside her while praying aloud for God to send them both "a good father."

Their house at 6248 Afton Place was at the periphery of a middle-class neighborhood in North Hollywood, and for the next thirteen years, James Pike would call this address home. Afton Place was a street of pastel bungalows with pepper trees in the yards, red-tile roofs, and a few other distinctively Hollywood features. Across an industrial boulevard at one end of Afton Place, within one block of the Pike house, were the buildings of the RKO and Columbia motion pictures studios. At the other end was located a small city park with an oversized bronze statue of a nude male climbing a world globe. This work of public art was entitled *Aspiration*, and had been erected in memory of Rudolph Valentino.

Their home was at the outmost periphery of conventionally practiced religion in Los Angeles. Only a short drive eastward on Hollywood Boulevard were places of urban worship profoundly disturbing to rural Catholics from Kentucky. There was, for example, the ornate Angelus Temple, the 5,300-seat religious auditorium that was also the penthouse home of the white-robed evangelist Aimee Semple McPherson, who nightly broadcast from the temple's radio station her religious services and her urgent appeals for cash. Or turning southward a few blocks from the Pike home, across the invisible line of the future Route 66, was the most sanctified building in the United States among Pentecostal Protestants. This was the Apostolic Faith Gospel Mission at 312 Azuma Street. The mission, although quiescent by the late 1920s, had attracted thousands of black and white Pentecostals in the first decades of the century, loudly celebrating what the *Los Angeles Times* dismissed as a "weird babble of tongues," or what the Pentecostals consider the divine gift of glossolalia. (When this phenomenon began to occur within the Episcopal Church in California in the early 1960s, then-Bishop Pike would issue a pastoral letter describing glossolalia as "heresy in embryo.")

The Roman Catholic Church by comparison offered to the young James Pike what he perceived as stability and a social respectability. The boy desired both. By the time he was a student at nearby Hollywood High School, Pike "had a regular routine," in his mother's words. Daily, he attended early morning mass at Blessed Sacrament Church, locally described as the "Church of the Stars," at 6657 Sunset Boulevard. After-ward, he would breakfast with his grandmother and aunt at their house directly across the street from the Hollywood High campus. (The two women had moved from Kentucky to assist Pearl financially in support-ing her son.) This morning worship usually was not Pike's only daily visit to Blessed Sacrament. In the afternoons on his way home from school, his mother recalled, Pike "would stop at the church to talk with a very fine elderly priest."

After Pike's death, two friends, William Stringfellow and Anthony Towne, speculated that his adolescent piety was a sublimation of his need for a father and his desire for a total intimacy with his mother, vic-ariously experienced by their shared Catholic faith. Possibly these claims are accurate; if so, Pike managed his adolescence with a minimal display of rebellion or turmoil. In 1924, the year he was at the cusp of age twelve, his mother married the second of her three husbands, a Los Angeles attorney named Claude McFadden. It was not necessarily a love match; McFadden was more than a decade older than his bride, and he was a Protestant to boot. (Pearl Pike in her old age and final widowhood remarked unapologetically that she had married both her second and third husbands primarily for the advantages they brought her son.) After his mother's second marriage, James Pike acted his part well; a lawyer friend of McFadden was pleased to note in the mid-1930s that the young Jim Pike displayed toward his stepfather "all the respect, love, and obedience due a father." But it is likely that Pike gave his first loyal-ties to the priests at Blessed Sacrament and to his mother, whom he con-tinued even in his late teens to call "Mommy."

While he lived at home and was a student at Hollywood High, Jim Pike was not unpopular with his classmates, but he suffered from the twin disadvantages of being physically smaller and a year younger than most members of his class, having been promoted one year ahead because of good grades. His senior photograph in the Hollywood High yearbook, *The Poinsettia*, is instructive both in its placement and in com-parison with those of other graduates of the class of 1930. Most of the young women in this school annual look directly at the camera with a startlingly frank sexuality, many of them affecting the gold-tinted marcels in their hair worn by Mary Pickford in the 1929 motion picture *Coquette*. The young men mainly appear as solidly built and wide-shouldered, with thick pompadours. One almost feels sorry for Jim Pike, whose photographic caption contains no college or vocational choice, and whose senior picture is sandwiched between the photographs of Richard "Dick" Pattee, who plans to enter the Army Aviation Corps, and Bill Rambo, who aims to study engineering and play football at Georgia Tech. By comparison, Pike appears puckish, narrow-chested, and scholarly.

Pike had in fact decided to become a Roman Catholic priest after graduation. He wanted to go directly into a preparatory seminary and thereby spare his mother the costs of an undergraduate education. "Well, Mommy," Pearl McFadden remembered her son arguing with her, "they [seminary priests] will educate me and you won't have that expense." His mother was adamant. "No, you must finish college first. You are too young to make a decision that serious." At her insistence, Pike enrolled for regular baccalaureate studies in 1930 at the University of Santa Clara, a Jesuit institution located in what was then a farming and ranching valley south of San Francisco. The school offered a soundly Catholic education, a rural remoteness from urban temptation, and a rugged, all-male student body best known for collegiate athletics. There he would join his classmates in being instructed, as the university's president assured Catholic parents such as Pike's mother, by clerical faculty who were "not merely clever men, not merely good men, but good men who are clever."

It was Pike's good fortune to find two outstanding mentors among the faculty at Santa Clara, Walter Kropp and James F. Giambastiani. Although neither was yet a priest, each finishing the teaching regency required of scholastics before ordination, Pike immediately called both of them "Father." Giambastiani was the more outgoing of the two. (He had studied at a seminary at Rome, and could be persuaded occasionally by the Santa Clara undergraduates to perform a wickedly humorous parody of Benito Mussolini.) He took an immediate liking to Pike. Nearly forty years later, Giambastiani clearly remembered teaching the "brilliant young Jim Pike," whose "ideas flashed through his mind with such rapidity that they collided." Both teachers nurtured their new pupil's talents in literature and journalism, and Giambastiani and Kropp, rather than any of his contemporaries at Santa Clara, became

Pike's most long-lasting friends and correspondents from his student days. Kropp would continue to write letters to his former student for the next three decades, and always wish him the blessing of "*Pax Christi.*" Giambastiani would live long enough to pray at mass for the soul of Pike's adult son, Jim, who died a suicide in 1966, and to pray for James Pike himself after his death in Israel in 1969.

These two instructors were encouraged by their promising student's early expressions of his intent to become a Jesuit; they apparently had no inkling, until Pike permanently left the school at the end of his sophomore year, that he had undergone a radical reversal of his Christian belief, and that in his second year of college found it no longer possible to believe in the Roman Catholic faith or to continue a Catholic education. "I left the college, the church, and my vocation to the priesthood and was a thoroughgoing agnostic humanist for some years," he later wrote of his decision in 1932. Such a decision was personally and spiritually a momentous one for the twenty-year-old Pike. Not only did it represent a rejection of the only moral authority he had known and previously obeyed literally for all of his childhood and adolescence, but it also was a declared spiritual separation from his mother. All the more unusual, then, is how varied and sparse were the reasons Pike later gave for this decision, as expressed by him throughout subsequent decades not only in his public statements but also in his personal letters to his mother.

Sometimes the decisive moment was described by him as a "second-year course in religion," when "the whole idea of evolution was indicated as improbable"; sometimes, the offending course was "Fr. Sheerim's class in cosmology," when the teaching father could not answer Pike's question on how to reconcile St. Thomas's idea of matter with the "electronic theory." (Interestingly, the only poor grade Pike ever received at Santa Clara was a D for a course in general physics.) Other times, it was his intellectual distaste, as described in a letter to his mother nine years after he had left Santa Clara, for what he considered to be the typical Roman Catholic college as "some ingrown institution that seeks to pour the man's life into a groove." But the most extensive and rationally considered explanation for his loss of faith in 1932 was published by Pike in the *National Catholic Reporter* in late 1968, which in an irony of circumstances was entitled "Speak Out Boldly and Stay In."

Addressed to those Catholic faithful who were troubled by the encyclical letter written that year by Pope Paul VI, *Humanae Vitae*, describing as "illicit" any artificial means of contraception, Pike took the occasion of this guest column to revisit in detail his own reasons for having left the Roman communion in 1932. He wittily noted that while he was urging Catholic clergy and laity who disagreed with *Humanae Vitae* to remain in their church and work for change from within, he was uniquely qualified by his own exit to counsel restraint to those who were thinking about leaving. "Under parliamentary procedure, a motion to reconsider must be introduced by someone who voted No on the issue," he wrote. Thus, by analogy, he was "highly qualified" because "on this precise issue I voted with my feet in 1932." He then gave further details:

> When I was a sophomore at the University of Santa Clara, in a course in theology the apologetic for the anti-contraception position of *Casti Connubii* [the papal encyclical of 1930 in regard to contraception] struck me as particularly unconvincing, and, although I had no practical interest in the subject, I came to the conclusion that I could not accept it intellectually.
>
> In those days it was generally assumed that the papal teaching in question was infallible, the subject matter falling under the "morals" half of the faith-and-morals rubric and *ex cathedra* being taken for granted from the solemnity of the encyclical and its unqualified mode of statement. Nor was there the slightest hint in the air that the doctrine might be reconsidered. Having learned in the first year of scholastic philosophy St. Thomas Aquinas' teaching that a negative particular destroys an affirmative universal, it dawned on me within a day or two that at the moment I concluded against the given principle of moral theology, *co instanti* and *ipso facto*, I had denied the doctrine of papal infallibility.
>
> This drove me to reading the history of Vatican Council I and then back to the early church fathers and the New Testament and I realized—to put it minimally (since my purpose here is not to argue that doctrine pro or con) that infallibility was not as simplistically supportable as I had assumed from the two customary truth texts—*Tu es Petrus* and *Pasce mea oves*. There is

such a thing as being too logical (but no one with a serious interest in scholastic philosophy could have thought so) and it may
have been unsophisticated of me to deem infallibility so central
a doctrine (though my teachers would not have thought so).

In any case, I left the college, the church, and my vocation
to the priesthood and was a thoroughgoing agnostic humanist
for a few years. It was a case of throwing out the baby with the
bathwater.

This version certainly is a fully intellectual account of why Pike left
the Roman Church (in his haste of composition he slightly misquoted
Christ's injunction in Latin, *Pasce oves meas*, "Feed my sheep") and the
incident he described is apparently the origin of his lifelong quarrel
with Roman Catholic doctrines on artificial contraception. However, in
the absence of any mention of his emotional distress or temporizing,
this story is a little too pat, a little too ipso facto. Two weeks after the
publication of Pike's account, Giambastiani wrote a lengthy letter to the
editor of the *National Catholic Reporter*. In it Pike's former instructor
described himself as in the "painful situation" of publicly contradicting
the printed statements of his favorite pupil:

> As close friends, Jim and I saw quite a bit of one another at
> Santa Clara. Never once did he bring up doubts of difficulties
> about the arguments against birth control, papal infallibility, or
> the Virgin Birth. As a trusted friend, I should think he would
> have occasionally spoken to me about these things. Jim was also
> the very close friend of another Jesuit scholastic at Santa Clara
> [presumably, Kropp] with whom he sometimes held very long
> conversations covering matters of intellectual interest. I
> recently asked this Jesuit if Jimmy had ever expressed any of
> these doubts or difficulties. His answer was, "Never once!" This
> particular Jesuit has kept in close contact with Jim Pike all these
> years.

Pike's version in 1968 of his exit from the Roman Church therefore
appears more an expression by the confident, fifty-five-year-old Episcopal bishop that he then was rather than by the uncertain nineteen-year-

old he was in 1932, away from his home and mother for the first time. The statement of religious disbelief, like the proclamation of religious conversion, usually is preceded by a long quiescence—what William James in *The Varieties of Religious Experience* called the process of unification: "We have a thought, or we perform an act repeatedly, but on a certain day the real meaning of the thought suddenly peals for the first time, or the act suddenly turns to a moral impossibility." To the young James Pike, emotionally vulnerable and devoted to his pious Roman Catholic mother, the devotional act of accepting Catholic doctrine was not yet a moral impossibility for him.

Pike did eventually give up his intention to be a Jesuit priest after departing Santa Clara, but his concurrent statements about leaving the Catholic Church and becoming "a thoroughgoing agnostic humanist for a few years" appear to have been hyperbole to emphasize his later conversion to the Anglican Communion. At least until the mid-1930s, he was more of a nonpracticing Catholic than an agnostic. Nor was his ambition for the priesthood irrevocably put from his mind. "I'm inclined to suspect that Jim is not so sure of himself as appears on the surface," Giambastiani wrote after Pike had left Santa Clara. Giambasiani further recalled how, when he briefly had stopped in Los Angeles before traveling to Rome in the fall of 1933, "Dear friend Jimmy paid me a visit. He was attending UCLA at the time. He told me he was thinking seriously of becoming a Jesuit. I encouraged him in this, and referred him to a Jesuit priest in Los Angeles whom he knew and could consult."

In sum, no sudden and absolute loss of religious faith his sophomore year was the sole cause of Pike's leaving the Jesuit institution. Instead, he quit Santa Clara partly because he was developing an independent and individualistic intellect, which he felt was incompatible with a strictly Catholic education, and also because he apparently was ambitious for a more marketable degree than this small church institution, surrounded by apricot orchards and cattle ranches, could provide. He was at times indiscreet at Santa Clara in expressing his new appreciation for his mental abilities and his ambitions to attend another, more selective university. Giambastiani remembered how Pike once publicly criticized the university's course work as insufficiently challenging to him, and subsequently was booed by his classmates when he entered the student dining hall.

But probably the most important reason for his departure was, simply, that Pike was homesick for his mother's company, and she homesick for his. "He wasn't happy at Santa Clara, he didn't like it," Pearl McFadden later remembered, and when her son would return briefly to Los Angeles during his school vacations, "Christmas and Easter, and so on," she said, "I spent most of those vacations crying." In 1932, she informed her son that she had become seriously ill. There was no question that, given the emotional intimacy between the two, he would return to her side at any announcement of her ill health. By the summer of that year, Pike was back living with her and his stepfather at their Afton Place house.

Shortly before James Pike left Santa Clara in the summer of 1932, he composed an essay for the student literary magazine that was sponsored by Giambastiani. From the perspective of his subsequent religious wanderings and his death by misadventure, this essay reads as almost prophetic in its description of his early experience. He relates how he had camped one weekend with his classmates at an isolated site in the Sierra Nevada. Leaving behind the other students, Pike "started out alone one morning, hoping to penetrate the woods and surmount one of the lofty eminencies." He soon became dangerously lost. "Entranced with the beauty of the things which God had made, I suddenly noticed that the path was no longer visible." Uncertain of what was ahead, but "not wishing to turn back," he continued walking into the wilderness for several hours, until he discovered that he had been walking in a circle. "Unconsciously I had constantly been changing my direction until I was back to where I had started." With startled insight, Pike realized he did not know where he was, and that he could fall through the underbrush and off a hidden cliff at any moment. Unlike his later wandering in the Judean Desert, this early misadventure in the Sierra Nevada ended benignly, with Pike returning safely to his companions. "Believe me," he wrote for Giambastiani, "the sight of our camp was welcome, indeed." That autumn, back in his Hollywood home, he enrolled in pre-law studies at the University of California at Los Angeles.

Pike's subsequent studies in law, culminating in receiving a Juris Doctor degree in 1938, were distinguished more by his diligence in the library and success at winning academic honors than for his political abilities or his vision of jurisprudence. After a year at UCLA, he transferred in 1933 to the University of Southern California, while continuing to live at home. Within three years at USC, he managed to obtain both his bachelor of arts and his postgraduate law degree by 1936. Whatever her personal misgivings about her son's supposed lapse from Roman Catholicism, Pearl McFadden continued to finance his education during these years, and he responded dutifully.

While at USC, Pike was remembered as something of an academic grind by his contemporaries. "When Brother James Pike receives the degree of LL.B.," as his fellow law students ironically eulogized him in a bulletin of 1936, "the Law School will seem different without his brisk footsteps in the library (he always walks twice as fast as anyone else) and his alert, yet absentminded, presence, and, of course, his rather malodorous pipe." The pipe, like the pencil-thin mustache he had recently grown, was perhaps an attempt by Pike to project an image of maturity; at age twenty-three in 1936, he was several years younger than most of the other law graduates of his class. Already, however, he evinced the scholastic and forensic skills he later would employ as a bishop. During his three years attending law classes at USC, only once did he receive a grade lower than an A, and while still a student there he published the leading article in the January 1936 issue of the university's *Law Review*, "What Is Second-Degree Murder in California?" His article, considering its subject from legal and psychological viewpoints, was highly praised by members of the state's bar.

He later described these university years as his attempt to fill a spiritual void in his life by substituting a secular humanism and a social liberalism for his lost faith. In a short autobiography published in *Modern Canterbury Pilgrims*, a collection of essays on Anglicism he edited in 1956, Pike described how at the end of his sophomore year at Santa Clara, "I sought the meaning for my life in career and in a zeal for social reform—more particularly through my eventual association, as an attorney, with the New Deal." But, as with his supposedly sudden loss of faith, Pike's personal journey to secular humanism and New Deal activism was a tentative and extenuated experience that he chose to recast, self-dramatizing, as a sudden decision. Nor were the alternatives in the early 1930s of a devout Catholicism or an economic liberalism mutually exclusive, as he later implied in *Modern Canterbury Pilgrims*.

Pope Pius XI's encyclical of 1931 affirming the right of Catholic workers to participate in industrial unions, *Quadragesimo Anno*, was widely distributed throughout American parishes, and the early years of this decade also saw the establishment in the United States of the Catholic Worker Movement. Neither seems to have offered Pike a sufficient balance between private piety and political action, and he left no written records of having noticed either the papal encyclical or Dorothy Day's new labor movement.

New Dealism also was a long time coming to his thoughts, or, at the least, his conversion to political and economic liberalism in the 1930s was not so dramatic as he later remembered. There was no immediate personal or economic impetus. His family was in reduced circumstances due to the Depression, though not desperate ones; both Pearl and Claude McFadden remained steadily employed throughout the 1930s, and there was never any danger of losing the Afton Place house to repossession, or of Pearl not being able to afford the university tuition for her son. In fact, Pike was comparatively conservative as a student. One of his earliest published efforts in college journalism, an editorial written in 1932 for Giambastiani's class and published in the student newspaper, was a pointed criticism of the perceived radicalism of an assembly of Catholic bishops, headlined "Is the N.C.W.C. Pink?" The National Catholic Welfare Conference (NCWC) was an advisory body of U.S. Catholic bishops convened since 1919—in its words, at "the utmost encouragement of Holy See"—to consider social and economic issues of interest to American Catholics. In its publication, *Catholic Action*, the bishops in 1931 described high unemployment in the United States as "due to the neglect of Christ" among capitalists and industrialists, and in 1932 they insisted that "federal and state appropriations for relief in some form will become necessary." These were scarcely radical notions in 1932, and only an erstwhile conservative college sophomore could have questioned them as being "pink."

The chairman of the NCWC in 1932, the year of Pike's editorial, was Archbishop Edward J. Hanna of San Francisco. It was unlikely that Archbishop Hanna would let pass unnoticed or unanswered a criticism of the conference appearing in a Catholic school newspaper from as near as Santa Clara. That summer Pike received at his home address a letter from the national office of the NCWC, emphasizing the officially recognized advisory role of the conference. In a tacit rebuke to his criticism, a packet of pamphlets was also enclosed, detailing the hardships of U.S. industrial and agricultural workers.

The student political activism at UCLA during the 1930s—and to a lesser degree at the University of Southern California—also seems to have bypassed Pike on either campus. Although at Santa Clara Pike had gained something of a reputation as a joiner and a student journalist, there exist no records of his participating in or reporting on the one-hour "student strikes against war," held annually on the state university campuses, or having taken a public side in a divisive campus controversy in 1934, when some USC undergraduates hired themselves out as strikebreakers. "Brother Jim Pike," in the recollections of his fellow students, seems to have spent most of his time on either campus quietly studying in the university library, or commuting to and from his mother's house. For Pike, the personally defining events of the early and mid-1930s were not economic, political, or religious; they were to be cultural and sexual. The occasion for these changes was his being selected, after his graduation from USC's law school, for the Sterling Fellowship for doctoral studies in law at Yale University. His winning of a fellowship to a prestigious East Coast university confirmed to Pearl McFadden her high estimates of her son's abilities. "That Jesuit school was not good enough for James," she insisted in later years. "James was much too smart to be at Santa Clara."

Pike was unable to cut his maternal ties when he relocated to Yale, in New Haven, Connecticut. His later biographers, Stringfellow and Towne, described how he had told them about "the terrible loneliness Jim felt in his separation from his mother when he went to Yale Law School." The ten months he studied at New Haven, from September 1936 to June 1937, were his longest uninterrupted absence from his mother. It was also his first experience of the predominantly Protestant culture of the eastern states. Despite his sometimes announced agnosticism, Pike was quick to notice the social and economic cachets of the Atlantic states' most liturgical Protestant worship. "Practically every churchgoer you meet in our level of society is Episcopalian," Pike later wrote to his mother, "and a R.C. [Roman Catholic] or straight Protestant is as rare as hen's teeth." At this same time in 1936—"about four years" after he had left the University of Santa Clara, in his mother's remembrance—Pike began occasionally attending Sunday morning services at Episcopal churches. He went, as he wrote in *Modern Canterbury Pilgrims*, more for the church's "aesthetic—and, in my case, nostalgic appeal"—of familiar liturgies and prayer books than for any specific attraction to the doctrines of the Anglican Communion.

It was also at this time that Pike probably first experienced adult homosexual intercourse, according to Stringfellow and Towne. They later wrote of being told by a third party that, "while he was a lonely law student at Yale," Pike had "succumbed to the blandishments of another [male] student." The two biographers had their own shared personal agenda for recording this assertion, but this early incident with an unnamed student was confirmed by Pike's third wife, Diane. A physical consequence of his scholarly loneliness, this single encounter does not seem to have been repeated by Pike either while at Yale or later, although he regarded both homosexual and heterosexual acts with equal casualness. While having sex with another man, he had felt neither guilt nor displeasure, Bishop Pike later recalled. "It was just that nothing seemed to fit together the way it should."

Whatever his emotional state, Pike succeeded in receiving his doctorate in law in 1937. His mother intuited that her son "really wanted to come home." Pearl McFadden added emphatically, "I wish he had." However, he chose to stay at his Orange Street apartment in New Haven throughout the summer of 1937 while he looked for legal work on the East Coast. He also was dating Jane Alvies, a former Hollywood High classmate with whom he had become reacquainted when she had also enrolled in the school of law at Yale in 1936. (Yale Law School officially had begun to admit women in 1919.) In January 1938, he was offered and accepted a position in the office of the general counsel of the Securities and Exchange Commission (SEC) and moved to an apartment in Arlington, Virginia, outside of Washington, D.C. Alvies for the time being stayed in Connecticut.

The following summer, he and Alvies together visited both their respective families in Los Angeles. Pike also took advantage of this occasion to stop by the Episcopal church nearest his mother's home and the favorite place of worship of the Episcopal stars working in the motion picture industry, St. Mary of the Angels. He and the priest in charge, the Reverend Neal Dodd, took an immediate spiritual and personal liking to each other. Dodd was a conservative Anglo-Catholic who preferred being addressed as "Father" and also had something of a dramatic side; he was known for having married Mary Pickford and Douglas Fairbanks Sr., and had played the role of a priest in the 1934 motion picture *It Happened One Night*, starring Claudette Colbert and Clark Gable.

With Dodd's blessings, Pike was officially confirmed into the Episcopal Church. Once "in," Pike was enthusiastic in his new beliefs as a High Church Episcopalian. As he later wrote privately about his decision, employing a telling metaphor for his conversion from an inactive Roman Catholic to a communicant in the Episcopal Church, "I had not thought through the faith very thoroughly—this was to come later when I went into the Navy—but I had a certain sense of being 'home' again." Indeed, there was much that was reassuringly familiar to Pike as a former Roman Catholic in his new church's use of vestments, liturgies, and prayers. The difference, of course, was that he was now a communicant of a church under an episcopal, rather than papal, authority. The Protestant Episcopal Church of the United States of America, as the national church was then known, was governed at its diocesan levels by bishops, just as Pike had experienced in the Roman Church. At the national level, however, decisions were determined not by archbishops and cardinals responsible to the Vatican, but by two collective bodies, the House of Delegates, composed of laity and clergy, and the House of Bishops. These two houses met in convention every three years, and changes in canon law required the assent of both bodies. The House of Bishops also assembled yearly for "the purposes of collegiality." (Pike often was to be a topic on the agenda of these meetings and a strain to their collegiality.) A nationally presiding bishop was elected from among their number as retirement or death opened this position. The presiding bishop of the U.S. church, which was known as a "province" within the international Anglican Communion, assembled with bishops of all national provinces every ten years at Lambeth Palace, England, under the authority of the Archbishop of Canterbury. This assembly, however, was not for legislating governance, but for consultation and fellowship. Hence, the organization and worship of the Episcopal Church offered to Pike degrees of both the Protestant independence he now desired and the Roman Catholic clerical authority and traditionalism with which he grew up. As one of Pike's fellow Episcopal bishops was to remark irreverently to him years later, apropos of their vestments and perceived authority, "We look like mother and talk like father." Such apparently was exactly what Pike needed spiritually in the summer of 1938.

There was also a practical advantage to Pike's being confirmed as an Episcopalian by the Los Angeles priest that summer. During this same visit with their families, on August 14, 1938, Pike and Alvies were married before a small side altar with the Reverend Dodd officiating, inside the Spanish-styled sanctuary of St. Mary of the Angels. Apparently little advance notice was given to their families of their decision, and there was no time for a honeymoon trip. The same day as their marriage, the couple boarded an airplane, then a comparatively infrequent means of travel, in order to return most quickly to Pike's job at the SEC in Washington. Pike's mother had been against the match from the start. "Jane was a highly intelligent girl," Pearl McFadden later recalled, but "she was just not for James." His mother's feelings of apprehension, however, did not preclude her giving the couple an expensive wedding gift of a buffet table before their return to Washington.

Among both his friends and his enemies—and a third, overlapping group including his three wives—James Pike would later be known for his rapidity in reinventing himself, for his pragmatic capacity to redefine who and what he was. His future biographers Stringfellow and Towne believed that the "single, casual homosexual episode" experienced by Pike had "prompted his eagerness to marry, as if marriage, by definition, would assuage his loneliness and protect his person." Their assertion, particularly as to "protect his person," probably is overstated. But the facts remain that the young California student of an uncertain sexuality, an unsophisticated politics, and an unresolved religious leaning, who had traveled east to law school in 1936, now returned to Washington in 1938 as a married man, a New Deal lawyer, and a Protestant churchgoer. Within six years and after a second marriage, Pike would radically redefine himself once more, as an Episcopal priest and a future bishop.

II

Becoming Jim Pike,
Lawyer and Priest

Thou madest us for Thyself,
and our heart is restless,
until it repose in Thee.

—*Confessions of Saint Augustine*, Book I

Pike began his legal career in Washington like a man anxious to make
up for lost time and money. Three months after joining the general
counsel staff of the SEC, he formed a private firm with another lawyer
in March 1938 and began a lucrative business selling manuals of federal
court procedures to other practicing attorneys. At the time, such an
activity was not considered a conflict of interest. Eventually, the shared
income from the firm of Pike and Fisher surpassed Pike's annual government salary. He also worked a third job in 1938–39, lecturing at
nights to law classes at the Catholic University of America. He began to
be recognized among his legal peers as an authority on federal court
procedures and, professionally, as a comer. Supreme Court Justice Felix

Frankfurter, an acknowledged talent scout for the Roosevelt administration, made a point of writing to Pike at the end of his second year at
the SEC. The justice noted that he had read the latter's recently published article, "Some Current Trends in the Construction of Federal
Rules." "I thought it a very good piece of work," Frankfurter wrote.

Pike apparently also tried to sustain this pace both in his marriage
and in his new commitment to the Episcopal Church. Jane Alvies had
been a nonpracticing Christian Scientist when they first met, but, after
Pike became a member of the Anglican Communion and their marriage
ceremony at St. Mary's, Pike insisted that his wife also study for Episcopal confirmation. Both found adjustment to marriage difficult, but he
was persistent in urging his new wife that together they could "help the
situation by increased religious devotions, in the form of spiritual reading together and more frequent reception of Holy Communion."

It was a pace perhaps only Jim Pike alone could have sustained. The
physical and religious demands made upon Jane Pike silently emerge
from a letter Pike wrote in early 1939 to "Dearest Mama." After
reproaching his mother for her claim not to have time to read some
Episcopal religious tracts he planned to send her, Pike wrote, in his own
italics and abbreviations:

> Lord knows Jane and I are busy enough, yet we *make* time for
> God and let other things find their place. . . . And as to being
> too tired—*e.g.*, I was very tired Tues. after a busy weekend and
> two hard days + class Tues. night. So I was tempted to rest on
> Washington's Birthday instead of making our annual parish
> retreat—but we talked it over and decided it was important to
> go. The next morning we got up early so that Jane could get
> some sandwiches made for the light lunch (she was on a com-
> mittee to take care of that) and so that I could practice the
> "Missa Penitentialis"—a mass I hadn't sung before. By 10 a.m.,
> when the retreat started (with ashes and high mass) we were
> awfully tired—By the end of the day (after Benediction at 4.00)
> we felt *fine* and have felt fine ever since.

There is a ghastly cheerfulness here ("we felt *fine*"). Nor did Pike
further help his domestic situation by his habit of sending and receiving

confidential letters, such as this one to and from his mother, and avoiding sharing the contents with his wife. Given the physical and religious exhaustions experienced by Jane Pike, it probably was inevitable that she would express her rage, and that her outburst would be directed toward the Episcopal practices being urged upon her by her husband. Pearl McFadden was by no means an unbiased witness to her son's first marriage, but her recollection of a particular scene with her son and daughter-in-law records the suddenly unrepressed violence of Jane Pike's animadversions toward the role she felt imposed upon her. Pike and his wife had gone together to a Christmas communion service, McFadden recalled, "and when the communion was to be served she jumped up and ran out of the church, screaming." Pike's mother also implied that there had been other scenes of Alvies's hysteria—and of her finding sexual comfort with other men—while she and Pike lived together.

There appears to have been a mutual agreement by James and Jane Pike within their two years together to end their short marriage as soon as possible. The couple returned to Los Angeles in July 1940 to visit their parents. (Despite being twenty-seven years old and having established his own household for four years, Pike always referred to these trips back to Los Angeles as "returning home.") On their arrival, the couple separated, returning to the house of their respective parents. On this visit, Pike told his mother that he planned to file for divorce. Pearl McFadden approved.

An initial judgment was granted in early September 1940, and the divorce was recorded as final in early October 1941. (Pike got back the buffet table his mother had given the couple.) With a lawyer's thoroughness, Pike kept the legal papers for his divorce in his personal files for the next two decades. Interestingly, he blotted out the typewritten lines on his copies describing his complaints for divorce, but he left undeleted on these copies the countercomplaint filed by Jane Pike, in which she described to the court how he had treated her "in a cruel and inhuman manner, and has inflicted upon her great mental anguish, pain, and suffering." Pike perhaps left her countercomplaint uncensored as a private rebuke to himself (just as he would later carry on his person the accusatory suicide note of his mistress). Or perhaps he left Alvies's court documents unaltered as documentary evidence of his long-suffering forbearance. Pearl McFadden always maintained her son could have sought divorce from his first wife on the grounds of her adulteries, and Pike later privately wrote a friend about "the decision my counsel and I had made not to seek a civil annulment or a divorce on the grounds of adultery, due to the inevitable publicity and harm to people, and the ease of a divorce in California on the grounds of 'extreme cruelty.' "

But whoever or whatever were the reasons for their divorce on the grounds of his alleged cruelty, it was his later actions to secure a church annulment of his first marriage that were to cause him his greatest trouble. The question of this annulment was to vex Pike repeatedly after his second marriage in 1942: for example, in 1946, when he wished to enroll at the General Theological Seminary in New York; in 1958, when he was considered for appointment as the Episcopal bishop co-adjutor of California; and in 1968, when he married for the third time. Not everyone by a long count within the Episcopal Church was sympathetic toward Pike's wish for an annulment or the means by which he eventually obtained it.

Pike was disarmingly vague with his later interlocutors about his motivations for this annulment. In one account, he described to a writer how, in the summer of 1940 after he first had been sued for divorce, "I was walking up the street from my lawyer's office [and] I passed St. Paul's Cathedral and saw the sign 'Diocese of Los Angeles' and it occurred to me to inquire what the status of things would be in the church." According to Pike, he impulsively then entered the diocesan offices "and asked for the chancellor (my Roman background suggesting that there would be some such officer on hand—not realizing that in the Episcopal Church the chancellor is a layman who is in legal practice), but the secretary indicated that the bishop was free and so I asked him about the situation. Once he heard the facts he volunteered the information that the marriage was ecclesiastically annullable."

Pike apparently considered an annulment to be his for the asking, and, beyond this first, purportedly casual meeting with Bishop Bertrand Stevens of California in July 1940, he did not immediately address his annulment beyond a letter he sent the next month to Stevens. The Episcopal canon law then in effect listed a number of "impediments," in addition to adultery, that prohibited a marriage from being considered sacramentally valid. It is a depressing list, including mental deficiency, impotence, venereal disease, and bigamy. The Church's general convention of 1937 had amended the impediments to also include the condition of "lack of free will and legal consent of either party." It was upon this comparatively recent impediment that Pike argued his case in a letter of August 5 to the bishop. "I believe that my case falls within 'lack of free consent,' " Pike wrote to Stevens. "Her consent to share my life and love was not given at all; my consent to share my life and love was given, but it was not 'free,' because induced by fraud. Or, to put it another way, there never was a real marriage between us." His reasoning seems to have been that some unspecified act or behavior committed by Alvies after the couple's espousals was a posteriori evidence that her consent to their marriage vows had not been given "at all," or honestly; that these presumed, premeditated intentions on her part constituted fraud; and, therefore, by the application of the impediments clause, her practice of fraud obviated their wedding vows and made their marriage annullable.

Bishop Stevens was almost persuaded. But in petitioning the bishop, Pike for the moment had met his match with an intellect as legally subtle as his own. For more than a year, the bishop, by canon law, took no action while the divorce petition made its way through the civil court; nor, apparently, did Pike initiate any further correspondence with him. Over a year after Pike's divorce was recognized as legally final in civil court, he received in Washington on November 27, 1942, the following note from Stevens:

My Dear Mr. Pike:

On November 5th I sent you a notice that I had restored you to communicant status. Apparently your bad mail arrangements have prevented you from receiving it. Anyway, you may consider yourself in good standing.

The scholasticism of this note was masterful. Stevens had *presumed*— but never explicitly stated—that Pike's first marriage was invalid. This invalid status could be inferred by Pike's being found as a communicant "in good standing." But it was evident that beyond this charitable inference the bishop at present would not go.

Pike had remarried in January 1942, before his receipt of this note. Confirming the vows for his second marriage in a civil ceremony before receiving any ecclesiastical resolution—however ambiguous—of annulment of his first marriage would cause him, as noted above, a great deal of future trouble. But at the time he sincerely believed himself to be both a practicing Christian and a pragmatic actor for the greater good of all people involved. His consequent disregard for the canonical process may simply have been an instance of his characteristic impatience. But, in the best interpretation, it also may be considered as his first risk as an ethicist in making decisions according to the *Sitz im Leben*, the situation in life, rather than to an absolute natural law or canon dictate. He was not yet, nor would he be for several decades, a self-proclaimed situational ethicist within the Anglican Communion, such as Joseph F. Fletcher or John A. T. Robinson. But he was certainly in the process of becoming the future author of *You and the New Morality*, the book that in 1967 would make Pike's name synonymous with situational ethics.

Interesting also is the argument in Pike's letter to his bishop in 1940, proposing that "there never was a real marriage" in 1938 because there was at present a need for that marriage never to have existed. This proposition also was an emerging characteristic of the James Pike that was to become famous in the 1960s—that is, his belief that each person is best considered as in a process of always *becoming* an identity, rather than as an expression of fixed character or a specific historical past. Indeed, Pike apparently would argue that the reality of "the past" is continually being redefined in our minds by the experiences and exigencies of the present. Because he wanted to be married without Church prejudice in 1942, it therefore became true to him that his prior marriage in 1938 was not "real" in a spiritual or a historical sense. In short, he wished it so, and, therefore, it was so. Both in his letter to his bishop and his personal behavior, he was logically audacious, spiritually pragmatic, rhetorically clever, and historically presumptive. He was becoming the James Pike of the 1960s.

All that was in the future, however. For the moment, after separating from Jane Alvies in 1940 and awaiting the civil resolution of their divorce, Pike returned to his Arlington apartment and his work at the SEC. He also continued to teach law classes at nights and, occasionally, date women he met through work. "I've started getting around a little," he wrote his mother, "which is very good for the ol' morale."

He also was beginning to mature professionally and socially. In late 1940, Pike was licensed to argue cases before the U.S. Supreme Court, and he was promoted to the position of senior trial attorney at the SEC. He also sensibly had shaved off his Ronald Colman–style mustache, and his face had taken on a rounded fleshiness that was not unattractive. He was witty in the presence of women, and he was known for his willingness after work to buy a drink or two. By 1941, when Pike was twenty-eight, he permanently had assumed the physique and personality that would continue to charm women and future parishioners—he had the appearance and manner of a slightly irreverent, highly flirtatious cherub.

One to whom Pike particularly directed his personal charm was Esther Yanovski, a dark-haired young woman who was attending the evening classes in civil procedure he taught in 1941–42 at George Washington University. Pike and this student first began arriving together apparently by coincidence at dinner parties given by other faculty or students; later, they dated openly as a couple. This manner of meeting eligible women was a pattern in Pike's life; he would meet his third wife while he was the teacher of a class she was attending. In 1941, Pike went out of his way to emphasize in a letter to his mother that this time she would be very pleased with his choice of a potential daughter-in-law. "She's *very* nice," Pike wrote to his mother, in his own italics. Pike and Yanovski were married in a civil ceremony in Washington by district court judge Bolitha Lawes, a friend of Pike's, on January 29, 1942.

Pike later commented that the date of his second marriage had been accelerated by the likelihood of his entering the military in 1942. He had been administratively detailed from the SEC in 1942 to the Office of Price Administration when that wartime agency had a sudden need for lawyers experienced in federal court procedures. Thereafter, he was transferred as a civilian employee to the Office of Naval Intelligence. Military service in the future seemed inevitable, and Pike applied for a commission in the U.S. Navy. He was accepted as an ensign on November 26. Although it seemed reasonable to suppose that Pike—with his myopic eyesight and his legal skills—would not be assigned to sea duty, his eventual military posting was anything but certain to James and Esther Pike in the first full year of the Second World War.

In the summer of 1942, the newly married couple made the inexorable vacation trip to Pearl McFadden in Los Angeles. Esther Pike had been a nonpracticing Jew when they first met, and, at Pike's urging, had been taking Episcopal religious instruction. Pike met again with Bishop Stevens to discuss further petitioning for an annulment of his first marriage. The bishop rather bluntly told Pike that he must do more "to clean the matter up."

Following their civil ceremony, Esther Pike for the duration of their union was able to hold her own against Pearl McFadden for the emotional control of Jim Pike. This accomplishment was no mean feat. She could do so first by taking control of Pike's correspondence with his mother once the couple returned to Washington. Letters back to California were now written jointly in their names by Esther, to which Jim added only short, personal messages. Pike's mother apparently complained to her son about this new practice, and he privately promised that he would try to send her furtive, personal letters "in between times" his wife corresponded. Secondly, Esther had sealed the emotional bargain with her husband by giving birth to their first child, Catherine Hope Pike, on February 23, 1943.

Pike by this time had received his noncommittal message from Bishop Stevens, informing him only that he was "in good standing" within the Episcopal Church. His wartime status, however, was not so ambiguous. He presumably was to remain stationed in Washington for the duration of the war. Following his commission as an ensign, Pike returned to his work at the Department of the Navy, reading and evaluating intelligence reports. He did well and remained stationed at this same post throughout 1943.

In a short spiritual autobiography within a later collection, *Modern Canterbury Pilgrims*, Pike later wrote how, soon after his second marriage and the birth of their first child, he and his wife "decided to give serious intellectual consideration to religion . . . out of an explicitly felt need for a more meaningful basis for our personal lives, for our marriage, and for our social concerns." Although Pike had become a communicant at St. Mary of the Angels in Los Angeles in 1938, he noted in this 1956 essay that up until this time he had been attracted to the Anglican Communion more by his personal nostalgia and the aesthetic appeal of the communion's liturgy. Now, in the winter of 1942–43, Pike set himself the task of seriously studying the major Protestant theologians. Since the paper traffic at his office in Naval Intelligence was sometimes slow, and as he frequently worked the third (midnight to early morning) watch, he took advantage of the quiet to do much of his reading there. This is perhaps the most attractive picture of James Pike that can be assembled thus far from the incidents of his life—Pike, alone in the early winter hours, dressed against the cold in a dark Navy uniform suggestive of the Jesuit he once had hoped to be, earnestly studying theology in order to become a better husband, father, and citizen.

In subsequently listing the theological works he had read, Pike placed at the top of his typewritten list *Nature, Man, and God*, written by William Temple, then the Archbishop of Canterbury. Pike certainly kept intellectually engaged with the Protestant and, specifically, Anglican theologies emerging after Temple's death in 1944, as his later sermons and books give evidence. He intended his 1967 book, *If This Be Heresy*, partially as an introductory handbook for laity in order to understand such postwar and contemporary movements in the church as process theology, which predicated a God who is an evolving reality, or the death of God theology, which asserted entirely the death of any transcendent higher being. But despite his reputation for modernity, much of Pike's theological thinking and assumptions throughout the 1950s and 1960s was centered in his study of the earlier lectures of the Canterbury prelate, collected in 1934 as *Nature, Man, and God*, considered by many as the archbishop's masterwork.

Temple argued in that scholarly work for the validity of "natural theology," the notion that, by the use of analogy to the natural world and right reason, mankind can learn certain verities about God. Such a scholastic argument was familiar territory for Pike, who had been trained in the Thomist system of natural theology as a student at Santa Clara. Where the archbishop of Canterbury departed, excitingly for Pike, from the received teaching of the Roman Catholic Church was in Temple's insistence of what he called the "sacramental universe." For

Temple, the Christian Church was not to set itself apart from the world as an anticipation of the Augustinian "City of God," but, rather, it was to be judged by how well it had engaged the world as a sacrament given by God in order to achieve its beliefs of justice and love among humanity. "It is a great mistake to think that God is interested only, or even exclusively, in religion," Temple wrote, an assertion to engage the concerns of the world that Pike subsequently quoted approvingly in his own book, published in 1955, *The Church, Politics, and Society*. Pike's characteristic insistence in his own church career on dissolving the boundaries between the sacred and the secular—by employing a liturgy and a theology that can be colloquially understood by the twentieth-century secular person, for example, or of his insisting that the Anglican Communion be engaged with the political issues of its time—such as advocating racial integration, the ordination of women, and acceptance of homosexuals—have much of their origins in his early reading of Temple. Even as Pike would rise in ecclesiastical office, this conviction stayed with him. As the dean of the Cathedral of St. John the Divine in the 1950s, for example, his public and earnest declaration that "nothing is secular to God, and any concern of the sons of man is a concern to God" affirms his belief in Temple's "sacramental universe." In sum, Pike found in Temple an encouragement to love both God and the language and conflicts of the secular world.

Having found within Anglicanism a tradition of scholasticism, a liturgy, and a prayer book with which he was somewhat familiar from his worship as a Roman Catholic, and at least a generalized approval of social and political activism by its foremost archbishop, Pike had but one more spiritual hurdle to leap privately before becoming a more fully committed communicant. This was to prove to his satisfaction that the Anglican Communion was *catholic*, as Pike had understood the word while a practicing member of the Roman Catholic Church: that is, historically part of the apostolic succession to St. Peter. The extraordinary effort that he personally put into proving this point reveals, once again, that he had been not so much a "thoroughgoing agnostic" before he became an Anglican as he had been an increasingly dissatisfied Roman Catholic. His confirmation into Anglicanism was, in his description, a move to worship in a communion "more Catholic than the Church which is colloquially referred to by that name," and he detailed in a letter to his mother written in the mid-1940s the results of his exhaustive research to prove that the Church of England was part of the same Church founded by St. Peter:

> I want to assure you that there is no break in episcopal succession and no loss of orders. There is no question into which I have gone more thoroughly—(unless you count the Federal Rules)—and I have spent many an hour in the Library of Congress reading secondary authorities of all shades of thought, R.C., Anglican, Greek, Protestant—also many of the primary source documents—and I was satisfied without question the apostolic succession has been continuous since the missionaries from the Greek Church planted the Catholic Faith in England in the fifth century. True, from about 1100 to 1550 or so the English Church was a good deal of the time under Papal domination . . . but all through it remained the same Church of England with the succession passed on from bishop to bishop.

He began referring to himself as an Anglo-Catholic in letters to his mother, and, indeed, it is somewhat inaccurate to speak of Pike's conversion to Anglicanism, as it could be argued that he simply had exchanged a Roman Catholicism for an English Catholicism. And in his newfound dedication to the Anglican Communion and the Episcopal Church, he suddenly developed a fervent dislike of his earlier Roman Catholicism. "The authoritarianism, the fear, the keeping of people in ignorance and superstition, the heartless cruelty to the individual—all that the Axis powers stand for has its spiritual expression in the Roman Church," he had written to his mother in 1941, in an ultimately successful attempt to persuade her to join him. This antipodal reversal of his earlier devout Roman Catholicism was characteristic of Pike's later hyperbolic enthusiasms in politics and theology; he was a natural partisan, either 100 percent in favor of an idea or spiritual movement, or 100 percent opposed. And, in his insistence that he had remained loyal to what he considered the true catholicism, he prefigured his later opposition to the Episcopal Church two decades later, when he claimed that his adopted communion also had obscured its original, first-century meaning with it insistence upon belief in later doctrines such as the Trinity.

Both his zeal in defending Anglicism and his insistence upon remaining historically and liturgically true to what he believed were the practices of the early Catholic Church can be seen in his sometimes barbed correspondence conducted at this same time with Walter Kropp in 1943–44. Pike's former teacher at Santa Clara had kept in contact with him throughout the war years, when Kropp was traveling frequently to the East Coast. In the fall of 1943, for example, Kropp had found time while passing through New York City to send a postcard to Pike at his Arlington, Virginia, home recommending that he read Karl Adam's *The Spirit of Catholicism*. Knowing of his former pupil's study of Protestant theologians, Kropp had penciled an additional brief message at the bottom of the card: "Stop reading heretics!" Pike's letter in response a month later began formally with the salutation "Dear Father Kropp"; gone, apparently for the time being, was the camaraderie of his undergraduate days when he had addressed his mentor as "Father Walter." Countering his former teacher's reading suggestion, Pike wrote Kropp that he in turn should read Temple, "whose depth as an orthodox theologian (I need only mention 'Man, Nature, and God') is only matched by the leadership he has given the English people toward measures of vital social reform." (Pike, apparently in the heat of this composition, transposed the first two words of Temple's title.) Referring pointedly to "we Anglicans," Pike asserted that "we now best represent primitive, orthodox Catholicism with the highest standards of intellectual honesty and freedom of spirit in its access to Him, and the best articulation of His message."

In Pike's conviction that he was a communicant in a church "more Catholic than the Church which is colloquially referred to by that name," the friendship was increasingly strained, but not irrevocably broken, between these two churchmen in their continued correspondence. For example, in an exchange of letters later in 1944 about evolution, Pike took to task the Roman Church for its "stubborn opposition" to Charles Darwin's theory, "when the facts of evolution were presented to the world." Such an action, he wrote, put the Roman Church in the same position "with the Bible-belt Fundamentalists" in not finding, "as our great Anglican theologians did, that the concept of evolution afforded great insights into the knowledge of God and His works." Slightingly, he once again encouraged his former teacher to read "Abp [Archbishop] Temple's 'Nature Man and God' re this relationship (if this book is not on the Index.)" Yet in this same scathing letter to Kropp, Pike was capable of closing with a remarkable grace note. As if he could not let pass unqualified his earlier harsh irony regarding Temple's book, Pike now wrote with an evident sincerity "to express my gratitude to you for remembering me at the Altar all these years." (Kropp had told Pike that he prayed regularly for the return of his favorite former pupil to the Roman Catholic communion.) Pike continued: "I am sure that that has played a part in God's giving me, entirely unmerited, the gift of Faith after so many years of searching. Please continue your prayers for me that I may continue to find many opportunities for expressing in works my gratitude for His saving Grace."

The "opportunities for expressing in works my gratitude" were taking the definite shape of a career as a cleric within the Anglican Communion. Although Pike remained what William James had termed a "first-born" practitioner of his faith, never truly having experienced a period of disbelief followed by conversion, he had felt growing within his consciousness another type of conversion—to the religious vocation—throughout 1942–43. In spring 1943, he formally applied to the Episcopal Church to be recognized as a postulant, the first step of religious study and reflection toward being ordained as an Episcopal deacon or priest. (The position of deacon within the Episcopal Church is an ordained order.) "I have for some time been firmly convinced that after the war I should not return to the law, but devote my full time to the Church," Pike wrote in his application for study. "I believe that I can be of greater use to God, especially in the turmoil of the post-war world," he continued, "if I am prepared, by training and commitment, to minister in the name of His Church to such of His people as come under my care."

Esther Pike was extraordinarily supportive of her husband's professional decision to enter holy orders after the war. After all, she had married Pike the previous year under the mutual assumption that eventually he would return as a layman and a civilian to his law practice, rather than to a less-well-paid Episcopal priesthood. She had also very effectively managed his legal publishing business while he was occupied with his navy duties and his reading, upon this same assumption. Nevertheless, she acquiesced, or actively concurred, with Pike's decision. She continued her Protestant religious instruction, and, on April 13, 1943, their marriage was solemnized in a ceremony at All Saints Episcopal Church in Frederick, Maryland.

This church ceremony was Pike's latest attempt to resolve the vexing question of the annulment of his first marriage and to satisfy the requirement of Episcopal canon law as expressed in that church's Book of Common Prayer: "Let the deacons be the husbands of one wife, ruling their children and their own house well." Before requesting his admission to the postulancy in April, Pike had again written to Bishop Stevens in California. On March 23, 1943, Stevens answered in a handwritten note. "Dear Mr. Pike," he wrote, "I am sorry that I have been so rushed during the past few days that I have not been able to answer your kind letter." The bishop then continued in a lawyerly style equal to Pike's own: "I can say that if you were now petitioning for the right to remarry, I would (with the necessary legal approval) give my consent." Pike was foxed again; he was a skillful enough lawyer to realize immediately that this note was not an official decree of annulment, but something analogous to a civil judge's advisory opinion. He privately noticed Stevens's careful use of the conditional: "*if* you *were* now petitioning" and "*with* the necessary legal approval" (italics added). That this message was handwritten and bore no indication that a copy was to be preserved in the diocesan archives, as was required by Episcopal canon law in decisions of annulment (which Pike surely knew) was another indication that Stevens was not speaking ex cathedra and was providing only a tentative judgment. In fact, in later years, the only proof of the existence of this note was Pike's word that he had received it. Philip Adams, the chancellor of the diocese of California during Pike's later tenure as bishop there, was said by Stringfellow and Towne to have had a letter written to him by Pike in which the latter quoted to the chancellor an excerpt from the Stevens letter of 1943; the two biographers reproduced the excerpt in their book about Pike. But apparently there is no record of the original letter in the Los Angeles diocese's archives. However, Pike's word from the bishop of Los Angeles apparently was sufficient documentation for him to have obtained his church's marriage ceremony a few weeks later that year at a parish in Maryland. With the unique flamboyance that seemed almost inescapable with Pike, their infant daughter, Catherine, was present among the wedding party in a baby carriage.

Pike later distributed to critical churchmen a typed statement of what he called "the basic facts" in 1943: "I wrote Bishop Stevens, caught him up to date, and asked for a formal expression of his decision as to the null character of the first union. He granted this request, and, following his direction, we had our marriage solemnized in the Church." Of course, "the basic facts" were nothing similar to what he so described. The bishop's "consent" was not his "direction" that the couple marry. Pike also neglected to note that the bishop's consent was given in answer only to hypothetical situations, and was also hearsay, as there was only secondhand word that the bishop actually had so given his consent. As a lawyer, Pike would have known that such statements were not legally credible. Yet, even if such "facts" were not accepted by his fellow churchmen, he later cleverly made use of his lack of a canonically legal annulment while he was being considered for the California bishopric; he argued that, like Augustine, his early lapses in moral and legal judgment contributed to the strength of his later Christian faith: "In short, I have experienced the meaning of St. Augustine's words, 'O *felix culpa*, O happy guilt, which brought redemption.' " He continued in this same message, "Incidentally, though I certainly do not aspire to his level of usefulness to the Church, it is interesting to note that, in spite of a 'past' much more colorful than mine (I am not busy preparing my 'Confessions'), St. Augustine was elected and consecrated a Bishop in the Church of God."

In any case, both Pike and his second wife were now in 1943 safely inside the Anglican Communion. And, once accepted that spring into the postulancy by the diocese of Washington, D.C., Pike seems to have been placed on a fast track for future ecclesiastical advancement. His rapid rise through the church ranks may have been due to the exigencies of wartime and also partly due to Pike's own restlessness, the almost compulsive physical and mental hyperactivity he exhibited once he had made a decision or chosen a new career. For instance, the usual academic requirement and residency tenure for the completion of a postulancy was, as specified by the canons of the diocese of Washington, "a certificate from seminary showing one year's work." Thereafter, a postulant was eligible to be admitted for further study as a candidate for holy orders. However, once Pike was accepted as a postulant in April 1943, he was admitted as a candidate for studying holy orders in September after only five months. Thereafter, he was ordained a deacon on December 21, 1944.

This rapid advancement also may have been due to the theological rigor and the clerical prominence of Pike's mentor in Washington during his postulancy and candidacy. This was Rev. Howard A. Johnson, then curate, or assistant minister, at what is called the "church of the presidents," the historic St. John's Episcopal, just across from the White House on Lafayette Square. At the time he met Pike, Johnson was already acquiring a reputation as one of the Church's most promising scholars. At his encouragement, Pike began taking his first Protestant seminary classes at Virginia Theological Seminary, where Johnson also taught part-time. Two years younger than Pike and also a former UCLA undergraduate, Johnson was comparatively self-effacing, but he did not allow a sense of Christian humility to prevent him from occasionally reminding his friend that he was Pike's ecclesiastical and academic superior. Johnson was one of the few who was not too intimidated to call Pike's intellectual bluff. He was Pike's intellectual "sustainer," in the diplomatic word of one who knew them both, and "he could make Jim face up to the absurd lines he was taking."

Their relationship continued into the next two decades and was described by their mutual acquaintances in the Church as being highly cordial and intellectually synergetic, rather than confrontational. Johnson would be named as godfather to Pike's first son; he would be among Pike's first choices to join his staffs at Columbia University and at the Cathedral of St. John the Divine; and he would coauthor two popular books with Pike in the 1950s. Those who knew both of them sometimes intuited that each man provided professionally or emotionally what the other most lacked. Pike needed the orthodox solidity of collaborating with Johnson, who had studied at Princeton University and at St.

Augustine's College in Canterbury, England. Johnson, considerably less self-aggrandizing for his part, seemed to relish the private excitements of regularly challenging Pike's intellectual and ecclesiastic enthusiasms and his association with a church and journalistic celebrity.

After tutelage under Johnson, Pike was ordained at St. John's in late 1944 by Bishop Angus Dun of the Washington diocese. Dun, who already was regarded nationally with an almost patriarchal affection by many Episcopalians, would continue to serve his church for the next two decades, and, ironically, would chair the so-called Dun Committee of bishops which in October 1966 evaluated the heresy charges considered to be brought against then-bishop James Pike. On Thursday, December 21, 1944, two days before the Fourth Sunday in Advent, Dun read the text for the ordination of deacons from the Episcopal Book of Common Prayer, exhorting Pike, " 'Likewise must the deacons be grave, not double-tongued, not given to much wine, nor greedy of filthy lucre; holding the mystery of the faith in pure conscience.' " To this assertion, and to further interrogations regarding his faith by his bishop, Pike answered, also reading from the text: " 'I will do so, by the help of God.' "

Within fourteen months of his ordination, Pike's second child, James Albert Pike Jr., was born on January 16, 1946. By that time, Pike had been discharged from the navy, had sold his interest in the legal publishing firm, and had accepted an $1,800-a-year appointment as a curate at St. John's, rather than returning to his law practice. This monetary sacrifice was a worldly testament to his religious honesty. From the sordidness of his first, failed marriage, the responsibilities following his second marriage and the births of his two children, and his private restlessness as a former government lawyer, Pike apparently had taken to heart William Temple's message in *Nature, Man, and God* that only from a sacramental, Christological point of view was life made bearable, that, in Temple's words, "There is given hope of making human both politics and economics, and of making effectual both faith and love." Parallel thoughts were expressed by Pike in a letter to his mother, who earlier had written to her son expressing her anxiety over his forsaking his law practice: "As to the law *vs.* the Christian ministry," he wrote back, "the law is a noble profession. . . . But if a person is granted the vision to see the realities of life and the only answer to persistent evil and maladjustment—that being the gospel of Jesus Christ—then he could never rate saving people's property & money—or gaining more of them—as high as bringing their twisted lives into the pattern of Christ."

His piety did not necessarily mean that he had renounced worldly ambition, however. As he had written to the Washington diocese, on first applying for candidacy, "as soon as I am released from the Navy, I will study one year at Oxford and one year in an American seminary before seeking advancement to the priesthood." A year's study of theology at an Oxford college would be a valuable cachet, he knew, for his financial prospects within the Episcopal Church; and, for other personal reasons, Pike was desirous of adding an Oxford residency to his curriculum vitae. Keenly aware of his western, provincial beginnings in academics, he was always ambitious to test himself, and prevail, at more prestigious universities, such as had been his experience at Yale University. Just on the cusp of his studying for the Episcopal priesthood, Pike perhaps can be forgiven for writing an exultant letter to his mother, favorably comparing the Episcopal Church's preparation of priests to that of the Roman Catholic Church. "They [the Episcopal Church] want our men to go to the very best universities," he assured her. His personal acceptance to the "very best" was thought by Pike also to be assured.

Pike's academic candidacy for the priesthood began with a lasting disappointment. Oxford University discouraged his idea of applying for theological study. "Dear Sir," a university official wrote in late 1944,

> I think it does not seem likely that you would be accepted to study for the degree of B.D., which is an advanced degree. For it, you must show that you are qualified, and then pass an examination of a high standard; it includes translation from at least two of the languages: Hebrew, Greek, Latin. [Pike had attempted to study and struggled unsuccessfully with the Greek lexicon while at Virginia Theological Seminary.]
>
> Further, you cannot apply now for admission at an indefinite period "after the war," but for admission in a particular term. I gather that you cannot yet decide that. And, after the war, Colleges will be very full of English students returning to

complete their interrupted studies. There will be very little room for overseas students unless they have a very good record—Yours sincerely. . . .

The casual bluntness of this reply always rankled Pike. He did not consider the score settled, or his intellectual worth demonstrably rewarded, until he was awarded a sabbatical to study theology, this time at Cambridge University, in the mid-1960s.

For the moment, however, he dealt with his disappointment by increasing his activities. While serving his curacy at St. John's in 1945, Pike also began a popular and energetic chaplaincy to the Episcopal students at Roman Catholic Georgetown University. And he applied—and was accepted—at his first choice among seminary schools in the United States, Union Theological Seminary, on the Upper West Side of Manhattan, in New York City. His American application was fortuitous. Although, unlike Oxford University's, the stone buildings of Union Seminary possess only one crenellated tower, and the tower overlooks not a river meadow but traffic on Broadway, part of Harlem, and the bricks of Columbia University, the faculty at Union during this time was perhaps the most intellectually distinguished at any Protestant seminary in the world. The professors included the well-known theologians Reinhold Niebuhr and Paul Tillich, and within immediate memory among many faculty was the face of their academic colleague Dietrich Bonhoeffer, who had left New York City voluntarily for Germany in 1939 and had been killed by the Nazis in 1945. By early fall of 1946, Pike had cobbled together a financial arrangement by which he took Old and New Testament classes at General Theological Seminary, also in New York City, and was paid as a tutor and fellow there while attending additional classes at Union. Esther Pike stayed intermittently at their Washington apartment, caring for their two children. There were other changes that year in the Pike family. In the summer of 1946, Pearl McFadden became a widow for the second time, when Claude McFadden died. Indomitable, Pike's mother would marry her third husband within two years, and also outlive him.

Pike worked that year with his usual fervor. By the end of his first semester in New York, he had completed a total of five classes and two tutorials, both at General and at Union. In a repeat of his academic excellence in the law school at USC, he received the grade of A in all but one of his seminary classes. But the old impropriety of his first marriage in 1938 also followed him to General, where, in Pike's later recollection, "someone raised the issue." He was requested in 1946 to defend the ecclesiastical validity of his second marriage and his suitability as a seminary student before a specially called committee consisting of the dean and selected General Seminary faculty. Angus Dun, who was a good friend to Pike until almost the very end, provided an opinion in which he stated that he would "without question" have granted Pike an annulment within his diocese under the same circumstances as the dissolution of his first marriage in the Los Angeles diocese. Pike subsequently was, in his triumphant words, "promptly confirmed" to his tutorship and fellowship at General.

He was a seminarian with an unusual history in other ways. Pike, while at Union, "seldom appeared in class," in one description, and fulfilled most of his academic responsibilities at that institution either by providing an essay at the end of term or meeting privately with the professor to discuss his readings. His attempts at establishing social and professional contacts were apparently at least equal in importance to him as his academic assignments. Pike's appointment book for 1946–47 records an active social life, including his introduction to the Right Reverend Charles K. Gilbert, then the Episcopal bishop for the diocese of New York State, and visits with Paul and Hannah Tillich at their home. This friendship continued until Tillich's death in 1965. (Pike's consequent "contact" with Tillich's postmortem spirit deeply angered Hannah Tillich.) But during their lifetimes their friendship resulted in a cordial "Dear Paul" and "Dear Jim" correspondence, mainly in regard to mutual friends and academic vacations.

The question of what Pike learned or how he was influenced intellectually by Christian thinkers such as Tillich and Niebuhr during his year at Union is more problematical. Other men's ideas and beliefs were like a concave, silvered vessel that Pike occasionally held up to his eyes; all he usually saw was his own features, reflected and enlarged. From the examples of Niebuhr and Bonhoeffer he probably gained his belief that the practice of Christian faith inescapably meant becoming engaged in political action, while at the same time having a deep distrust of any positivist, liberal theology that society by its own volition can make itself any better. Pike, though politically activist and usually socially liberal, remained conservatively Anglo-Catholic in his liturgical practices and distrustful of secular authority. The influence of Tillich is more traceable in Pike's writings and life. Pike attended at least one seminar on Martin Luther led by Tillich at Union, in February 1947, at a time when Tillich was fully expounding his theory of the *kairos*. This transcendent experience was, in Tillich's words, "a moment in which the eternal breaks into the temporal, shaking and transforming it," and creating a new order or a new possibility of religious belief.

Tillich was certain that he and his religious associates had shared an experience of *kairos* at Berlin from 1919 to 1924, when the old European social and religious order was collapsing after the Great War. Similarly, Pike was to spend much of his subsequent clerical career in search of experiencing this numinous self- and history-transforming moment. This theological quest explains many of his later writings and his religious enthusiasms. The conviction that he was living at a unique "moment of truth" in the history of Christianity prompted Pike in the mid-1960s to write two of his most controversial books, *A Time for Christian Candor* (1964) and *What Is This Treasure?* (1966). His later interest in spiritualism was perhaps a desperate grasping after *kairos*, and the contemporary publicity regarding the recent discovery of the Dead Sea Scrolls was further proof to Pike that he was practicing his religion in a new Axial Age (the name given by Karl Jaspers to the period from 800 B.C.E. to 200 C.E. when nearly all the world's major religions appeared).

For his part, Tillich had almost perfectly anticipated both the temperament of his future seminary pupil and Pike's later experiences when he had written, ten years earlier in his *Interpretation of History*, of what he then defined as the "demonic," the "power in personal and social life that is creative and destructive at the same time. In the New Testament, men possessed by demons are said to know more about Jesus than those who were normal, but they know it as a condemnation of themselves because they are divided against themselves."

The contradictory impulses within Pike probably were most balanced throughout 1946–47 at Union Seminary. On the one hand, there was the luxury of independent study and of solitary, contemplative walks within the beautiful garden of the seminary's courtyard; on the other, there were the student cafés, the crowded, postwar campus of Columbia University, and the drinking dives along Broadway. But however intellectually stimulating or physically sensuous it was to study at a seminary, there was also Pike's compulsion to succeed, particularly by the Ivy League eastern standards of his contemporaries. With his usual willingness to work two, three, or sometimes even four jobs simultaneously, Pike in the fall of 1946, in addition to his tutorship, fellowship, and academic classes, also provided pastoral services to a small Episcopal church in upstate New York. Before he had completed his requirements that fall for his B.D. degree from Union, he additionally began looking for full-time church employment.

The pickings were slim. The best that was offered Pike from out of state was the position of "Episcopal Chair of the Bible" at the University of Texas, at Austin. The candidate was expected, as described in a letter to him, to "interest college boys and girls in the Episcopal Church at this state university," where a majority of the students at that time were nonecclesiastical Protestants, while the university itself was at best only regionally distinguished. The annual salary was less than $4,000, although "living quarters" were possible on campus. (The Episcopal Church official in Texas who extended this offer, John E. Hines, was later to become the presiding bishop of the Episcopal Church when Pike was accused of heresy.)

Pike turned down the offer. He had on January 26, 1947, accepted the position of rector at Christ Church, the Poughkeepsie church where he had been preaching and providing some pastoral services. He was not necessarily biased against a calling to a western Episcopal church, but he also had his personal ambition, and he had his pride at demonstrating his mastery for high place and honors. He was determined that he and his family would not return west until he was—one way or another—an unqualified success.

III

Making It: From Poughkeepsie
to Columbia University

Are you going to that salesman downtown?

—Reputed remark of a Vassar College professor
of religion in reference to the Reverend James A. Pike

Christ Church, incorporating a neo-Gothic nave built in 1888 and a
Tudor-styled rectory added in 1903, is located in what was then an old-
money neighborhood of Poughkeepsie, New York. Both structures are
substantially constructed of rose-colored sandstone. The churchyard, a
block wide and defined by the intersections of Barclay, Academy, Montgomery, and Carroll streets, is, even today, like the unexpected green
space of a proprietary park within a crowded neighborhood. In Pike's
day, the houses facing the churchyard on its four sides were single-
family, and many were owned by the descendants of the first industrialists of Poughkeepsie, who after the Civil War had moved up the
southeastern hills of the city to Academy Street. By the time of the

Pike's arrival in 1946, the old Tudor rectory had become the parish house, containing the church's offices.

One street away from the church was a comparatively modest, narrow two-and-a-half–story frame house at the intersection of Academy and Barclay streets. Although perhaps not as finely appointed or as spacious as some of the houses in the neighborhood, the new Episcopal rectory at 15 Barclay Street nevertheless had an outstanding view of the churchyard and buildings. In sum, the benefice at Poughkeepsie appeared to be a promising first appointment for this thirty-four-year-old, newly ordained Episcopal priest, his intelligent and vivacious wife, and their two small children. (Pike continued intermittently throughout 1946–47 to attend classes at Union Seminary, but did not graduate either year.)

Once he had settled in Poughkeepsie with Esther, Jim Jr., and Catherine, Pike lost no time in imposing his personality upon the style of worship practiced at Christ Church. There was, for example, the instance of the altar candles. Pike's predecessor, Rev. Alexander Griswold Cummings, had for forty-six years been an advocate of Low Church Episcopalianism and determinably kept the altar at Christ Church physically bare except for a simple crucifix and ceremonial vessels. The absence of altar candles apparently had not risen as an important issue at Christ Church, and a majority of the congregation had been content with, or at least tacitly accepted, Reverend Cummings's bare altar. Pike, however, wanted candles.

This difference in the liturgical furnishings preferred at Christ Church by the new rector in contrast to his predecessor was an instance of the "High Church" and "Low Church" parties that had emerged within the Anglican Communion in the late seventeenth century and had continued within the Episcopal Church to Pike's time. Generally speaking, High Church Episcopalians such as Pike emphasized the primacy of apostolic succession, preferred to see its clergy dressed in formal surplices and other elaborate vestments, favored the use of incense, bells, and candles during worship, and considered the public administration of sacraments a much more significant means to God's grace than the individual's private experience of salvation. They made up the Anglo-Catholic wing of the Church. But there was a significant and long Low Church tradition within both the English and American communions that declined the use of the "smells and bells" liturgical style of the Anglo-Catholics, emphasized the importance of effective preaching and evangelism, and was profoundly uncomfortable with the idea of a decorated altar. This party of the Anglican Communion had its historical origins in Calvinism, and its expression within the Episcopal Church was fully illustrated by the nineteenth-century Low Churchman Bishop Manton Eastman of Boston, who on a visit to one of his diocese's churches had noticed that the rector there had placed two vases of flowers on the altar, and thus rebuked him: "Mr. Steemstra, although I know that you make no idolatrous use of these flowers, I cannot on principle take part in a service with them on the holy table." It is a testament to the Anglican Communion's successful practice of "a middle way," or honorable compromise among its communicants, that two such disparate parties had remained within Anglicanism.

The presence or absence of altar candles had been a point of contention unresolved by compromise between the High and Low Church parties within the Episcopal Church since the nineteenth century; the Church's general assembly considered petitions in 1868, 1871, and 1874 to prohibit their use. Within the twentieth century, altar candles as a general rule were favored by Episcopalians of a more Anglo-Catholic tradition, such as Pike, and at Episcopal churches where the priest and the congregation also favored votive candles. The use either of votive or altar candles had been strongly resisted by Low Churchmen such as Reverend Cummings.

Pike resolved this self-created issue without further consultation with the vestrymen by making a special trip to New York City in order to buy two brass candleholders. He privately placed them in Christ Church on an evening preceding an Advent Sunday. (In High Church Episcopal worship, four candles are successively lit weekly to represent the four Advent Sundays of the season preceding the birth of Jesus Christ. A fifth "Christ candle" may be lit at Christmas.) It would have been difficult, even churlish, for any Low Church advocates within the congregation to have protested this special illumination in the four weeks preceding the celebration of Christ's birth. And, in a politic and charming concession to the anti-candle faction within his congregation,

Pike had the two brass candlesticks bought at church expense beautifully engraved with a verse from Revelation 22:5: "They shall need no light or lamp or sun, for the Lord shall be their light."

The public response to such a take-charge ministry was favorable. A remarkable increase of activity at Christ Church was reported after Pike became the priest in charge. He summarized and publicized these activities at Poughkeepsie in the church newspaper, the *Christ Church Courier*, which he established during his tenure there. A total of 108 souls were listed by the *Courier* as having been confirmed by Pike in the Episcopal Church, plus 63 others who transferred into the congregation, plus 18 others who were received by Pike as converts "from Rome." Thirty-four members, for whatever personal reasons, transferred their memberships to other parishes. There was thus a net gain of 155 Episcopalians at Christ Church. These figures later would be seriously contraindicated by the diocese, but, for the present, there seemed to be much in favor of this new rector.

Pike also convinced this previously unassertive congregation to sponsor a daily nursery school open to the public, to begin radio broadcasts of the Sunday services (radio programs by mainstream denominations were unusual in the 1940s), to organize dating and social clubs for the younger parishioners, to establish a parish lending library open to the public, and to create Christ Church's own theatrical troupe, the Canterbury Players. Both the diocese and the congregation had known before Pike's arrival that his intellectual and theological credentials were impressive; what they subsequently discovered to their pleasure was that, spiritually or socially, inside church or outside it, Jim Pike also was *fun*.

"It has been truly said, 'People travel miles to hear Dr. Pike!' " the *New Hampshire* [Episcopal] *Churchman* editorially enthused, in a visible sign that the fame of Pike's preaching—and his personality—was spreading among Episcopal churches up and down the East Coast. Pike himself apparently thought of his sermons more as improvisational performances than planned literary acts, and, despite his lawyerly habit of keeping copies of his later writings, his sermons from the 1940s exist only as sparse typed or handwritten notes to be used as memory aids in the pulpit. Nevertheless, the extant notes of the sermon Pike delivered on an Advent Sunday in 1946, entitled "Repent Ye," intimate the intellectually nervous, hyperactive energy Pike must have later projected on Sundays from the Christ Church pulpit. His theological positions in this sermon are borrowed from Paul Tillich's concept of "the eternal now" and Tillich's definition of God as "the ground of all being," but the thoughts grouped into imagistic clusters are Pike's own, and his typed notes for his sermon, transcribed and indented as in his original manuscript, are concrete poetry:

> *HELL is NOW* Van Gogh (prisoners in circle—walls)
>   insanity; suicide
> Doom in OT—Hiroshima
> Tantalus—yearnings
> Stephen Crane's poetry
> Eccl 12:6
> What worse has Hell to offer—separation from
> the ground of meaning—God

> *HEAVEN IS NOW*
> integration with the overarching meaning of life
> —unity with God, man—What more has Heaven to
> offer than life like that?
>   INSTALLMENT PURCHASE OF TAXICAB
> The Kdom of God has come upon you/Thy kingdom come
> (1st and 2d Comings of X)
>   REPENT YE
> JUDGMENT IS NOW—Wolsey, Henry; Niagara falls

. . . .

> 'The Kdom of Heaven is within you'?
> No, IN YOUR MIDST

. . . .

> Child at Xmas (dull, sharp-tongued aunts, etc.
> Wouldn't seem like Zmas—to God wouldn't see[m] like
> Heaven without us.

Thus preached Pike. Certainly by the late 1940s there were rivals in the public performances of homiletics; for example, the U.S. Senate's Presbyterian chaplain, Rev. Peter Marshall; the Roman Catholic bishop Fulton J. Sheen; and the popular Protestant evangelist, Billy Graham were then arrived at or reaching their rhetorical heights. But in his combination of cutting-edge Protestant theology, of images apparently wrested with great personal effort both from depth psychology and the daily newspapers, and of High Church celebrations, Reverend Pike must have sounded and appeared irresistible.

Of course, not everyone was charmed. "Oh, he had a scalpel-like wit," one faculty member at Vassar College remembered of him, and it was noticed by other female faculty there how frequently Pike turned this scalpel-like wit upon his wife, Esther. "We sometimes wondered how she put up with him," this Vassar professor added. Also, both men and women who socialized with the Pikes saw how avidly the new rector consumed his glasses of wine and his frequent cocktails. It was not that Pike at this period of his life drank unhealthily or embarrassingly, but his consumption of liquor was noticeable to his associates even by the relatively alcohol-tolerant standards of eastern town-and-country society of the late 1940s.

But, all in all, Rev. James Pike and Christ Church were a good match. A survey from 1947 to 1949 of Pike's weekly column in the church newspaper, "Parish Notes," is a testament to his intimate involvement with his parish in all the little domestic emergencies, the daily banalities, and the forgivable venial sins by which humans manage to live and love among one another. On October 1, 1948, Pike was pleased to report to his congregation that the church's recent Men's Club clambake was "a great success numerically, *gustatorially*, and—we suspect—though the report is not yet ready, financially." On March 7, 1947, he good-naturedly complained that "there are never any books in our Circulating Library. They are borrowed just as soon as they are purchased." On August 27, 1948, he found it necessary to announce in his column, "A couple of recent incidents in the life of the Parish family make it necessary for the Rector to preach this Sunday on 'Why People Gossip.'" On January 21, 1949, he found it useful in his newspaper to quote without further comment from St. Chrysostom on drunkenness:

"If you say, 'Would that were no wine because of the drunkards,' then you must say, going on by degree, 'Would that there were no steel because of murder' . . . and 'Would that there were no women because of adultery.' " And on May 6, 1949, with no apparent improvement in the inventory of the lending library, or of the habits of some of its patrons, there was "*A Special Request from the Rector*" (Pike's italics): "Would any who have borrowed books from the Rector's library or Parish library please return them soon?"

In November 1948 the *Christ Church Courier* reported "the first baby to be born in Christ Church Rectory." This was Esther and James Pike's third child and second daughter, Constance Ann, born on November 18, 1948. "Mother and daughter—and father—doing fine," the newspaper reported. (Esther Pike, having postponed her own legal studies, was seldom out of the nursery during their time in New York State. Their next child was also born at a two-year interval, in 1950.)

After the birth of his third child, a less ambitious minister, or at least a more circumspect one, might have chosen to perceive in his appointment to Christ Church an instance of God's tender mercies. If not mercy, there was at least good fortune. The financial aspect of living in Poughkeepsie for a beginning minister with a wife and three small children certainly was preferable to that at an unestablished ministry at a campus in Texas. James Pike, however, had grander ambitions beyond his parish.

The earliest documentation of his agenda was a letter Pike received dated February 3, 1947, even before he had been officially installed at Christ Church, from Rev. Arthur L. Kinsolving. Kinsolving was the latest prominent member of a Baltimore family whose name had been formidable within the Episcopal Church's history since the late eighteenth century, having repeatedly provided the Church with bishops and priests. Indeed, the male Kinsolvings appeared to the episcopacy born; when Arthur Kinsolving, himself the grandson of a bishop and a cousin to another, became a deacon in 1923, he had been ordained by his paternal uncle, also an Episcopal bishop. At the time he wrote to Pike, Kinsolving was the rector at Trinity Church in Princeton, New Jersey, and within the year he would be appointed rector to the even more prestigious St. James Church at Madison Avenue and 71st Street, where many of New York's wealthiest Episcopal families worshiped. In sum, Kinsolving was a member of that social and religious class whom Pike had emulated upon his first trip east, when he had written to his mother that "practically every churchgoer you meet in our level of society is Episcopalian."

Kinsolving's letter of 1947 was both complimentary and preemptive. "Dear Mr. Pike," he wrote, the absence of a clerical title perhaps a deliberate reminder to Pike that, despite his being a social acquaintance with Paul Tillich and a soon-to-be-rector, he was also at present just a tutor at General Theological Seminary who did not yet possess his divinity degree. "The other day I heard that you had been called to the big parish in Poughkeepsie," Kinsolving began. "As a former Vassar trustee, I have been particularly interested in that because I have long hoped to see a clergyman of your caliber at Poughkeepsie." Kinsolving then came to his point. "Vassar draws a splendid group of girls of religious background, but the Episcopal Church has never provided them leadership." What was wanted by Kinsolving—and, by implication, by others of like mind and prominence within the Episcopal Church—was a rector of Anglo-Catholic sympathies who could identify with the students at Vassar during their crises of faith. Kinsolving noted, in an interestingly ambiguous comment to Pike, "You know what college students are like in their oblivion of churches at a distance."

The letter closed with an intimation of money. "The Committee for the Procter Foundation has seemed to me to be strangely inactive," seemingly apropos of nothing regarding Vassar College, since the William Alexander Procter Foundation paid the salaries, benefits, and office expenses for Episcopal chaplaincies at two universities. "We meet next Friday, and I am hopeful that we may get a move on, and also to look in your direction, if you are not already signed up. My warm wishes to your wife and to you, Yours sincerely, Arthur Kinsolving." Kinsolving then added a handwritten note at the bottom of the typed letter, in a tone both imperative and familiar: "Jim—You better call tonight if you get back in time, since they meet tomorrow."

Pike's response was not kept in his files. But soon after his arrival at Poughkeepsie, he began what he called an "aggressive" ministry to the Episcopal students at Vassar, accompanied by an equally aggressive criticism of the college, both from his pulpit and outside it. Strangely, his harshest comments were ideological, not religious. Pike sounded like a strident Cold War warrior. From 1947 to 1949—a period when the House Un-American Activities Committee indicted the "Hollywood 10" and the first perjury trial of the accused spy Alger Hiss dominated much of the nation's headlines—Pike adopted a similarly prosecutorial style toward Vassar. He publicly described the faculty there as "Unitarian, humanist, materialist, and Marxist." The campus itself was a speaking ground for "avowed Communists." And when a Vassar student published an article questioning the reality of the Virgin Birth and, in Pike's opinion, was insufficiently chastised by the college president, the rector was quoted in the local newspaper, "Dr. Pike said that at the Alger Hiss trial, 'It came out that Whittaker Chambers wrote a similar article in his student days at Columbia. A stand was taken. He was dismissed.' "

Pike may or may not have picked this quarrel in 1947 in a deliberate attempt to gain the patronage of some conservative and powerful figures within his church. But the resulting controversy, however it may have arisen, certainly advanced his career within his diocese. Pike reflected back on these early controversies in 1953, after his elevation to the deanship of the Cathedral of St. John the Divine in New York. The occasion was an interview for the national Sunday newspaper supplement *This Week* magazine, in which Pike was described in the headline as "The Outspoken Dean." Pike, who was misleadingly identified within the article as the former Vassar chaplain, was quoted as declaring that "the churches should 'clean house' of any clergymen that are Communists or fellow travelers," and that his own "battle against 'humanist secularism' began six years ago at Christ Church, Poughkeepsie."

In the subsequent decade of the 1960s Pike gained something of a reputation as a social and political liberal, and during that time he seldom made reference to his confrontational activities in Poughkeepsie in the 1940s. The damage he had done there, however, was long-lasting. It resulted in the resignation under duress of the college chaplain (*not* James Pike) and a troubled administration for that college's first female president. Even more than half a century after these events, retired Vassar faculty and administrators—some of whom Reverend Pike had characterized as "sub-Christian"—remembered his political attacks and public confrontations in the late 1940s with a sense both of puzzled hurt and of abiding anger.

Vassar College, at first glance, did not appear to be the irreligious institution that Pike in the mid-1940s accused it of being. In the spring of 1946, Paul Tillich had accepted an invitation to speak on campus, followed by a semester during which the college's registrar had noticed enrollments in religion and philosophy courses had "increased sharply." Vassar was attended by 1,366 women in 1948, of whom all but 43 identified themselves as members of a church or synagogue. The Episcopal Church had the most numerous representation on campus, with about 500 who described themselves as members—"45% are ours," as Pike emphatically expressed it. The Jewish faith was the second most populous on campus, with about 200 students. An ecumenical religious service was held on campus for all students every Sunday at the Vassar Community Church by the college's chaplain, Rev. Charles McCormick. It was he, two years younger than Pike and just as well educated, whom the rector soon came to see as an impediment to Christianity at Vassar College and, possibly, as a rival to Pike's own religious leadership.

"The Rev. Charles G. McCormick rides bicycle to his class in 'Development of a Personal Philosophy' at Vassar College," read the caption of the three-column photograph that accompanied the flattering interview in the Sunday Poughkeepsie newspaper the first week of July 1948. Pike scarcely could have missed noticing this article, which was headlined "Meet the Clergy." There was also the prominently displayed quote: "Head of Vassar Community Church deplores accusation that college is 'community of secularism.' " The photograph showed a darkly handsome Chaplain McCormick bicycling energetically across campus dressed in a style both casually English and Ivy League: wearing a tailored, two-button tan suit, rather than the usual American businessman's double-breasted jacket; and an Oxford-collar shirt framing a tartan necktie. The book-filled wicker basket attached to his bicycle provided a donnish look.

McCormick, like Pike, had been raised a Roman Catholic, and became active as an undergraduate in local Episcopal and Unitarian churches. Like Pike, the chaplain was a highly personable and intellec-

tually arresting figure, with an interest in the theater and a flair for ama-
teur dramatics. He also was married with small children. After receiving
his undergraduate degree from Amherst College, McCormick attended
Union Theological Seminary where, unlike Pike, he obtained his B.D.
degree, as well as a doctorate in education from Columbia University.
At their first meeting in mid-1947, at a gathering of the Poughkeepsie
ministerial association, Pike seemed to take an instant dislike to
McCormick.

"Mr. McCormick does not regard any religion as something that
one ought to persuade others to believe," Pike wrote privately to
Charles Profitt, the administrator of the Columbia University Press,
and fellow Episcopalian, in November 1947. And equally provocative to
the rector was the reported way in which McCormick and another Vassar professor referred among themselves to Pike—as "that salesman
downtown." Their derogatory description of course got back to Pike. It
doubly stung. Pike interpreted the "salesman" label as an intellectual
dismissal of his proselytizing and social work at Christ Church; secondly, and more personally, he probably perceived in their verbal slight
an Ivy League–East Coast rejection of himself as a philistine lawyer-
cum-huckster from Los Angeles. Both McCormick and the other Vassar
faculty members consistently denied ever having described Pike in these
terms, but more than two years later, after he first claimed to have
learned of their remark, Pike was still bitterly complaining in 1949 to
the college president about the insult to his position.

Pike got a revenge of sorts on November 16, 1948, a date on which
the Vassar president happened to be absent from campus. He turned up
at the college that Tuesday afternoon in the company of the traveling
Anglican evangelist, Bryan Green, who was then conducting a New York
diocese preaching tour. On short notice, Pike pressured McCormick
into allowing Green to speak to a hastily assembled group of students at
the college's principal building, the Aula. McCormick himself gave an
uneasy introduction of Green. As Pike surely must have known—having
invited Green to preach at Christ Church the earlier week—the Reverend Green was no accomodationalist, and in fact prided himself on a
proselytizing and confrontational style of preaching more frequently
associated with Nonconformist chapels than with Anglican parishes.

"I know you will say that I am only an Englishman who knows nothing about conditions on campus," Green then, and later, told the students, in one of his favorite phrases of self-description. But this was not an expression of his false, much less real, modesty. Green removed any possible doubts about his authority by addressing his audiences as an exacting schoolmaster: "All I would ask you to do is to read the Acts of the Apostles; the first eight chapters will be quite enough," he told them. He then proceeded to warn the young women, including the Jewish students among them, about the dangers of their ecumenicity: "There does seem to me to be a danger in obtaining a pleasant, conciliatory spirit at too great a cost; it can mean allowing those who hold definite non-Christian convictions to prevent the making of definite and decisive Christian statements. This seems strange to me on a campus."

A majority of students left the talk at the Aula offended or puzzled; their chaplain, McCormick, was greatly nonplussed. Green took his usual position that, as he later stated to the college president, "whether people like me or dislike me is of no consequence to me, to society, or to God." Pike seemed pleased, both with himself and the way the talk had been conducted; and Vassar president Sarah Blanding when she later returned to campus and was told of the content of Green's speech, was furious.

"My Dear Mr. Pike," she wrote the following week to the rectory office, "a situation has arisen which I cannot allow to pass without presenting to you a vigorous protest. It involves the Reverend Bryan Green and is the result of his recent visits to the Vassar campus." (Green had returned later to the campus area, without an official invitation, after his Aula talk.) Blanding objected to Green's use of "pressure tactics, which I heartily dislike," and pointedly reminded Pike that "we have many Jewish students on our campus whose beliefs we respect and whose principles we certainly would not try to shake." Blanding curtly concluded her letter by noting that, if the action of Pike and Green had been accurately described to her, "the most generous statement I can think of at this point is that, if true, it was an unmitigated breach of hospitality."

Pike's answer on December 1, 1948—three days before the year's first Advent Sunday—was vociferous. His letter was composed of five and a half single-spaced typed pages detailing what he considered the anti-Christian bias among faculty and administrators at Vassar College, where "what is desired is an un-Christian influence." He denied that

Green's remarks at the Aula were intended as anti-Semitic, and claimed that Green in fact had "won the respect of several Jewish students whose respect Mr. McCormick has failed to attain." Pike complained again of his old hurt, that "the professor of religion with whom I have the most pleasant contacts referred to me as 'that salesman downtown.' " More ominously, he told Blanding that he had revisited the campus within the last week "to investigate" reportedly anti-Christian remarks made by Chaplain McCormick.

Writing four years after his forced resignation, Charles McCormick recalled that Vassar College's tacit policy from 1948 to 1949 was of "not dignifying Mr. Pike with a reply." But as Pike's multipage letters continued to be sent to President Blanding throughout 1949, it became increasingly difficult, and politically dangerous, to ignore the local rector. On April 5, 1949, Pike sent a five-page, single-spaced typed letter to Blanding again complaining of the reputed "salesman" remark; in a concluding paragraph he rebuked, and then forgave, Blanding for "our conversation [in] which you blamed me for the divisiveness and conflict which has occurred." He added: "However, I am hurt that you have so quickly forgotten that the first gun was fired by Mr. McCormick." On April 28, Pike wrote to Blanding that he had arranged for "one of my parishioners" to take shorthand notes of a talk given at the local YMCA by a Vassar professor of religion, thereby providing evidence, in Pike's opinion, that this professor "does not hold the Christian faith." (It was within six weeks of sending this letter that Pike was quoted in the Poughkeepsie newspaper comparing documents in the Alger Hiss perjury trial as equal in moral offense to the published essay by a Vassar student regarding the unlikelihood of the Virgin Birth.)

McCormick later recalled that, during this period, "it was harmful enough to have the name 'humanistic secularism' used by Dean Pike to describe a college program which differed from his own preferences," but that "the use of that gross representation in the context of Communism" was an act on Pike's part of "extreme irresponsibility." The ex-chaplain then dryly noted: "The results possible are obvious."

Pike was always extreme in his political rhetoric—as when, a new convert to Protestantism in the early 1940s, he in a letter to his mother equated Roman Catholicism with European fascism—but he was acting in 1948–49 on concerns that other, less dramatic Episcopalians also shared about the displacement of the subject of Christianity in secondary and higher education. The U.S. Supreme Court's decision in 1948 in *McCollum v. Board of Education*, which had banned religious instruction within public school buildings during time reserved for extracurricular activities, was viewed with alarm by national and regional Episcopal publications such as *The Living Church* and *The Southern Churchman*, and by some Episcopal educators within Pike's own diocese. Even the tactless, ubiquitous Bryan Green had received with Pike's encouragement an invitation to preach from the prestigious pulpit of Trinity Church, Wall Street, on the dangers to Christianity. By late 1948, Pike emerged in his diocese as the leading man for advocates of Christianity within higher education.

In the autumn of that year, Christ Church parish received a large grant in order to fund an assistant for Pike in his self-described "mission" to the Episcopal students at Vassar. On June 3, 1949, he announced to his parishioners that he had been appointed by their bishop to serve on the diocese's Commission on College Work. Two weeks later, Pike exulted in an interview with the local Poughkeepsie newspaper that by virtue of "the appointment of the Rt. Rev. Charles K. Gilbert, Bishop of New York," Pike now had "charge of Episcopal student work at Vassar College."

Pike thereafter acquired the habit of referring to himself in his official biographies as the Episcopal chaplain to Vassar College and, sometimes, "at" Vassar College for the years 1947 to 1949. Such was the description also provided for use in the alumni directory of Union Theological Seminary. This choice of wording implied an administrative connection to the college. The *real* chaplain at Vassar during those years, Charles McCormick, found this presumption to be particularly vexing. Even after Pike's assumption to the deanship at the Cathedral of St. John the Divine, McCormick was still trying to set the record straight, as when he wrote to *This Week* magazine following the favorable interview with Pike in 1953: "The assumption of the title 'Chaplain to the Episcopal students at Vassar' was in no sense official," McCormick wrote. "Dean Pike had no appointment from the Vassar trustees. From the college's point of view, all local pastors were potential resources for the students."

But as James Pike, the attorney, could have replied, the question of who was the college chaplain between 1947 and 1949 was becoming a moot point personally for McCormick—because Pike had arranged by 1949 that whoever occupied the Vassar chaplaincy, it would no longer be Charles McCormick. McCormick was out of his job. Without notifying the chaplain or the college's president, Pike had circulated a letter to the college's trustees, including Mrs. John D. Rockefeller Jr., urging that at their next meeting in September 1949, "steps will be taken to correct a situation in which the 'dice are loaded' against Christianity." The trustees at that meeting offered, and McCormick consequently accepted, a year's administrative leave, with the understanding that his employment contract would not be renewed after June 1950. Pike was noticeably indifferent to the possible unemployment of this father of two. As he wrote to the wife of a trustee on June 10, 1949, "Jesus said, 'You who are not with me are against me,' and the foolish remarks of Mr. McCormick and Mr. Howson [a Vassar religion professor] which I have quoted in the enclosed letter show how true this statement of our Lord is."

But the assumption of the title of chaplain to the Episcopal students at Vassar College was also becoming a moot point to Pike by the end of summer 1949. There was another chaplaincy in which he had a greater interest. Columbia University had been in contact with Pike since early 1948, in regard to filling the vacant post of university chaplain and assuming the chairmanship of an expanded department of religion. For the remaining two-thirds of that year, Pike and the university's provost had corresponded over terms of his salary, housing allowance, and teaching duties. Finally, in January 1949 (just as Pike's multipage missives to President Blanding had begun accelerating), Pike and Columbia University closed the deal: Pike was to become, officially, the university's chaplain and the religion department's chairman at an annual salary and housing allowance of $10,000, with duties to commence on September 1, 1949. The offer meant that, for the first time since he became a curate at St. John's in Washington, Pike's annual income was approaching what he had once earned as an attorney.

This appointment also may have been a deliverance to Pike in other ways. By his last year at Christ Church, he was accumulating significant administrative problems and a number of personal opponents. Foremost among the difficulties was what Pike described to his parishioners, only half-jokingly, as "the seamy side"—that is, the ledgers at Christ Church. The plain fact was that Pike had badly overspent his church's budget in enacting his new plans and programs. In midsummer 1947 he pointedly reminded his parishioners that "the new activities we are launching cost money—more than our budget or present income will cover, particularly since we still have to pay for the new boilers and the rectory repairs, and our Easter offering fell way below our necessary goal." On November 14 of that year, Pike used the *Christ Church Courier* to declare a financial crisis to his parishioners. Although in the last twelve months the church had collected $10,500 in planned gifts, he told his congregation that "our minimum need this year *to maintain our present programs* [Pike's italics] is $16,000—that is, 50% over last year." On June 10, 1949, Pike reported to his parish that over $29,000 had been spent on improving the furnishings of the church and rectory office. Only $5,000 for the expense had been available from the church's income. Fortunately, a wealthy donor made up much of the difference.

Second, there was the matter of an accurate tabulation of church communicants during Pike's tenure. Pike had prided himself (and publicized) the number of new members he had brought to Christ Church. In 1948, a total of 1,270 communicants at the Poughkeepsie church had been reported to the diocesan office in New York City. But the following year, there was a startling loss. In 1949, the number of Christ Church communicants was reported as 730—a reported drop within twelve months of over 40 percent.

Of course, these missing persons were not active members who had left the church because of personal differences with Pike. What became obvious to the diocesan office was that under Pike's predecessor, Reverend Cummings, an effort had begun to strike from Christ Church's roll of active communicants those who were no longer alive or living in the parish. Commendably, Pike had continued this project to its completion in 1949. But the result was that the number of Pike's added communicants no longer seemed quite as impressive when contrasted with such a large net loss, and the accurate lower figures for the congregation made Pike's programs and expansion appear even more financially unrealistic.

Nor had his harsh criticisms of Vassar from his pulpit or his ambitions for a post at Columbia University passed unnoticed in Poughkeepsie. A Vassar faculty member who had attended services at Christ Church the first Sunday of May 1949 had been so shocked by Pike's statements from the pulpit—a "thoroughly evil reflection on Charles McCormick"—that he wrote to President Blanding the following Monday to warn her of Pike's "cruel, thoughtful, unprincipled, jesuitical approach to the truth." Nor were public opponents limited to a circle of Vassar faculty. The September meeting of the Vassar trustees regarding McCormick's continued employment as chaplain had become community knowledge. On September 12, Rev. Philip Swartz, the minister since 1940 of the First Congregational Church in Poughkeepsie, wrote on behalf of "a number of local ministers" to President Blanding, stating that they "deplore the investigation of published criticisms by our colleagues on the Vassar faculty by one of our number who was terminating his pastorate." Swartz and his like-minded ministers offered to circulate among other local clergy a public letter in support of Blanding, McCormick, and other faculty. "We realize that some of our colleagues in the local ministry may not be able, because of absence or other reason, to join with us in this communication," Swartz added. This was a restraint not usually characteristic of Pike's letters to the Vassar president.

But by this time Pike was absent from Poughkeepsie. At his request that spring, Columbia had predated his employment contract so that he could assume his new duties on campus two months earlier, in July 1949. This resolution of his rectorship at Christ Church was of a piece with his later careers. Whether as a chaplain and academic department head at Columbia, the dean of the Cathedral of St. John the Divine, or the Episcopal bishop of California, the pattern in James Pike's careers was the same—the exuberance and novelty of new ideas and programs, the inability to pay the bills as the costs of the new programs came due, followed by personal disputes and Pike's voluntary departure, usually due to a promotion or a radically different endeavor, as the situation he had created reached its crisis.

Pike was on the Columbia campus by late July, seeing out the last days of the summer term and helping Esther move into their new residence at 445 Riverside Drive, on the Upper West Side of Manhattan. From August 15 to September 15—when McCormick was dealing unsuccessfully with the Vassar trustees, and Reverend Swartz was trying to gain pastoral signatures for his letter of protest—Pike vacationed with his wife and children at Cape Cod, Massachusetts, before resuming his new duties in Earl Hall at Columbia. From his successful arrival in New York City, he effectively edited out any self-consideration of the disruptions that his earlier actions at Christ Church may have caused in the lives of others. Pike practiced what he preached.

He who was not with him was against him.

Pike's appointment at Columbia had auspicious beginnings. The university's president, General Dwight D. Eisenhower, supported the policies of an expanded department of religion and a prominently active chaplain; the general had delegated to the provost the task of finding the right man for the job. (Since no mainstream denominations at that time ordained women as clergy, only men were considered.) As news of the Columbia position spread among the academic and clerical communities, Reinhold Niebuhr at Union Seminary, three blocks away, made a point of speaking to the provost on January 15, 1948, stating that he "thought Columbia should give real consideration to the Rev. James Pike." (Niebuhr was then at the height both of his academic and his popular prestige, and later in March 1948 would be selected as *Time* magazine's "Man of the Year." He had approached the Columbia provost at the request of the Episcopal Church official who had ordained Pike as a deacon and priest, the bishop of Washington, Angus Dun.)

Pike subsequently met with the provost, Albert Jacobs. The two quickly took a liking to one another. Jacobs, like candidate Pike, was an attorney and a former navy officer, and he was an active Episcopalian. Pike, on his part, knew that Eisenhower regarded Jacobs with an extraordinary trust, and that the provost frequently was Eisenhower's ex officio spokesman on matters both private or academic. Together, Jacobs and Pike agreeably defined the new duties of the Columbia chaplaincy as the two practiced attorneys they were. Pike was to participate in and encourage public Episcopal worship at St. Paul's Chapel on campus and, in effect, personally invigorate the dedication, *Pro Ecclesia Dei*, inscribed above the chapel's doors; he would oversee all the college's religious counselors to other faiths on campus; and he was to assume the title of "executive officer" of the soon to be expanded religion department.

Pike was officially installed as chaplain on October 11, 1949, but he had lost no time in preaching his first sermon on the campus; on October 3, he presided over that Sunday's services at St. Paul's and gave from the pulpit an impassioned sermon to the assembled students, administrators, and teachers. Standing at the chancel under the ninety-one-foot domed ceiling of this Italian Renaissance chapel—and looked down upon by nineteen distinguished Columbia alumni portrayed in stained-glass windows—Pike described to his congregation his ambitions for religious instruction at the university. There was to be, he declared, "the maximum flowering of each great tradition." Toward that end, Pike urged his congregation to support his future choices of professors who were to be both ordained and zealous believers in the faiths they were to teach. Pike's insistence upon this policy was a direct rebuke to what he had characterized as the religion of "the lowest common denominator" taught at Vassar. "We want to see Roman Catholics, full-blooded Roman Catholics," Pike told his Columbia audience, so "that their great insights and devotions may help in the salvation of the rest of us." Pike also eagerly sought "articulate" Jews, as well as Episcopalians "to express the full heritage of the Anglican tradition." Perhaps as an afterthought, Pike added, "We also want Lutherans to be Lutherans."

Pike did succeed in bringing a diverse and distinguished faculty to the university's religion department, including such former mentors and teachers as Reinhold and Ursula Niebuhr and Paul Tillich as adjunct professors. (Pike tried without success to hire his former theological mentor, Howard Johnson, but Johnson was happy in his position at the University of the South in Sewanee, Tennessee.) He also succeeded in his mandate from the provost and the president to increase the number of religion courses offered to undergraduates at Columbia. "More Courses in Religion," announced the headline in the *New York Times* on April 4, 1950, introducing the news story that, according to "Dr. James Pike, the university chaplain," thirty-six new religion courses would be offered at Columbia that autumn. Also, in observance of the university's religious origins, Pike would begin regular services at St. Paul's in accordance with the Episcopal ecclesiastical calendar, and by 1952, the chapel additionally would provide as many as thirteen services a week for students of other faiths.

The two year-period from 1949 to 1951 was a time of personal creativity for Pike as well. On March 5, 1950, his fourth child and second son, Christopher, was born, and that year he also completed the manuscript of what was to be his first published book on a religious subject, *The Faith of the Church*, coauthored with W. Norman Pittenger, his teacher and colleague from the General Theological Seminary. Pittenger was still a decade or so away from formulating the radical Christian process theology that Pike later embodied personally, and their popular exposition of the Episcopal creed in the book was an expression of what Pike later termed the "smooth orthodoxy" of his religious thought at this time. From its first publication in 1951, *The Faith of the Church* had an extensive circulation and use within the Episcopal Church, and more than 130,000 copies were in print by the mid-1970s.

In sum, Pike's accomplishments at Columbia between 1949 and 1951 were little short of extraordinary. From nominal beginnings of only a few courses, the university was offering the largest number of undergraduate religion courses in the nation by 1950. In view of his rising success, Pike perhaps can be forgiven for writing an exultant letter to Sarah Blanding on December 9, 1949. "We have harmony all round in developing for next fall a full curriculum in the Department of Religion," Pike wrote, "with Roman Catholicism and Judaism, Eastern Orthodoxy, and Protestantism, all represented by those who speak 'from the inside' of these traditions." Pike enclosed for Blanding's further study "a copy of our [departmental] offerings for 1950–51—all of which will be available in Barnard [College] as well as Columbia." (He also noted in his letter to Blanding that, in regard to recent events at Vassar College, "I am especially glad to learn that the present chaplain's tenure will be concluded.") All events seemed to be falling Pike's way.

But then the bills came due. "I am very embarrassed to report that it appears that I have exceeded one of my accounts, Chapel Services, by $816.43 as of May 31," Pike wrote in a memorandum to the university's financial vice president on June 9, 1950. "I hardly know how I could have avoided the expenditure involved," as there had been "extraordinary items" associated with his assuming the chaplaincy. These expenses included "outdoor signs for the [campus] court in front of the Chapel and for the Amsterdam Avenue side, announcing the day's services"; display advertising in the *New York Times* to promote the same services;

and an "autograph master machine and attachments" for use in "taking down my sermons."

On December 15, 1950, Pike reported once more to the university's vice president that despite the "flourishing" state of the department of religion, "I ran over $1,200 last year" and "that the same thing is bound to happen again next year." Pike attempted to temporize these deficits, however, by pointing out that the expanded religion offerings had resulted in "many adults in the community enrolled in our courses though the School of General Studies," and that these new enrollments "represent new money to the University." Pike here was far ahead of his time. He intuited that in higher education success in fund-raising can cover a variety of administrative and academic sins.

In early 1950, Pike worked with a new provost, Grayson L. Kirk, who had succeeded Jacobs, and from that year through late 1951 Pike persistently lobbied Kirk for permanent increases in his departmental and chaplaincy budgets to provide an assistant for Pike and secretaries for the four religious counselors he had recruited. At this same time, he pointedly reminded Kirk, in a memorandum of December 15, 1950, that "my salary is set at $8,044.96, and the cost of living (and raising and schooling four children) has not gone down." These requests continued, though in the summer of 1951, Pike was obliged to report to the provost at the end of fiscal year 1950–51 that the chapel's account "is overdrawn about $1,000," and that, including other debts, "we will run over about $1,500."

There was no doubt that Pike was becoming overextended, both physically and fiscally. On October 5, 1950, he received a welcome note from the assistant provost's office informing him that "I have today requested transfer of the sum of $1,742.00 from a fund at the President's disposal," in order to pay the salary for a part-time assistant for Pike for one year. Others within the university community, however, were not so kindly disposed toward Pike. Joseph L. Blau, who was at that time a professor of philosophy at Columbia, complained in his unpublished history of the department of religion of the "expansionist, imperial policy" under Pike. Another contemporary professor, a little friendlier to Pike, remembered the tendencies of his colleague to politically stumble into "pitfalls of not having done groundwork with people."

One of those pitfalls was Pike's failure to have completed the requirements for his divinity degree at Union Theological Seminary—a failure potentially embarrassing to Columbia in consideration of Pike's assumption of the title "executive director" of the religion department. Acting upon either meticulous record keeping or, possibly, the complaint of another faculty member, the secretary to the university faculty privately asked Pike the first week of May 1951 about the absence of his degree. Pike wrote back on May 22, informing the secretary that, "for the sake of the record," he—quite fortuitously—had received his divinity degree from Union that very same date. Pike explained that he had "tidied up this matter with a couple of research papers which fortunately corresponded to work I was engaged in anyway." With a typical Pikean double entendre, he wrote of his relief "to be legitimate"—at least, "in this regard." Pike's explanation satisfied the secretary, but a bureaucratic and political notice had been served to the executive director of the religion department that not everyone at Columbia was willing to accept his improvisational style or his authority without credentials.

Later that academic year, uneasiness at Pike's professional methods and his comparatively freewheeling spending led the university's Committee on Instruction to vote down several curricular changes for his department proposed by Pike. His reaction was of a piece with his earlier reaction to criticism at Poughkeepsie. He announced his intention to resign from the chaplaincy and the department of religion at Columbia University. His resignation was accepted January 31, 1952.

He was by no means jobless. Pike had been in contact with a potentially new employer since October 1951. (Pike's friends Stringfellow and Towne recounted that after the faculty committee's vote that fall Pike threatened to publicize his resignation as a protest against the university's lack of support for the religion department. According to them, Grayson Kirk personally dissuaded Pike from making public his discontent.) Characteristically, Pike's resignation in the middle of an unresolved controversy effected a move not only physically outward but professionally upward. Although this move would be the third change in his employment within four years—and the third such change for Esther Pike as well—a greater stage awaited his talents.

Columbia University's chapel certainly had been an impressive platform for the chaplain to deliver his sermons, but there was an even more impressive site just a few blocks southward, its spire visible above the university's buildings from the chapel's rear entrance on Amsterdam Avenue. This was the Cathedral of St. John the Divine, on West 112th Street, the principal building of the Episcopal Church's New York diocese, the cathedral close containing the residence of its bishop. An uncompleted but still massive landmark of neo-Gothic architecture, St. John's by the fall of 1951 was in need of a dean, the priest delegated by the bishop to be in charge at the cathedral. Pike had emerged that autumn as the leading candidate.

His preferment was the result of Pike's own hard political and religious work for the past five years, which had brought him from a small parish in Poughkeepsie to the Morningside Heights neighborhood of Columbia University. Pike's acceptance of Reverend Kinsolving's advice, his appointment by Bishop Charles Gilbert in 1949 to the diocesan Commission on College Work, and his subsequent strong advocacy of an Episcopal presence on campus had been noted approvingly by the Church's general convention and by Gilbert's successor, Bishop Horace Donegan. Pike had also made a good name for himself with the financial patrons and trustees of the cathedral, such as Charles Profitt (the Columbia University Press administrator to whom Pike had complained about Reverend McCormick), Rev. Frederic Sydney Fleming (rector of Trinity Church, Wall Street, where Bryan Green had been invited to preach), and Albert Jacobs (the former provost at Columbia who had hired Pike). Donegan in early 1951 had put Pike's name before the cathedral's board of trustees, and the board subsequently agreed with the bishop's nomination. The former Columbia University chaplain was soon to become Dean James Pike.

IV

The Deanship at St. John the Divine

He didn't have to worry there about money or power.
He had a perfect spot to be heard and seen.

—REV. DARBY BETTS, canon precentor of
St. John's, on Pike's appointment as cathedral dean

Paul Tillich and Reinhold Niebuhr had their admirers at Union Seminary; Grayson Kirk had his chancellery at Columbia University; but a deanship at the largest cathedral in Christendom trumped them all. James Pike liked to make these comparisons, particularly in regard to his former faith of Roman Catholicism. After his installation as dean, Pike was fond of boasting, not at all facetiously, that the Basilica of St. Peter's in Rome, although physically larger than St. John's, was not technically a cathedral. That venerable Vatican City building, however large, was not the ecclesiastical residence of a bishop or a dean, and therefore was, in his Pike's argument, simply a *big church*.

The Protestant cathedral over which the dean took such pride was, like Pike himself, an expansive and unfinished project. Begun in 1892, the construction of the Cathedral of St. John the Divine remained uncompleted in 1952, but the finished nave—the longer axis of a cathedral built to resemble a large cross—is an awe-inspiring monument. From the narthex, or entrance area, to the altar where Pike would celebrate the Eucharist, the nave at St. John's stretches 601 feet or slightly more than the length of two American football fields placed end to end. Yet it was not simply the interior dimensions of St. John's that led one scholar to describe it as a "mini Vatican." The cathedral and grounds then included seven chapels, a baptistery, a choir school, a cathedral school and staff, a landscaped close (or green space), a cathedral house, a study and office known as the deanery, the bishop's residence, the Pike family residence, the diocesan offices, and a staff of nearly three dozen lay professionals. Pike's energies could play themselves out here organizing what was in fact a miniature clerical city. The five and a half years that he was to stay at this appointment, from 1952 to 1958, were to be the most productive and happiest of his restless church career.

The ambitious spending and political overreaching that had brought him criticism at Columbia could be accommodated at the cathedral. St. John's had been well endowed by some of the wealthiest Episcopal families in New York City since the generation of J. P. Morgan, an original contributor. After Pike became dean in 1952, the annual endowed income for the budgets of the cathedral corporation approached a half million dollars. Pike spent these budgets magisterially, and with few constraints. The cathedral's dean operated under the financial supervision of the diocesan bishop, but Bishop Donegan's financial crosier was gentle or absent. There were also greater opportunities for political action and publicity than at Columbia. John Krumm, Pike's friend and his successor as the university's chaplain, later compared Pike's career as an academic at Columbia unfavorably with his deanship at St. John's. "When he pretended to be a reflective scholar, which he certainly was not by temperament, the effort did not succeed," Krumm recollected. "In my opinion, Jim was more effective as dean of the cathedral. . . . In a position where he could be frankly a preacher and, in a sense, a propagandist, he was at his best."

Pike was installed as the fifth dean of St. John's on the afternoon of Saturday, February 16, 1952. The day had begun with a public celebration of Holy Communion at 7:30 a.m., and again for the cathedral clergy at 10:30 a.m. A congregation of three thousand spectators then gathered inside the cathedral. At promptly three o'clock, Pike, wearing the vestments of the dean-designate, began his processional walk toward the altar steps, proceeded by a crucifer, the choir of St. Paul's Chapel, the combined faculties of the departments of religion at Columbia University and Barnard College, and two bishops. A third bishop and a crucifer bearing the Cross of New York came behind. Before the installation, a liturgical questioning by the senior bishop was required of Pike, during which the candidate affirmed that "by diligent study and sound learning," he as a dean would "labor to make this Cathedral Church a center of intellectual light." There followed, among other celebrations, three hymns, an offertory anthem, the recitation of *Ecce quam bonum!*, a sermon, four prayers, and two blessings, and he was thereafter Dean Pike.

He kept his word to make St. John's a center of Episcopal intellectual activity. Soon after his installation, Pike set to work increasing significantly the number of books in the cathedral's library. He also studied the customaries, or the ceremonial practices, of the oldest Church of England cathedrals and brought traditions at St. John's into accordance. The new dean additionally revived the positions at St. John's of the four cathedral canons, or assistant priests. Pike also quickly registered with the secretary of state of New York the corporate title "The New York Cathedral." The Roman Catholic archdiocese of the city was thereby denied the legal usage of this phrase to describe that *other* New York City cathedral—St. Patrick's, at Fifth Avenue and 50th Street. This coup so soon after his installation "privately delighted" Pike, his friends recalled.

The new dean also wrote prodigiously. In addition to composing and delivering a sermon about once every two weeks, Pike set about producing dozens of published articles, essays, and book reviews from the deanery, as if his waking mind were a type of ceaselessly running Minerva press. Sometimes he sent his articles to church publications or to comparatively obscure academic journals; more frequently he chose larger audiences, and articles bylined by him appeared throughout 1953 in popular and secular magazines such as *Vogue*. His two book-length manuscripts completed that year, *Roadblocks to Faith* and *The Day After*, were conceived and composed just as rapidly, and they, too, were acquired by commercial publishers and distributed nationally. Krumm, the coauthor of *Roadblocks to Faith,* soon got a firsthand experience of the dean's quick dispatch of literary business. Krumm recalled how, at a reception at Bishop Donegan's house in 1953, he had suggested to Pike that the two coauthor this book. The dean asked a few questions, then excused himself to talk with other guests and, later, to dine with the bishop. That night about ten o'clock Krumm received a telephone call at home from Pike, who verbally outlined their proposed book and informed his listener that he had obtained a firm commitment by a commercial publisher to take the manuscript. He had also arranged for radio broadcasts by the American Broadcasting Company of future sermons the two would give in anticipation of their book's publication. "Somehow he had managed to make some telephone calls," an amazed Krumm recalled of Pike that night, "and the whole project was thus launched in a few hours during which he also kept up his usual brisk conversations with guests at the reception and at the dinner party."

The new dean was also noted for the brisk number of public quarrels he picked and won in 1953. He began in January by denouncing as "un-American" the current opposition by Roman Catholic charities in New York City and Brooklyn to membership by the Planned Parenthood Committee on the two cities' Welfare and Health Council. Pike's rhetoric contributed to an irremediable breach—Catholic charities soon withdrew their participation from the council—but his advocacy of an open discussion of birth control was favorably reported that month by the *New York Times* and publicly supported by such prominent Episcopalians as Arthur Kinsolving.

The next month, Pike's name became linked nationally to the issue of nondiscriminatory admissions to higher education for black Americans. On February 10, he declined as "a degree in white divinity" an honorary doctorate to have been awarded him that spring by the University of the South in Sewanee, Tennessee. This was a protest against that Episcopal university's refusal to accept black seminarians or to allow faculty dissent to its admissions policy. He made his public disavowal of the degree only after some temporizing, however, and at a hazard to his church career. The University of the South and its adjunctive St. Luke's Seminary, known collectively as Sewanee, had been reverenced since the Civil War by a succession of prominent southern bishops who served as trustees and whose dioceses literally owned the university and its property. These "owning dioceses," as they were known in the parlance of the school, were formidable opponents to any outside changes. Pike earlier had expressed his opinion that the bishops of the owning dioceses "would rather be swallowed up in the earth than admit Negro students." He also knew the Sewanee administration had been unmoved by the proffered resignations of eight religion faculty members, to take effect at the end of the academic year 1953, should the seminary not open its admissions to black candidates. Among the eight who had offered their resignations was Pike's friend and former theological tutor, Howard A. Johnson, who had taught there for three years. Nevertheless, when Pike was invited by Sewanee's vice chancellor to preach the baccalaureate sermon and receive an honorary doctorate at the university's commencement ceremonies scheduled for June 1953, he had at first accepted, telling the vice chancellor he would "very much like to have a Sewanee degree."

There were to be un-Christian surprises for both sides. On February 6, Johnson privately informed Pike that the bishop trustees had declined to meet or to discuss any changes in the seminary's admissions policy and that the Sewanee administration that day summarily had accepted his resignation, as well as those of the seven other pro-integrationist faculty. Pike subsequently wrote a letter dated February 10 to Sewanee's vice chancellor declining the university's invitation to the June commencement. "I cannot in conscience receive a doctorate in the white divinity which Sewanee apparently is prepared to offer the church hereafter," he wrote. Apparently by honest mischance, Pike made public the text of his letter to the *New York Times* and other newspapers before the original was received in the mail by the vice chancellor in Tennessee. That university official learned Pike would not appear at the school's commencement ceremonies only when the *Times* telephoned on February 12 to ask for comment on Pike's public refusal.

The possibly unexpected publicity occasioned by Pike's making the letter known certainly contributed to Sewanee's decision that summer to reverse its admission policy and open its seminary to black candidates. "It's a masterpiece of writing and a masterstroke of strategy!" Johnson enthusiastically wrote to Pike the day after excerpts from the letter appeared in newspapers nationally. "Already this morning one of the students was flashing an old, three-inch 'I Like Ike' button—to which he had added the letter 'P'!" Even after the university's reversal of policy, however, Pike let stand his refusal to accept a degree, nor was he reinvited to speak at commencement by the school's administration. In acting to effect this change in admissions, Pike had received the strong approval and support of his bishop in New York. But for the dean to have refused the university's honors and to have evulgated what the' Sewanee administration considered to be a private discussion among gentlemen on race had made some chronic and powerful enemies for him. Foremost among them was Henry I. Louttit, the bishop of southern Florida. Pike would have later opportunities to learn from Louttit and his peers that bishops can make good friends but bad enemies.

More fortuitous as a result of the Sewanee controversy was obtaining the services of Johnson as the canon theologian at the cathedral, responsible for directing research and academic programs. After his resignation, Johnson had been appointed, at the invitation of the archbishop of Canterbury, to a visiting fellowship at St. Augustine's College, Canterbury. Pike was able to entice Johnson, after his year's study in England, to join the clerical staff in New York. The appointment was part of the dean's continuing determination to make the cathedral, in his words, "an international center for Anglican culture and teaching" by appointing notable scholars to the four canon positions under his direction. The dean had already filled two canonries by 1953. Rev. Edward West was in place as the canon sacrist, with oversight of all the cathedral's worship services, and Rev. Darby W. Betts was the canon precentor, acting as headmaster at the cathedral's school and director of all the cathedral's community activities. By his adding Johnson as canon theologian and also appointing Rev. John W. Pyle as the canon pastor, the priest in charge of the cathedral's counseling services, St. John the Divine by the fall of 1954 had begun to fulfill Pike's ambition of making the cathedral under his direction the center of Anglican social activism and scholarly research in the United States.

Johnson and Betts both were close friends of Pike. Betts was the urbane, sometimes cynical companion who was to stay at Pike's side on his rise to celebrity, both in New York State in the 1950s and San Francisco in the early 1960s. Johnson, although he remained at the New York cathedral after Pike became a bishop, was the embodiment in his friend's mind of the high-minded, scholarly seminarian who in a different world he himself might have become. The dean's relationship to Johnson was emotionally mixed. On the one hand, Pike acted with a noticeable deference toward his nominee for canon theologian, aware of Johnson's superior academic accomplishments, including his fellowship at Cambridge. He earlier had advanced Johnson money to travel to England, and, after his friend's acceptance of the St. John's canonry, the dean was quick to assure Johnson that he would be free to study and write without interference from the cathedral's administration. "As a matter of fact," he wrote his friend at Canterbury, "one of the principal reasons we want you here is so that theological scholarship of the rest of us will have better direction." On the other hand, Pike was sometimes imperious toward his former seminary teacher, acting in the manner of a worldly older brother, as when he again wrote Johnson, who was at times socially unprepossessing, reminding him that "black tie" would be the expected dress at receptions at the New York cathedral, and "I would suggest that before you leave England, you procure same at Whipple's [tailoring shop] or somewhere else." Yet whatever the vagaries of being Pike's personal friend as well as his clerical associate, the dean was to have no more loyal defenders than Betts and Johnson, and he was pleased to be able to reward Johnson for his outspokenness in the Sewanee controversy.

The same month as the Sewanee seminary quietly accepted its first black student, in July of 1953, Pike became engaged in a new dispute with the staff executive director of the Senate Permanent Subcommittee on Investigations, chaired by U.S. senator Joseph R. McCarthy. The dean had been deeply angered when this assistant to the senator's subcommittee on subversive activities had asserted that "at least 7,000" Protestant U.S. clergymen were members of "the Kremlin's conspiracy." In a July 4 sermon entitled "If This Be Treason," Pike ridiculed the accuracy of this statement and belittled the subcommittee investigator, Joseph B. Matthews, by name. "I know from personal experience that what Mr. Matthews has said is simply not true," he told his St. John's congregation. The dean's objections carried political favor perhaps unavailable to other prominent Protestant clergymen also disturbed by the statement. "I will only mention the fact that I am a good friend of President Eisenhower's," Pike wrote to a conservative critic of his actions, adding, "I had a visit with him two nights before his inauguration, and the bishop and I had lunch with him during the campaign this fall." Four days after Pike's sermon on Independence Day, Eisenhower made the first public comments of his presidency on the activities of McCarthy's subcommittee, labeling as "deplorable" statements that "condemn such a vast portion of the church or the clergy," and declaring that "such attacks portray contempt for the principles of freedom and decency." Matthews, under such presidential pressure, resigned from the committee on July 8.

Of course, as Martin Luther once observed, it makes a difference whose ox is gored. Pike had not hesitated, when it served his purpose, to employ accusations as unsubstantiated as Matthews's, as when he had described Vassar College as a haven for "avowed communists." But for Protestant clergy to stand accused of being communist conspirators was to Pike a different issue. The dean chose to believe that the charges were motivated not by anticommunism, but by sectarian jealousy. "It is not surprising that the Roman Catholic hierarchy, not adverse to taking positions on other moral issues (for example, for their particular view of birth control) has been silent on McCarthyism," Pike declared from the guest pulpit of the National Cathedral in Washington, D.C., on March 21, 1954. He noted in this same sermon that, "entirely apart from the fact that the senator is a Roman Catholic," the "Roman Catholic newspapers with huge circulations have been pro-McCarthy in influence." Pike later tempered slightly his public remonstrance to the Roman Catholic Church's press, but he continued throughout 1954 to criticize McCarthy's investigations.

Pike's skills at sermonizing on McCarthy, racial discrimination, birth control, and other controversial subjects from 1954 onward made him a celebrity preacher in New York City. Congregations of 3,000 to 4,000 were not unusual when Pike preached at Sunday services at St. John's, and sometimes double these numbers—6,000 to 8,000— attended on Christmas Day or Palm Sunday. His homiletics were impressive. Quick in wit and gesture, both hands describing images in the air as he preached, elegant in his clerical robes, Pike spoke in a rapid, clipped rhythm, his diction curiously free of any particularly Californian accent or other regionalism. The numbers who came to hear him are even more impressive when it is remembered that St. John's is a cathedral with no designated parish. The thousands who come each Sunday do so by traveling from other churches within the city, or are part of New York City's "unchurched" population. These popular sermons in turn became gist for the dean's books, usually catchily titled and distributed by commercial publishers rather than by the Episcopal Church's Seabury Press. Between 1952 and 1958, Pike wrote or coauthored seven books, or an average of about one per year, including the widely read *Beyond Anxiety* and *Doing the Truth*.

The content of these sermons and books was not startling theology. Pike was not original in his theological assertions in his writings, just as in the 1960s he would not be original in his supposed heresies. His greatest talent in the 1950s was for what seminarians call apologetics, which Pike defined well in his 1955 book, *The Church, Politics, and Society*, as "the reasoned commendation of the Christian faith to the secular mind." He argued for Christianity like the forensically skilled attorney he was, employing case studies, logic, eloquence, and topical comparisons. He enjoyed reminding his audiences that, in his words, he was still a licensed attorney and that he simply had "exchanged clients."

Only occasionally did he write in the mid-1950s about the theological ideas that were then exciting students and professors alike at Protestant seminaries and that, in the early 1960s, would begin to divide Episcopal churches. The new theologies questioned, for example, whether accounts of the Virgin Birth or the bodily ascension of Jesus after his death should be considered as describing actual historical events and church credo or as poetic communications and peripheral to the *kerygma*, or proclaimed truth, of the Christian gospels. Speaking in 1957 for the traditionalist view, *The Living Church*, an influential and usually conservative Episcopal publication, editorialized against the "startling departures from the official teaching of the Church," which it described as "the concept of 'demythologizing the Gospel' and distilling out the 'Kerygma,'" an effort associated with the name of Rudolph Bultmann and other advanced theologians today." Probably influenced by talks with Johnson, who was now in place as his canon theologian, Pike tentatively approached demythologizing biblical texts, as in this passage from another 1955 book, *Doing the Truth:*

> People usually think that a myth is something that isn't so. Actually, a good myth is the picturing of something that *is* so—generally a complicated and paradoxical truth about a situation which can be better portrayed in a story than in a series of logical propositions. The critical question to ask of such a narrative is not, "Is it historically true?" It may or may not be; such elements of historical truth as it may contain do not destroy its value or its preeminent function as a myth. The proper question to ask is, "Does it adequately hold together the facets of truth in the situation it seeks to portray?"

He was not totally committed to what *The Living Church* had called "advanced" positions in his church's thinking, however. Theologically, he was testing the waters to see how far he might tread. Five months after *The Living Church*'s anti-demythologizing editorial, Pike wrote his friend Norman Pittenger describing his personal position on the traditionalist versus advanced theologies of the Virgin Birth. "I think that during this period it is just as well that some people are able to say, 'I hold to the historical Virgin Birth, but don't think it's important,' alongside those saying, 'I don't hold to it and don't think it's important.' I think of it as strategy."

The popular success within Pike's books and sermons of these situationalist strategies—why so many of his readers or listeners throughout the 1950s found so convincing his "reasoned commendation of the Christian faith to the secular mind"—was because he himself embodied so many secular traits apparently reconciled with his Christian faith. Within the next decade, Harvey Cox, a popular theologian contemporary to Pike, would describe the twentieth-century secular man in terms totally applicable to the dean. The modern secular man, in Cox's description, is highly pragmatic and comfortable with "this world" realities; he views experience "not as a unified metaphysical system, but as a series of problems and projects"; and he "can live with highly provisional solutions." In making his apologetics, Pike was largely a secular mind speaking to other secular minds. He made full use of what he called "strategies" such as pragmatism, relativism, and technologies, so long as the general excellence of Christianity was proposed. In the fall of 1955, Pike intuitively adapted one of the latest technologies of the secular world in order to make a long-running "commercial for God" on the new medium of television.

VIDEO	AUDIO
Fade in:	*Music*:
Exterior of the Cathedral	An Important, Dignified Theme, Dip it for:
PAN: Across the Cathedral Close to the Cathedral House	*Anncr*: (Live, Voice-over) From the Cathedral Close of the Cathedral of St. John the Divine, on Cathedral Heights in New York City, the American Broadcasting Company brings you the Very Reverend Dr. James A. Pike.
DS (dissolve) to: Dean's study, LS (long shot) interior of Cathedral House . . .	
SUPER(imposed) Card "Dean Pike"	Ladies and gentlemen, . . . Dean Pike
DS (dissolve) to: Close shot: Dean Pike	All: Ad Lib Conversation

The above script, written for the premiere of the *Dean Pike* program and broadcast on the ABC network on Sunday afternoon, October 9, 1955, marked the first successful program hosted by a Protestant clergyman on national television. In 1951, the young evangelist Billy Graham had attempted a weekly broadcast, *The Hour of Decision*, but national viewers apparently were not yet comfortable with Graham's nondenominational proselytizing; the program did not last beyond that year. Fulton J. Sheen of the Roman Catholic Church had enjoyed an initial success competing against Milton Berle on Tuesday nights from 1952 to 1955 with his homiletic program, *Life Is Worth Living*, but the bishop's broadcaster, the DuMont Network, was defunct by 1955. By contrast, *Dean Pike* would continue to be aired nationally by ABC for the next six years.

Pike's natural ease in front of a television camera as an occasional guest or moderator on infrequent "spot" programs of religious content had been noted by ABC producers, and he was approached early in 1955 about his interest in hosting a weekly talk show. The format eventually agreed upon by Pike and the network was a novel combination of a kaffeeklatsch and a pastoral session. ABC technicians, early each Sunday afternoon, brought their cameras, cables, and lights into the cathedral house at the grounds of St. John's in order to broadcast that week's program from what the dean had specified should be an informal gathering in a "living room setting, or dining room, or whatnot." James and Esther Pike would then chat before the cameras, live and unrehearsed, for half an hour, with usually no more than one or two guests. The topics were what Pike specified as the "various social and personal problems in the light of the general Judeo-Christian perspective."

Pike called upon his significantly large circle of acquaintances, including celebrities and public officials, in order to provide guests for his program. Although he occasionally invited notable theologians such as Tillich, more frequently his guests were politicians, diplomats, or other secular figures. For the ABC network, *Dean Pike* was a convenient means to satisfy the Federal Communications Commission's requirement that broadcasters provide a required minimum of what was then defined as public service programming. But for Pike, both the weekly program and its content were a natural extension of his ministry, and, as he later emphasized, "This was not to me just being on TV as a business on the side." A televised meeting of Christians in a living room, he insisted, was as appropriate a form of worship as the public rituals enacted inside a cathedral, as "nothing is secular to God, and any concern of the sons of man is a concern to God."

For its first two seasons, *Dean Pike* was on the weekly schedule of ABC with *Life Is Worth Living*, after Bishop Sheen was invited to move his program from the disbanded DuMont Network. However, Sheen never seemed to have understood, as Pike did immediately, that success in this new medium of television required the appearance of intimacy and informality with the unseen audience. Sheen, who dressed in a cassock and full-length cape for his Thursday evening broadcasts, stood in front of a stationary camera on a theater stage before a set composed of bookcases, a statue of the Madonna, and a chalkboard. The result of this style of "straight-in-camera preaching" was that, in Pike's description, "a lot of people just flip it off." Sheen's program was not renewed by ABC after its second season. By contrast, there was the apparently unstudied familiarity of *Dean Pike*—Esther and Jim frequently invited daughter Catherine to join in conversations with the adult guests, as a later television host, Jack Paar, did with his daughter. The dean's broadcasts from 1955 onward remained a steady favorite on ABC. Pike usually let his guest, or wife and daughter, do most of the talking; then, "about five minutes before the end, I would take over with a summary, which was not a sermon," Pike recalled in 1961. "We called that little five-minute end, jokingly, the commercial . . . the commercial for God, exactly, our client as it was."

These appearances and low-key "commercials" together made the dean by 1956 the most popularly recognized Christian apologist on U.S. television. *Dean Pike*, unlike other religious broadcasts of the early 1950s, such as *Life Is Worth Living*, *Frontiers of Faith*, or *Lamp Unto My Feet*, was forthrightly named for its genial host; and Pike demonstrated on other occasions his affinity for combining his name and clerical title with maximum exposure in the mass media. There was, for example, the *Baby Doll* controversy in late 1956. This motion picture, scripted by Tennessee Williams and starring Carroll Baker in the title role as the nineteen-year-old southern bride of a sexually frustrated older man, was far and away the most notorious U.S. film of that year upon its premiere in New York City. Much of the notoriety was the result of the "Baby Doll of Times Square," a 135-foot-long promotional billboard set above 45th and 46th Streets picturing a scantily dressed Baker lying in a crib and sucking her thumb. The movie and its advertising became a public issue for Pike after Francis Cardinal Spellman denounced the film from the pulpit of St. Patrick's Cathedral on December 16 and forbade Roman Catholics from viewing it "under pain of sin." Spellman and Pike, by this time having repeatedly clashed over birth control and other issues, literally "hated" each other, in the recollection of St. John's canon sacrist, Edward West. On December 18, two days after Spellman had spoken ex cathedra, Pike and his wife were photographed that evening by news reporters, along with other celebrities such as Henry Fonda and Lee Remick, entering the Victoria Theatre at Broadway and 46th Street for a special, fifty-dollar-a-ticket showing of *Baby Doll.* Prominent in all the printed photographs was the giant billboard overhead. Although later that week, in his Advent sermon at St. John's, Pike criticized the "brazen advertising" by the movie's producers, newspaper editors nationwide had found irresistible, as he knew they would, the image of the jaunty dean walking by the seventy-five-foot bare legs of "Baby Doll." Afterward, Pike remarked publicly, "I don't think I sinned in seeing it." Spellman in effect had been upstaged by the dean, and the cardinal's earlier prohibitions received diminishing press attention thereafter.

The dean was not simply the media's gadfly, however. He spoke out publicly on more substantial issues throughout 1956, as in a sermon at St. John's on November 11, when he declared to his congregation of three thousand that "the blood of the Hungarians is on our hands" after the U.S. government declined to intervene in their revolt the previous month against Soviet rule. In another sermon at St. John's, given earlier that same election year, Pike criticized the Eisenhower administration's "secret" approval of arms shipments to Saudi Arabia, a nation he described as "intent upon exterminating" Israel. He had warned his congregation against a future U.S. policy in the Middle East disproportionately influenced by "campaign funds from oil interests."

Pike's use of his celebrity in the pulpit to dramatize his position on contemporary political issues "was basically prophetic," in the words of his canon precentor, Darby Betts. Betts's adjectival use of the word *prophet* was meant not in the sense of a seer but in the Hebraic tradition of calling the corporate church or the political state to God's judgment. The prophetic temper in Pike's sermons at St. John's—as well as his frequent defense of the modern nation of Israel—was more noticeable after his first trip to Israel and Jordan in early February 1956. Pike later described his twelve-day visit as "a religious experience." Spiritually, he had, as he described it, "felt much more my own Jewishness, if I may use that phrase, which also meant that I became a better Christian." While he was visiting Jerusalem, an exceptional privilege also was extended to the dean by the curators at Hebrew University to view the Dead Sea Scrolls, including the earliest extant scroll of the Book of Isaiah.

The visit seems to have confirmed in Pike's mind that he himself and his ministry were a continuation of the prophetic tradition. Even before going to Jerusalem, his thoughts had been turning toward the prophetic direction, as in this description of the "vocation" of believing in God from *Doing the Truth:*

> Thus through all the history of the Church, of the Old and the New Israel, men have sought to delimit the scope of such a vocation. . . . This has required two special roles among God's servants. The *priests* codify the applications of the claim [of belief in God] according to the best insights they know, and men (including the priests) very rapidly assume that this is all that is expected of them. Then *prophets* are raised up to proclaim that this isn't enough, and, in fact, swing over in the other direction and show contempt for the codification [italics in original].

Pike's love of controversy, his instinct for publicizing his messages, his egoism, and his occasional contempt for those who disagreed with him all could be considered—at least, in his mind—as the paradigm of his move from priest to prophet, of becoming more concerned with the needs of social and political justice than the mere "codifications" of an Episcopal priest.

Pike may have felt himself becoming a Christian prophet, but by the late 1950s, he was also beginning to feel some heat. His practice of a liberal Anglo-Catholicism, combining a High liturgy with an openness to liberal theology, contemporary psychology, and social criticism, was no longer as pleasing as it once had appeared to many Episcopalians. High Church practices combined with a liberal theology was what had helped attract Pike from being a nonpracticing Catholic to becoming a converted Episcopalian in the first place. Norman Pittenger approvingly recalled the 1940s as "a time when Anglicans, especially Anglicans of the 'Catholic' sort, rejoiced to be known as 'liberal Catholics,' " but by 1957 High Church liberalism was losing its popularity among Episcopal laypersons. An early, indicative straw in the wind was the "demythologizing" editorial appearing that year in *The Living Church*. Among the Episcopal laity, High Church sentiment was beginning to align itself squarely *against* many of the liberal initiatives—such as the questioning of Marian or Trinitarian doctrines, or the practice of an outspoken political activism—that were personally of most interest to Pike. Pittenger openly warned his friend of "this anti-liberal mood" in the church.

There were also troubles closer to home. The dean set a hectic schedule for himself that seldom allowed uninterrupted time with his family, and his emotional intimacies with his wife and four children suffered accordingly. Nor were they the only ones who perceived his absences as excessive. A probably apocryphal but persistent story among the staff at St. John's recounted how Pike, arriving by taxi at the Amsterdam Avenue entrance of the cathedral after a trip out of town, hurriedly approached a crowd of tourists at the cathedral steps in order to greet them and introduce himself, as was his custom. In midconversation, the dean suddenly realized that he was shaking hands with his own wife, who, with their children, had been waiting for him among the crowd. Another incident at the deanery, more credibly witnessed, also revealed how Pike was becoming a stranger to his family. His eldest daughter, Catherine, happened to pass by the open door of a room in the deanery on a day when an ABC photographer was taking publicity stills there of her mother and younger sister for *Dean Pike*. Catherine, in her words, "seeing a man with dark hair and tortoise-shell glasses" holding a camera to his face, stopped at the room and asked, "Why, Daddy, what are you doing with a camera?" The ABC publicist lowered the camera and then bluntly told the child, "This is not Daddy." Catherine Pike recalled, "I ran from the door in hysterics, shouting to Jimmy [her brother] about the funny mistake I had made."

The children were amused, but Esther Pike probably less so by the mental reflection that her older daughter had mistaken a stranger for her often-absent father. There were also other stresses in their marriage. Pike's consumption of alcohol, always enthusiastic, had become noticeably excessive during his years in residence as a dean. In the following decade, after he would acknowledge his drinking problem and join Alcoholics Anonymous, he dated his abuse of alcohol to the beginning years of his celebrity in the 1950s. There were also rumors, persistently

repeated among some of the staff at St. John's, of the dean's marital infidelities. Clearly what was wanted—at least by Pike's understanding—
was a change in locale and vocation. Always before, when faced with
personal, financial, or professional difficulties, he had resolved them by
taking a new job or promotion at a different location, thereby redefining
his professional roles and his private life.

On the evening of February 4, 1958, James and Esther Pike were
hosting a cocktail party at the deanery when he was summoned to the
telephone for an urgent long-distance call. There followed an excited
exchange with an Episcopal churchman in San Francisco. Within fifteen minutes of Pike's putting down the receiver, the telephone rang
again—this time the call was from a reporter at the *New York Times* asking for comments—and the telephone continued to ring almost constantly thereafter with messages of congratulations throughout that
happy, confused night. Pike had just received the news that he had been
nominated to be the Episcopal Church's next bishop in California.

He had known by mid-1957 that, within a few years, he might claim a
bishopric for himself. Bishop Donegan, his next-door neighbor at the
cathedral close, was said to favor Pike as his eventual successor at the
New York diocese. On the other coast of the national episcopacy, when
Bishop Karl Morgan Block of the diocese of California had instructed a
nominating committee to consider possible choices for his succession,
Pike's name had been added to the list of out-of-state candidates by May
1957. Block's diocese was a covetable appointment. Although one of the
three Episcopal dioceses in the western state—the cities of Los Angeles
and Sacramento also had bishops in residence administering their
sees—the inclusively named "Diocese of California" was centered at
San Francisco and was considered the most prestigious and best
endowed among the state's bishopries. Almost three times larger in area
than the diocese of New York, the San Francisco see administered Episcopal parishes and missions within the ten counties surrounding the bay
city.

Pike had kept his distance politically and geographically, remaining
in New York during this selection process, but Howard Johnson, a
UCLA graduate, and others of his friends had urged the dean's nomination to acquaintances in California as delegates from the diocese met at

Grace Cathedral in San Francisco in late January 1958 to choose their next bishop coadjutor. (The Episcopal Church provides for the positions both of a bishop coadjutor and of a suffragan bishop to assist the foremost, or diocesan, bishop, but only the coadjutor has the automatic right to succession after the death or retirement of the diocesan bishop. Block, then age seventy-three, planned to retire soon after the selection of his coadjutor bishop.) For the convenience of the voting delegates attending this convention, the nominating committee assembled one- and two-page biographies of the final eight candidates to distribute among the attendants at Grace Cathedral. There was one exception— Pike's dossier of recommendations was over seven times longer, at fourteen pages, than that of any other candidate. "*Everyone* likes to write about him at length," the committee had prefaced its section on Pike, employing its own italics for emphasis.

Described by his supporters at the convention as "a man with singular prophetic gifts," Pike was presented as a "brilliant lawyer, bureaucrat, teacher of law, distinguished scholar in divinity, pastor, administrator, counselor, preacher, author, lecturer, and 'television personality' with a national audience." This encomium was perhaps expected, but with remarkable honesty and insight, the dean's partisans also put his name into nomination by praising what was called the "versatility" of Pike's personality: "Every stage of his career has called for a complete break with the preceding phase, a striking out in new directions, the mastery of new forms and techniques," the delegates were told.

The resulting votes were razor-thin. By prior agreement, the delegates cast their ballots for the coadjutor in two separate groups, voting either as clergy or as laity, with majorities in both required to win the nomination. After six inconclusive ballots, late in the afternoon on February 4, Pike was nominated by a majority of just one vote among the clergy. The final tallies were 221 lay votes for Pike, with 193 required for nomination, and 57 clerical votes, with 56 required for nomination.

Back at the deanery, Pike learned the evening of February 4 that he had successfully been named the nominee, but he knew that he was not yet out of the woods. The San Francisco vote had to be approved in another national round of balloting by the Episcopal Church's bishops and the diocesan standing committees, also voting in two separate groups, with majorities required within each. Receiving two majorities in this second round of ecclesiastical voting was by no means assured. Among certain bishops, clergy, and laity in the Deep South, memories still rankled over his prominence in the racial integration of the Sewanee seminary. (Even should some of the bishops of the Sewanee owning dioceses prove forgiving, more recalcitrant numbers of southern clergy and laity composed their standing committees.) Another complication was that the repeated balloting and speeches at San Francisco had led to a public revisiting of Pike's claimed annulment of his first marriage to Jane Alvies, the ambiguity of which disqualified him from consideration as a bishop in the eyes of some members of his church. Embarrassingly for Pike's chances, in the weeks following his San Francisco nomination, much of the adverse information regarding his actions for annulment was provided to the standing committees by the most prominent Episcopalian in the city of his former residence, Los Angeles.

Bishop Francis Eric Bloy, diocesan bishop of Los Angeles, had not approved the decision in the neighboring see of having Pike proposed as the church's next coadjutor bishop. Bloy had succeeded the now-deceased Bishop Bertrand Stevens, whom Pike represented as having approved in 1943 the annulment of his marriage to Alvies. Bloy "must have known," in the opinion of Pike's friends Stringfellow and Towne, that no document unambiguously confirming Stevens's approval of the annulment could be produced from the Los Angeles diocese's archives should Pike be challenged on his version of the details. All that was at hand in these archives was Stevens's letter to Pike of November 27, 1942, stating that the bishop had restored Pike "to communicant status." There was also a handwritten note—apparently with no file copy placed in the diocesan archives—that Pike said he received from Stevens, dated March 23, 1943. This note informed Pike that "if you were now petitioning for the right to remarry I would (with the necessary legal approval) give my consent"—but such a document was, by church law, insufficient documentation. Under canon 18, "Of Regulations Respecting Holy Matrimony," in effect since 1937, "any member of this Church in good standing, whose marriage has been annulled or dissolved by a civil court of competent jurisdiction," might apply to the diocesan bishop "for a judgment as to his or her marital status in the eyes of the Church." Immediately following this text was a section plainly written: "Every judgment rendered under this Canon shall be in writing and shall be made a matter of permanent record in the Archives of the Diocese or Missionary District."

To a secular mind, aware of Pike's civil court divorce judgment, granted in 1941 and placed into court files, this absence of a diocesan record of annulment might appear to be an inconsequential legalism; but to those who profess the sanctity of canon law, such as bishops or would-be bishops, Pike's casualness in this matter implied, at best, an insufficient respect for marriage as a sacrament. Bloy was unmoved by any proffered justifications in the dean's favor. He was adamant in his public insistences that Pike did not qualify according to the biblical standard of I Timothy 3:2, that a bishop be "the husband of one wife." The Los Angeles bishop found an ally with a priest active in the Sacramento diocese, and, by late February 1958, these two began a national letter-writing campaign to their Church's standing committees, "expressing shock and concern over the election of Dean Pike in the Diocese of California." Their letter continued, "If he is consecrated and this trend continues, what effect will it have on the Church, and the general concept of the office of bishop?" Bloy and his disciple then answered their own query, declaring that "the Church will suffer more in the long run if he or anyone else in such a position is consecrated bishop."

Pike wanted this new job, and he was willing to fight for it. Soon aware of Bloy's campaign, he called upon friends in the clergy and the legal profession to write letters of rebuttal to the standing committees and the bishops. For the next three months, from late February to April 1958, the details of his first marriage and supposed annulment were reopened for view by practically the whole episcopacy. Considering the unprecedented resistance to his nomination outside the California diocese, his comparative happiness while living in New York State, and the emotionally awkward position into which Esther Pike was placed by this public revisiting of her husband's prior marriage, one cannot help but wonder why Pike persisted. "He should never have become a bishop," Betts later recalled ruefully. "My wife and I fought that for all we were worth. His great podium was the Cathedral of St. John the Divine. He should never have left it. He didn't have to worry there about money or power. He had a perfect spot to be heard and to be seen." Betts had an insight, however, into what had made his friend so restless in his ambitions. "At heart, he was a Californian. He had grown up with the idea that San Francisco was it. The idea of being bishop there had an over-whelming fascination for him." The canon precentor, who was both a compassionate and, at times, acerbic observer of Pike, then added, "Nothing in heaven or hell could have stopped him."

Pike did compose a compassionate note for his wife to read pri-vately, in which he told her that, regardless of the consequences for his election, he "remained grateful for 15½ years of a genuine marriage and four children, and 13 years in holy orders with what appeared to be a useful ministry." He then also composed a public statement, indicating that he had no intentions of abandoning his fight for the position. Writ-ing in private collaboration with John Rauch, the chancellor, or chief legal advisor, of the diocese of Indiana, Pike arranged on March 13 to have a letter signed only by Rauch mailed to the Church's other chan-cellors. Rauch presented in this letter a detailed defense of Pike's annul-ment, arguing on the four legal grounds of res adjudicata, full faith and credit, double jeopardy, and ex post facto. Pike himself by the end of the month circulated a signed, four-page statement, headed "The Basic Facts Are These," among the standing committees. While not address-ing the lack of diocesan records, Pike recounted how Stevens had "stated spontaneously" to him in 1940 that his marriage was to be con-sidered annullable, and how, after his second marriage in 1941 in a civil ceremony, "I wrote Bishop Stevens, caught him up to date and asked for a formal expression of his decision as to the null character of the first union." According to Pike, he "granted the request, and, following his direction, we had our marriage solemnized in the Church." These two letters may not have persuaded any wavering voters in Pike's favor, and they may, unfortunately, have contributed to his reputation for sophis-try and legalism.

Meanwhile, back at the deanery, Johnson was keeping an updated tally as reports reached him of pro- and anti-Pike sentiments expressed as the standing committees debated their votes. Factoring out dioceses in which consent to the dean's nomination was assured, Johnson divided the remaining standing committees into three categories: Likely, Doubtful, and Declined. Troubling to Johnson and others at the cathe-dral was the growing number of committees entered in the Declined column. Bloy's letter-writing campaign had found receptive readers, not only in the South, but also in other areas of the national episcopacy. By the third week of March, committees from dioceses in Colorado, Michigan, Nebraska, and Wisconsin had been added to the Declined column. The diocesan standing committees of Los Angeles and Sacramento were also recorded against Pike. Sometimes these refusals of consent to his nomination were phrased civilly and regretfully; the members of the diocesan committee of Fond du Lac, Wisconsin, for example, after declining to support Pike's nomination, wrote to their counterparts in the California diocese, "We wish it understood that this action does not imply any reflection upon his faith or morals." Bloy and Henry Louttit, however, harvested a wide resentment of Pike's nomination among the Sewanee owning dioceses. For example, the diocesan committee at Charleston, South Carolina, not only refused to confirm Pike's nomination but also phrased its refusal in a fiery, two-page letter to the California diocese, in which the Book of Common Prayer was quoted on the examination of bishops. The South Carolinians in their letter underlined the final passage of the examination: "Will you deny all ungodliness and worldly lusts, and live soberly, righteously, and godly in this present world; that you may show yourself in all things an example of good works unto others, that the adversary may be ashamed, having nothing to say against you?" Obviously, they thought the answer was no.

But by the first week of April 1958, Pike had begun to pick up consents from diocesan committees in border states, including Sewanee owning dioceses, such as Missouri, North Carolina, Texas, and Virginia. A tier of standing committees and bishops in Massachusetts, New Jersey, New York, and Pennsylvania also voted in his favor. On April 8, 1958, the *New York Times* reported that the presiding bishop of the Episcopal Church the previous day had officially notified Pike of his election to the California bishopric. Once again, the vote had been close, although not as perilously narrow as his nomination at the California convention. The division among the church's bishops in his favor was not publicly disclosed, other than the announcement by the presiding bishop that Pike had obtained a majority. But among the fully reported votes of the Episcopal Church's seventy-five diocesan standing committees, forty-six had voted their consent, eight more than had been needed for a majority. Potentially troubling for Pike's future, however, was that nineteen committees, more than one-third of the church's total, had voted opposition to Pike's elevation as a bishop.

But bishop he was, or soon was to be, after his confirmation in ceremonies scheduled at Grace Cathedral. There were both congratulations and regrets arriving at the deanery for what was to be Pike's move to a California bishopric. Pittenger and Krumm were delighted at the promotion of their friend and coauthor, Pittenger writing in italicized enthusiasm that "you would be such an addition to the House of Bishops" by virtue of having "*both* brains and sense." Esther Pike was not as emphatic in her celebrations. The Pike family had averaged a household move about once every three years since her marriage, and this time she was faced with traveling across the nation and relocating herself with the couple's four children, two now of middle school age, in a new city and new classrooms. There would also be the relocation of Pike's formidable mother closer to their new home. After the death of her second husband, Pearl McFadden had married a retired railroad official, Clarence Chambers, and they had lived at a comparatively noninterfering distance from the Pikes' New York City household in a small town in North Carolina. But having become widowed a third time and exultant at her son's nomination, Pike's mother planned to move to California in order to be closer to her son.

It fell to former Canon Betts to express the deepest misgivings, before and after the fact, about his friend's elevation to the California bishop's chair. Betts, by the time of the confirmation of Pike's nomination, had left the canonry at St. John's and obtained a deanship of his own at a cathedral in Rhode Island; but two years later, in 1960, when the bishop invited Betts to move to California and become the diocesan archdeacon and canon to the ordinary, Betts agreed, and he did his best there to protect Pike, professionally and personally. The consequences were mixed. "You cannot be a bishop *and* a prophet," he later recalled with his own emphasis after Pike's death. "That is even truer without a strategy. He had no strategy whatsoever. It was just run on to this, to that, to whatever came along." Betts then tersely summarized in a 1973 interview the repeated calls for heresy presentments, the divorce, the suicides and near suicides, and the other scandals attendant to Pike's assumption of the office. Betts put it plainly: after Pike became a bishop, he said, "people were hurt."

V

An Unconventional Bishop
on Nob Hill

A mitre doesn't look good on me.

—BISHOP PIKE, in correspondence with the editors
of the Episcopal publication *The Witness*, September 1959

On the morning of May 15, 1958, Pike had the remarkable experience
of hearing a cautionary sermon directed at him personally from the pulpit of Grace Cathedral, an uncompleted structure of concrete towers
and spires overlooking San Francisco from the elevation of Nob Hill.
He listened among a congregation of about two thousand. The occasion
was his consecration service as the fourth Episcopal bishop coadjutor of
the diocese of California.

The morning's ceremonies, on Ascension Day by the ecclesiastical
calendar, had begun at ten thirty with all the liturgical pomp for which
his Church is noted. A processional, with a total of sixteen bishops in
attendance, entered Grace from the completed area of the eastern
narthex and advanced westward along the nave toward the altar, passing

underneath stained-glass windows, columned bays, and the cathedral's neo-Gothic arches. Pike had been among them, wearing the white, comparatively unadorned liturgical tunic called a rochet. He seated himself near the pulpit and by the presiding bishop's chair. In an innovation appropriate to Pike's personality, the ceremonies were broadcast live by television throughout San Francisco.

The order of service called for a sermon to be delivered before Pike received the laying on of hands by other bishops present to legitimize his election. The preacher was John Coburn, academic dean of the Episcopal Theological School in Cambridge, Massachusetts, and an old friend of Pike's. The two had vacationed together with their families during summers on Cape Cod, and there had successfully obtained funding to build an Episcopal chapel in Wellfleet for visitors and local residents, the Chapel of St. James the Fisherman. Coburn spoke that morning on the general duties of a bishop for about two-thirds his allotted time; then, in a remarkable apostrophe, he turned in the pulpit to face Pike directly and address his concluding remarks to "Brother Jim," as Coburn familiarly called him. His message came "with the hope that, although you would not heed my words as a friend to remain as the dean on the heights of Morningside, you might take to heart the words of God delivered as a preacher as you are elevated to the office of bishop on Nob Hill."

The words subsequently delivered were a praiseful rebuke. Coburn began by noting to Pike that "there has never been any question about your being a bishop. The only questions have been when, and in what diocese? In God's providence, the time is now, and the place your native land." He then honestly characterized his friend. "You speak the language of the people of the world," and "you are a controversial person." Pike's enthusiasm for controversy, Coburn said, "is part of your strength." The bishop-elect also was told, "You are at your best in controversy when you have been able to incarnate in yourself the principle which is at stake for which you would fight. . . . Witness the issue of segregation in the Church, and your part in it." Yet the preacher worried aloud that Pike was not sufficiently aware that his past controversies had occasioned his church "damage and separation not always necessary" and that his talent for putting his spiritual causes into worldly terms might lead him to lose that spirituality to the world. Coburn concluded,

"Your strength as a bishop will be determined as you engage in controversy as a last, and not as a first, resort."

If Pike was nonplussed on hearing these words, he gave no outward sign. Coburn remained a close friend for years after his consecration sermon (although Pike did confidentially tell an acquaintance in late 1958 that Coburn, although "definitely tops," also "has a candor that might seem to be negative"). But whatever his personal feelings, there was a liturgical ceremony to complete, and one of the great advantages of ritual is that it keeps everyone moving nicely along. Pike, by prearrangement, now stood and was escorted toward the altar by a small procession of suffragan and diocesan bishops. Awaiting them was the Church's presiding bishop, the Right Reverend Henry Knox Sherrill. Pike was formally introduced to him with these words: "Reverend Father, in God, we present unto you this godly and well-learned man, to be ordained and consecrated bishop." After a questioning and response of his beliefs, from the Book of Common Prayer, Pike received vestments over his rochet, including a bishop's stole placed about his neck. He then knelt, while nine consecrating bishops formed a circle about him and solemnly laid hands upon his head. Their number included Eric Bloy of Los Angeles and Arthur Barksdale Kinsolving of Arizona, close relative of Arthur L. Kinsolving of New York. Sherrill bid their newly vested brother to rise, and Pike was a bishop. The cathedral's carillon of forty-four bells pealed the good news to San Francisco, the congregation dispersed cheerfully down the building's outside steps and onto its plaza, and Pike and his family were honored guests at a luncheon at the Mark Hopkins Hotel.

He charmed his new diocese, and there were few misgivings when Pike as the bishop coadjutor succeeded to the higher office of diocesan bishop after Bishop Block's unexpected death on September 20, 1958. Such prominent Episcopalians as Goodwin J. Knight, the state's Republican governor, and William W. Crocker, a powerful San Francisco banker, did not see their new bishop as the divisive church controversialist described by Coburn in his sermon. By contrast, what the vestrymen and major financial contributors saw—at least until the first year of the 1960s—was an urbane, witty bishop, apparently happily married, noticeably affectionate toward his mother, fond of his cigarettes and dry martinis, and spiritually comfortable with California's economic and political establishments. Their view of Pike was not the result of his dissimulation; his ministry shifted for one or two years after he moved to California. The political activism and social prophecy espoused by theologians on the East Coast such as Reinhold Niebuhr and practiced by Pike when he was the dean at St. John's gave place temporarily to newer, politically less threatening interests. Pike was a creature of the moment. "My notions are all derived from other people," he honestly told a *Saturday Evening Post* interviewer at his bishop's office in 1961. "I just get behind the ones I like." From his consecration in early summer of 1958 until approximately the fourth week of Advent in 1960, Pike's new interests were not primarily political or social prophecy, but ecumenism and secularism.

His latest enthusiasms were at least partly a consequence of commissioning from the Stanford Research Institute a "market survey" of the California diocese in December 1958. This demographic investigation was one of his initial official administrative acts as a diocesan bishop, and he was perhaps the first bishop in the 1950s to consider his diocese as a marketplace to be studied. The findings confirmed the assertions announced that same month by the U.S. Census Bureau. "Six of the nine counties in our diocese now constitute the fastest-growing area in the country," Pike announced, the state of California itself having increased its population, according to the bureau, by 35 percent between 1950 and 1958. This influx of residents—with large numbers of both nominal Protestants and the unchurched—was seen by the bishop as an undeveloped market, or, as he emphatically announced, "Every Sunday there are new people, Episcopalian and non-Episcopalian, taking a 'look-see.' " It was evident to Pike that his personal success and that of his Church in California would be the result of what he described as "throwing out as wide a net as possible." His energies therefore were occupied throughout 1959–60 in attracting to his diocese the expanding market of what he personalized to other Episcopalians as "the lapsed Methodist or [the] secularist 'seeker.' "

His methods were as unconventional as the growing population of the Golden State. In mid-May 1959, Pike rented what formerly had been commercial space in the Mills Building in the heart of San Francisco's financial district—at an annual cost of $30,000—to open a chapel for the "secularist seekers" among the stockbrokers and traders in the adjoining offices. *Time* magazine, sensing a good story, sent a reporter and a photographer to the building on the day that Pike, dressed in his vestments, first opened the chapel's doors to the public. "This is a place," Pike told the delighted reporter, "designed to attract the 'money-changers' back into the temple." Later that summer, in August, Pike again cast his ecclesiastical net as wide as possible, this time for "lapsed" Protestants, by instructing his rectors to provide communion to any confessing Christian who attended services, rather than limiting the participants to confirmed Episcopalians. He reminded his diocese that "the altar in one of our churches is not a 'Protestant Episcopal' altar; it is the Lord's Table," and that "many visiting non-Episcopalians" were "much more likely to consider coming into the Church via confirmation if they are accepted at the Lord's Table."

Finally, on November 1, All Saints' Day, Pike "broke through a man-made barrier," in his description, by formally recognizing a Methodist minister, Rev. George Hadley, as having dual ordination in both the Methodist and Episcopal churches. The ceremony included a symbolic laying on of hands by the bishop upon the Methodist clergyman. Pike justified his actions—"I wasn't a lawyer for nothing," he told surprised laity—by his reading of what he described as the "somewhat controversial" canon 36 of the Episcopal Church. That canon allowed reordination of clergy into the Episcopal Church if the church considered that the earlier ordination had been "doubtfully authentic"; for example, if an ordained Presbyterian minister wished to leave his denomination and enter the Episcopal clergy as a priest, the minister would be reordained by a bishop of the Anglican Communion considered by the Episcopal Church to be in the apostolic succession from St. Peter. A reordination could also be performed, according to the canon, if a proposed clergyman of another organized church wished "to remain as minister and function in his original denomination," as Pike and Reverend Hadley had explicitly agreed.

Once again, Pike's unconventional actions received national publicity, reported at length in both *Time* and *Newsweek*. But whatever the immediate appeal for publicity intended by Pike, the significance—and the presumption—of this ecumenical action cannot be underestimated, coming as it did at the end of the 1950s, a decade during which American churches were much more denominational and when distinctions among Protestant mainstream churches were considered by both laity and clergy to be of much greater import than they would be in following decades. Pike in effect had given his blessing to a possible new church, which was to be neither the "Protestant Episcopal Church of the United States of America," as his church was known, nor the "Methodist Church," the official name of the denomination to which Hadley had been ordained. Pike seemed to be visualizing the creation in this country of a combined and much larger "Episcopal Methodist Church."

These actions were not without their Episcopal critics. *The Living Church*, at times Anglo-Catholic in perspective, wrote in a worrying editorial that Pike's actions that year were attempting to establish a "super-Protestantism" in the nation's second most populated state. But more important, within his own diocese Pike encountered few public objections from conservative-to-moderate churchmen to his encouragements of a more "open" communion or clerical union with Methodist clergy. The reason for his success was twofold. First, before proceeding with these actions, Pike had obtained support for his legal arguments from such lay leaders within his diocese as William Crocker and Casper Weinberger, a prominent lawyer and a member of the diocesan council of advisors. Second, from a broadly Episcopal viewpoint, the bishop was attempting to persuade *them* to join *us*, and not vice versa.

In fact, the most truculent criticism in California of Pike's recognition of dual ordination within his church came not from the state's Episcopalians, but from its Methodists. Particularly vocal in opposition was a Methodist professor of the Old Testament at the Pacific School of Religion. In an article published in *Christian Century*, this professor heaped scorn upon what he termed the "in-groupness among some Episcopal clergymen and laymen which makes them unwilling to accept the ministry of anyone who has not been sanctified—properly or improperly—according to their own traditions." Pike was annoyed by this criticism from the academy, and he displayed a flash of intellectual arrogance when he answered his critic, in a response published in a subsequent issue of *Christian Century*, written in the style of one who had studied under Tillich and Niebuhr and was forced to address his theological inferior. The Methodist critic "missed the distinction that is almost boringly obvious in modern theology," Pike wrote, "that between the essential and the existential." Whatever the essential total-ity of orders within the Methodist or Episcopal churches, Pike declared, "existentially not one of us operates as a total minister of Christ." Therefore, since "no man's orders are totally valid," there was an urgency for both Methodists and Episcopalians to minister "across the board" by ecumenical and unconventional methods.

This "existential" justification of forms of worship was a new way of thinking for Pike, apparently apropos of his move to California with its shifting demographics. Gone were the certainties he had found while studying back east the writings of Archbishop William Temple, who had assumed that right reason and a study of the natural world inevitably would bring mankind back to an established Christian church. New ideas now fascinated the bishop, including the existential urgency of his church engaging secular men and women as they actually live in the world. The fullest expression of Pike's new thinking in 1959 was the then so-called California customary.

Customaries in the Episcopal Church are the written descriptions of the ceremonial practices accompanying the act of worship at a partic-ular church or congregation, and Pike enjoyed writing them. He and Coburn together had written a customary for the Chapel of St. James the Fisherman in Cape Cod, and one of Pike's first acts after becoming the dean at St. John's was studying the customaries of the historic cathe-drals of the Church of England and writing one to bring the New York cathedral into accordance. Practices according to a customary could vary noticeably between Low Church and High, that is, between a "Protestant" Episcopal church and a more Anglo-Catholic one. Prior to his writing the California customary in midsummer 1959 for use by his diocese's mission churches, or those churches that could not yet support a full-time priest, Pike consistently had displayed a High Church, Anglo-Catholic preference. For example, in the customary prepared in 1953 for St. John the Divine, he had taken pride in restoring to use the traditional vestments of the cathedral's clergy, requiring such attire as the chasuble decorated in liturgical colors; this was an outer sleeveless garment worn by priests celebrating the Eucharist and derived from the outdoor cloak of the Greco-Roman world.

All the more remarkable, then, were Pike's instructions to his priests in the California customary of 1959 that they encourage a member of the laity, attired "in a business suit," to participate in their church's processionals and that they themselves obtain their bishop's approval before donning such liturgical clothing as a cope, another long, cloak-like garment with Roman origins. Both in writing his five-thousand-word customary and in justifying its usage, Pike made another of his calculated breaks with his past, this time in reference to his own Anglo-Catholic origins. This once newly ordained rector who in Poughkeepsie had insisted upon placing candles on the altar of Christ Church now told his fellow Episcopalians in California that too much emphasis upon keeping lit candles inside the church building was a sign of " 'Zoroastrian' light worship." Another instance of his changed views was his pragmatic answer to the question of whether an Episcopalian present at Eucharist should merely bow toward the sanctified elements or perform the High Church act of genuflection. "I don't think God cares," Pike responded. Formerly a "smells and bells" Episcopalian, he now judged the appropriateness of burning incense by observing the response of the congregation. "In the churches of which I am the rector," the bishop declared in defense of his customary, "I won't let a whiff of anything cause them to start for the door; but if they like it, they can have it until they can't breathe."

The new customary was criticized by both Low and High Church Episcopalians, although, once again, the brunt of the criticism came from outside his diocese and the state of California. The most frequent complaints were that, in addressing such liturgical details as the wearing of a business suit or a cope, Pike was attempting to impose his own legalistic and authoritarian rule upon his diocese's methods of worship. "Prelatic" and "pontifical" were words used to describe the customary in articles published that autumn in the Low Church publication *The Witness*, which objected not to the details of the customary but to Pike's autonomously imposing it. The High Church publication *The Living Church* also questioned in an editorial whether Pike was attempting to create in California an Episcopal clergy "functioning securely and happily only under a set of blueprints supplied from above."

These criticisms missed the point. Pike wrote the California customary not simply, or even largely, out of his egoism, but in an attempt to attract to his church the growing secular population of his diocese and state. These were the people who, in Pike's description in a defense of his customary published in *The Witness*, would be attracted by "bigger and bolder" and "less priest-centered" ceremonies than the Episcopal Church was accustomed to providing in the more settled, and presumably more sedate, Atlantic seaboard states. He insisted in this article that the California customary's critics—specifically "the eastern authors in relatively more static areas"—possessed "no hint of the existential situation" in the fifty mission churches for which it was intended.

The customary also had a significance within the context of Pike's spiritual life of which its critics were unaware. Prior to writing it, Pike had been comfortable containing a philosophically liberal theology and mildly progressive politics within High Church Anglo-Catholic liturgical practices. This combination of liberal modernism and Anglo-Catholicism was an established tradition within the nineteenth-century Episcopal Church, and long before Pike's ordination as deacon its seminarian opponents had described it, satirically, as the belief of "Hegel in a chasuble." (Their point was that the Hegelian idea of God is incompatible with belief in the Trinity and other Christian dogma, but the Anglo-Catholic modernists, schooled in continental philosophy and German biblical criticism, thought they could reconcile the differences.) Pike's new customary was the expression within his mind of his growing unease at identifying a modernist, existential church with high liturgical practices. For him, Georg W. F. Hegel was coming out of the chasuble—as were Søren Kierkegaard, Dietrich Bonhoeffer, and other existential and unconventional thinkers who were attractive to Pike.

Despite complaints about his customary published that fall of 1959 in the church's national press, Pike retained the doctrinal trust of many conservative and High Church Episcopalians within his diocese. As he himself pointed out, his eastern critics had misstated the applicability of the customary; its usage was required by the bishop only within the diocese's mission churches, and not within any of the established parishes, which were free to follow more traditional usages. Also, he did not articulate any disturbingly new theologies based upon his changing views of the liturgy until late in 1960, and, remarkably for Pike, he engaged in few high-profile political controversies until after that year. As an exception, he did continue his old quarrel with the Roman Catholic Church over the issue of birth control, most notably in December 1959 when he publicly asked whether the papal policy against artificial contraception "is binding on Roman Catholic candidates for public office." The nation's most prominently Roman Catholic office seeker, presidential hopeful John F. Kennedy, subsequently was described by *Time* that month as being "burned at being put on the spot" by Pike's question. Asked about his personal opinion of the bishop and his question, Kennedy brusquely responded, "That's my business." Yet such occasional confrontations with the adherents of the Church of Rome over the issue of birth control cost Pike little in popularity or authority with his fellow Episcopalians on Nob Hill.

Contributing also to his good repute within his diocese and his national church was the fact that the bishop had, at least initially, a nice touch for collecting money. When in late 1958 Pike assumed the office of diocesan bishop, the diocese of California reported total receipts to the church's national office of $2,903,586.56. Twelve months later, under Pike's bishopric, the diocese announced nearly a 15 percent increase in its receipts, to $3,327,038.26. Much of this new revenue came in the form of contributions to the Golden Anniversary Committee, established by Pike in 1959 and chaired by William Crocker, for fund-raising to complete the unfinished eastern entrance of Grace Cathedral. Pike also succeeded in changing his diocese's method of collecting revenues for its operations from the area's parishes, substituting in 1960 a voluntary tithe in place of a fixed assessment for each parish. Vestrymen and parishioners were very pleased with this change, and responded at first by generously tithing; but perhaps unconsidered by Pike in making this change was that he had linked the diocesan finances permanently to his own popularity, and that a steady receipt of budgetary money was assured only so long as he remained for the parishes a charismatic and well-liked bishop.

But, generally, for the first two years of Pike's bishopric money was generously given and the press clippings were good. By these outward signs, it might be assumed that Pike in 1960 was a happy man, or at least a content one. Such was not the case. His heart—what St. Augustine considered one's personal, worldly, and religious aspirations—remained as restless as ever. Partially, his troubles that year resulted from his personal finances. Despite his success in raising money for the diocese, Pike and his wife were having trouble making ends meet at home. They were unable, for example, to afford their usual vacation that summer to Cape

Cod. Early that year, Pike wrote to his friend Coburn saying not to expect the Pike family to join the Coburns at the beach. "[W]e had hoped," Pike wrote candidly, that "our financial situation would seem to better itself, but even with some honoraria and [book] royalty advances, the situation has continued pressing, since the cost of living is higher here than in New York, the school tuitions for four children are higher—and the cost of maintaining the bishop's house is much higher than maintaining the deanery." The children were a growing concern for Pike, or, perhaps more accurately, he was involving himself personally for the first time in their upbringing. He worried that his elder son, Jim, seemed unable to perform with academic confidence, despite attending a succession of carefully chosen schools. His elder daughter, Catherine, also was away from home that year, having received Pike's permission—which he regretted almost immediately—for an exchange-student trip to Borneo and Indonesia.

His daughter returned safely, but there were darker domestic troubles for Pike. Rumors of marital infidelity were repeated more insistently and more frequently after the family moved to San Francisco. "It was a constant whisper in the diocese, in the House of Bishops, and everywhere he went," Darby Betts recalled. These rumors also had made their way inside the 2510 Jackson Street residence of the bishop and his wife. He dealt with them, and his wife's increasing anger, by doubling and then tripling the amount of time he spent at his job, and, in a familiar pattern, began a plethora of new programs and spending.

He increased the number of his diocesan staff—and the employees and programs for which he ultimately was responsible—by hiring four directors for the newly created departments of education, social relations, stewardship, and promotions. By March, the *Pacific Churchman*, an Episcopal newsletter within his state, reported "record spending" that year in the diocese of California. Also that year, Pike invited Betts to move to San Francisco and become the archdeacon of the diocese and the canon in the ordinary, or personal advisor, to the bishop. His invitation was perhaps an attempt, unconsciously or consciously, to bring to his side one of the number of East Coast teachers and acquaintances who previously had acted as preceptors to his enthusiasms and excesses. Betts accepted the offer, but discovered soon after his arrival at the California diocesan offices that his unspecified duties also included acting as a majordomo to Pike, attempting to prevent the bishop from publicly embarrassing himself with women or alcohol. Betts was shocked, for instance, to discover Pike's new habit of concealing liquor bottles "in extraordinary places" inside his study. "I would find them and hide them in other places," Betts recalled.

As a result of Betts's discretions and his wife's forebearance, Pike was able to continue throughout the early 1960s at his usual frenetic pace. With the donated use of a Piper Cub airplane and pilot, the bishop traveled speedily over what he liked to describe as his "vast" diocese. Twice each month, he also commuted by commercial airline to Los Angeles in order to spend several hours at a Hollywood studio taping two shows at one sitting of his ABC national program, now titled *Bishop Pike*. (None of this activity was hindered by a serious hernia operation, which necessitated that his wife be his chauffeur for his trips throughout San Francisco.) Additionally in 1961 he assumed the responsibility of the chairmanship of the state's Advisory Committee to the U.S. Commission on Civil Rights, and he also served on the confidential committee convened by the House of Bishops to study "the problems of maladjusted clergy." A particular emphasis was placed upon the consequences of alcoholism and homosexuality. Pike signed in approval the committee's remarkably foresighted final conclusions, including the assertion "When we elect a president of the United States, hire a yardman, or select a mechanic to work on our car, we do not ask him what he does with his genitals. We want him to do what he is hired to do well; we tacitly agree that his sex life is his own affair."

The committee's report was kept at its request from most Episcopal laity on a "need to know" basis, but Pike also continued his usual production of polemical public writings. He coauthored with Richard Byfield, a newly hired executive assistant and chaplain, a partisan book, *A Roman Catholic in the White House*, published before the November presidential election. The two authors openly questioned "the degree to which a Roman Catholic president would really be able to enter into the occasions reflecting our pluralistic society." The bishop also agreed to provide a lengthy personal essay on his latest theological thinking to *Christian Century* later that year. And in a nationally publicized sermon and announcement at Grace Cathedral on December 4, 1960, Pike joined with Eugene Carson Blake, the stated clerk of the United Pres-

byterian Church, in a call for their respective national churches to com-
bine into one national congregation. The Methodist Church and the
United Church of Christ also were invited to join the proposed union.
The consequently named "Blake-Pike proposals" created what the
Christian Century described in a headline the next month as the "Big
Bang" of American ecumenism.

Yet even all this extraordinary activity could not allay the bishop's
restlessness, or his increasingly self-destructive consumption of alcohol.
Betts witnessed a frightening instance of the latter. "Just after the Blake-
Pike proposals here in the cathedral," Betts later recounted, "he had to
go to New York to be on the radio about the proposals. I went with him."
Their flight having been diverted to Boston as the result of a sudden
snowstorm, Betts and Pike were reduced to traveling to their destination
on a night bus. Pike carried aboard a half-pint of bourbon kept in his
pocket—"He usually did in those days," Betts observed—and drank it as
their bus slowly made its way in the direction of New York City. While
the bus stalled beside a railroad embankment, Pike suddenly was possessed by the idea that he might run to the tracks and flag down the next
passenger train to New York. "Let me out!" he shouted without pream-
ble, and, before Betts could restrain him, he "tore his clothes open,
exposing his purple vest and began waving his pectoral cross." The
amazed driver opened the bus door. Pike ran up the embankment, and,
in Betts's horrified emphasis, the intoxicated bishop "stood in the *middle*
of the tracks, waving that cross." Sure enough, a passenger train soon
came speeding on the tracks. There was "a screeching of brakes and
whistles blowing frantically and sand and snow flying all over the place."

The train stopped before it ran over the bishop. Pike, who was
"delighted," in Betts's word, joined the rest of the bus's passengers in
transferring to the faster train. The bishop made his radio broadcast on
schedule. Pike was unfazed by his near miss and apparently unrepentant
of the shock he had given to his archdeacon. Betts was to witness other
instances of dramatically self-destructive behavior while Pike was
drunk. Chronic drinking was becoming for Pike an act of attempted suicide, and there were to be many curtain calls.

Pike ended the year 1960 facing his first serious criticisms as a bishop.
Negative publicity greeted *A Roman Catholic in the White House*. The

Saturday Review dismissed it as "a highly biased account" of Kennedy's religious unsuitability to be president, and other critics complained of the two authors' specious reasoning and selective use of Vatican documents. One reviewer asserted that the passages in the book written by the bishop had the "earmarks of haste."

More detrimental to Pike's position in his church were the hostile reactions to the article he had written for the December 21 issue of the *Christian Century* describing his latest theological convictions. This article had been commissioned by the editors as part of their ongoing series, "How My Mind Has Changed," in which prominent American religious figures were invited to compare their past religious assumptions to their present spiritual beliefs at the opening year of the new decade. Pike's assertions of his changed beliefs, published in the fourth week of Advent, were an unconventional Christmastime declaration for the readership. "When Norman Pittenger and I were writing *The Faith of the Church* (a semiofficial Episcopal book on doctrine)," Pike began, "he did not find reason to accept the historical Virgin Birth; I thought I did." Pike then declared, "Now I am with him."

A secular reader might wonder why Pike's public declaration of doubt about the reality of the Virgin Birth, as with his prior questionings of the Triune nature of God, subsequently were judged so objectionable by his fellow Episcopalians in 1961. Few in the twenty-first century, even among Christian believers, trouble themselves any longer over the issues of parthenogenesis or the Triune nature of ultimate reality that had so occupied the early Church in the Council of Nicene in 325 C.E. and the Council at Chalcedon in 451 C.E. But if modernist Protestants—including many within the Anglican Communion—tacitly have cast aside the literal concepts of the Virgin Birth and the Trinity as "excess baggage," in Pike's subsequent phrase, then their discard of these ideas is directly a consequence of Pike's and, later, Bishop John A. T. Robinson's, controversial proselytizing against these doctrines throughout the early 1960s. However, at the time of Pike's *Christian Century* article these doctrines were considered essential theological baggage and had been for more than a millennium and a half. Indeed, an integral part of the liturgy of the Book of Common Prayer was—and is—the recitation of the Apostles' Creed and its public affirmation of belief in Jesus Christ, "Born of the Virgin Mary." Pike's apparently casual denial of this doctrine of the Virgin Birth therefore struck many in his church at that time as a deliberate blow against the sanctity of the *Symbolum Apostolorum,* or Apostles' Creed, and against biblical scripture itself.

But for all its incipient controversy, had Pike followed his statement with a few paragraphs of justification and then simply concluded the *Christian Century* article, the bishop's candor might have been better received. Skepticism over the literal truth of the Virgin Birth had not been unusual among liberal Anglican clergy since at least the beginning of the twentieth century, and so long as its denial was not expressed provocatively, this skepticism was within the accepted boundaries of the church's thought. Even the late Archbishop William Temple before his ordination had experienced difficulties in accepting its historical reality. One of Pike's perennial failures, however, was that he never had learned either in print or in person when to stop. He dilated upon his disbelief in the next paragraph that he could "no longer regard grace, or the work of the Holy Spirit, as limited explicitly to the Christian revelation," seemingly unwitting that many of his churchmen would consider this statement as apostasy. In concluding his article with an emphasis that "the *kerygma* is, was, and shall be primary," he wrote with an infelicitous crudity. "The church was centered around the truth of the gospel," Pike explained, "but the Bible came along as a sort of *Reader's Digest* anthology."

The critical responses were swift. "Is Bishop James A. Pike undermining our Christian faith?" was headlined on one-thousand fliers anonymously mailed in early January 1961 to other dioceses by "Episcopalians for the Faith," an ad hoc group of conservatives organized in Oakland, California. Their flier posited seventeen specific "questions we *must* ask" (italics in original), including, "Is James Pike presuming to be a prophet and bringing us a new word that Joseph is the human father of Jesus?" Outside the California diocese, fifteen Episcopal clergy in Georgia gathered on January 28 into a local convocation, known as a clericus, to assert that Pike's article "calls into grave doubt his suitability for exercising jurisdiction as a bishop of this church." They formally petitioned their diocesan bishop that charges of heresy be considered against Pike the following September at the triennial general convention of both the House of Bishops and the House of Delegates. The Georgia clericus specifically objected to Pike's expressed "disbelief in the Virgin Birth of our Lord" and his denial of "the necessity of salvation through Jesus Christ."

To both his critics and supporters, Pike responded to this first heresy crisis of his career by frequently quoting John 3:17: "But he that doeth truth cometh to the light." (The verse apparently was one of his favorites, having provided the title for his 1955 book on ethics, *Doing the Truth*, and having received a special exegesis by his former teacher Tillich in the latter's book *The Shaking of the Foundations*.) Pike's biblical point is best taken as meaning that, by late 1960, the bishop could no longer fully occupy himself with liturgical and proselytizing duties. Pike now felt compelled to proclaim his religious doubts as necessary to his being spiritually honest and his "doing the truth." His public statements on doctrine immediately before the heresy crisis precipitated by his article had been, in fact, increasingly confessional and impulsive. One month before the appearance of the *Christian Century* article, Pike had reacted strongly in Dallas, Texas, at the annual meeting of the House of Bishops to a proposed pastoral letter, supported by Bishop Louttit of South Florida, affirming traditional teachings on the Virgin Birth and the Trinity. Heatedly addressing his fellow bishops, Pike declared that if such a pastoral letter were accepted as an official statement of their church's belief, he himself would be found heretical. Promised the opportunity for further debate on the letter in the future, he finally signed it along with his fellow bishops.

The *Christian Century* article in December subsequently displayed signs indeed of a confessional impulsiveness. Pike had not consulted during its composition with his usual theological mentor, Canon Johnson; and, disregarding the presence in his diocesan office of Betts, he had discussed the contents only with his younger assistant, Byfield, with whom he had authored the unfortunate book on Kennedy. Byfield cautioned Pike that parts of the article were, in his words, "rather far out." In response, Pike had made some revisions, but, in his later recollection, he "didn't spend much time on it," and just "sent it out."

Despite his apparent casualness, Pike's public relations response to his critics was nimble. The same day, January 28, 1961, as the Georgia clericus sent to national newspapers a copy of their request for heresy charges to be considered against him, the bishop granted a telephone interview from his San Francisco home with the *New York Times*. His comments "as a bishop and a lawyer," in Pike's self-describing phrase, were published in the newspaper the following day. He insisted in this interview that the *Christian Century* article had been "within the bounds of doctrinal orthodoxy" as prescribed by such prior Episcopal works as *The Faith of the Church*, which he now identified as a publication "officially issued by the national council of our church." Pike then pointedly redirected his interviewer to a revisit of the Sewanee controversy of 1953. "It would be interesting for the *New York Times* to inquire of this [Georgia] clericus as to how many of their churches are racially integrated," he said, thereby shifting the argument away from the question of his heresy and strongly implying that the clericus's complaint against him was simply an instance of continuing animosity from racially prejudiced clergymen within Sewanee's owning dioceses. The *Times* pursued this inquiry. The spokesman for the Georgia clericus subsequently was placed—or placed himself—into a loser's corner. The newspaper reported the next day that the Georgia clergyman "could not be reached for comment on Bishop Pike's statement."

Two days after the publication of this *Times* interview, delegates from the California diocese met in San Francisco on January 31 to hear their "Bishop's Address" to the diocese's 111th annual convention. Pike once again publicly cast his doctrinal disputes into political terms, in this instance reminding the convention of his opposition while dean of St. John's to Senator Joseph McCarthy's investigations in 1953–54. He now told the California delegates of "an increasing development in the grass roots of people who believed as he [McCarthy] believed." Without explicitly identifying his doctrinal critics with McCarthyism, Pike nevertheless emphatically warned his diocesan convention against "those within the church who would seek to impose their particular interpretations—which they are free to hold and promulgate—upon others, being quick to cry 'heresy' and to seek the censure and discipline of those with whom they disagree."

These imputations of heresy and Pike's political counter-accusations continued in public throughout the first months of 1961. On February 11, Pike wrote a questioning pastoral letter, entitled "What Is Doctrinal Orthodoxy?" in defense of his doubts, and required it to be read the following Sunday from each of the 111 pulpits in his diocese's parish and mission churches. In response, the Episcopal bishop of Long Island, New York, the Right Reverend James P. De Wolfe, issued his own pastoral letter in April to the 210 churches within his diocese, in which he proscribed that "no single bishop has the authority to revise the faith of the church." (De Wolfe had been Pike's predecessor as the dean at St. John's.) Although while writing ex cathedra De Wolfe had not mentioned Pike by name, the New York bishop, when questioned later by a journalist, declared that "obviously" he was referring in his letter to the bishop of California. This public debate had its effects. As September 17 approached, when the members of the House of Bishops were to assemble at Detroit in national convocation with the House of Delegates for the Episcopal Church's sixtieth triennial general convention, Pike's actions clearly had set much of the upcoming agenda. The future of the Blake-Pike proposals, the validity of dual ordination, and the deposition of heresy accusations against the bishop himself were issues that the national Episcopal Church was obliged to discuss in its congress.

Pike traveled to Detroit enjoying substantial support from the California diocese and his former New York State diocese, despite the public stricture of the Long Island pastoral letter. "Churchmen here feel that the heresy charge will never be aired," the *New York Times* wrote of New York's Episcopal delegation prior to the convention. "It would require a presentment to the church's House of Bishops calling for an ecclesiastical trial. It is extremely doubtful, they maintain, that Bishop Pike's peers would countenance such action." In the days following the convention's opening session on September 17, the bishops and delegates gathered were able to resolve the Pike-occasioned issues using the "middle way" of honorable compromise for which the Anglican Communion can be noted. On the one hand, the convention declined to support dual ordination, by recommending that canon 36 be revised restrictively and that the Blake-Pike proposals be further studied; on the other hand, the diocesan bishop of Georgia, the Right Reverend Albert Stuart, was persuaded not to present to his fellows in the House of Bishops his clericus's complaint against Pike. Instead, the bishop and his state's church representatives in the House of Delegates were encouraged to sponsor together a general resolution, offered on September 20, and subsequently adopted by both church houses, reaffirming the traditional beliefs "as expressed in the pastoral letter issued by the House of Bishops meeting in Dallas in the year of our Lord, 1960." A heresy presentment against Pike was thereby avoided, and the bishop of California could vote in good conscience for this joint resolution along with his Georgia brethren. After all, Pike previously had approved this Dallas pastoral letter, albeit with promises of later debate.

Both the houses adjourned on September 28, 1961. The convention's giving him a bye on the Georgia clericus's accusations was accurately interpreted by Pike as confirmation that his doctrinal denials were within a broadly Episcopal belief. The lack of support to bring a presentment of heresy charges against him also implied that he successfully had argued his case to his peers that the accusations were a "phony frame-up," as one of the bishops at the convention told the *New York Times*, in retaliation for Pike's past controversy with Sewanee. The California bishop also interpreted his church's forebearance at Detroit as license to continue preaching and publishing nationally his expressions of a demythologizing, modern theology. The week after the adjournment, an interview with Pike was published in the *Saturday Evening Post* in which he spoke confidently of his Church's desired theological position. "Our loyalty should not be to particular formulations of past centuries," he said, "but rather to the truth they are seeking to express." Rather acidly, he then added, "When a person enters a church, he shouldn't be asked to park his education outside." The bishop's career as an iconoclastic, though popular, theologian was just beginning.

Pike's reinvention of himself in late 1961 as a controversialist did not result in his losing diocesan support or even preferment among his church's other bishops. Partially, his continuing good repute was the result of his success in raising money. The Golden Anniversary Committee, founded by Pike, had advanced sufficiently toward its three-million-dollar goal that on November 14 construction began at Grace Cathedral on the South Tower and the final bays of the building's eastern nave. This unfinished area of the cathedral had been covered with an unsightly wall of sheet metal for the past three decades, the economic Depression of the 1930s having abruptly ended the laity's abilities to honor financial pledges for its construction, but now, after barely three years in residence as bishop, Pike had garnered enough money that completion of Grace Cathedral was foreseeable before the national church's next triennial convention.

In securing financial and political support from the California diocese, Pike also fell back upon the strategies that he had used successfully years before in Poughkeepsie. At Christ Church he had championed from the pulpit the establishment of a department of religion, proactively Christian, to counter what he called the "lowest common denominator" worship practiced at Vassar College. Pike now reintroduced the higher education issue of religious instruction in public universities in California in a Thanksgiving sermon at the cathedral on November 23, 1961. Specifically criticizing the University of California at Berkeley for its lack of a department of religious studies, he warned of this university's failure to provide its students "the same opportunity to understand the principal religious traditions at the same level of maturity at which other aspects of knowledge have been presented to them." This sermon won him favorable and continual press coverage both in the *Pacific Churchman* and the *San Francisco Examiner.* "Pike Again Raps UC on Lack of Religious Education Department," the *Examiner* headlined in a follow-up story.

Also reenacted that year was the quarrel with an educational chaplain who had not performed to Pike's standards. He had found a convenient straw man for his political uses in Robert Morse, the Episcopal chaplain to the Berkeley campus, who in April 1961 had been fired by Pike. Morse had not cooperated well with the "presbyters," a unique innovation by Pike, partly modeled after the organization of the Presbyterian Church, composed of clergy selected by the bishop as his special administrators. A "presbyter" is also the Episcopal Church's official name for a priest, but Pike in the tradition of the Presbyterian Church had made these appointees "ruling presbyters," who in this instance administered areas midway in size between a mission and a deanery. He had become enamored with the idea after attending the Lambeth Palace gathering of bishops in 1958 and participating in ecumenical discussions with the Church of Scotland. However, he had not adopted the Presbyterian Church's organization eliminating the office and title of bishop. These California presbyters reported directly to Pike. Morse had a point in his opposition to Pike's latest innovation. He was, after all, a member of a Church under episcopal—not presbyterian—authority. Pike himself had boasted that he personally had created "the first presbytery (to my knowledge) in the Anglican community." Morse's traditional ecclesiastical authority had been further eroded by the bishop's establishing the "Bishop Berkeley Presbytery" in "the university community across the bay," in Pike's words, "to make it more possible to speak as one voice in the Episcopal Church."

In firing Morse, Pike had chosen to emphasize the ex-chaplain's inactivity rather than his unease at fulfilling church orders from a hand-picked presbytery of a questionable Anglican tradition. The bishop specifically had chastised the chaplain, in a letter circulated among other clergy, for "not reaching out to the entire academic community" and for not having supported the diocese's and presbyters' approval of a "large-scale building program" and "the location of the college work center" on the Berkeley campus. Morse's public dismissal thereby covered a variety of Pike's possible sins. Whatever the objections by potential critics to his theology, no one in his diocese would be able now to accuse the bishop of not being sufficiently a defender or a proselytizer of his church.

There was, meanwhile, growing trouble at home. Esther Pike announced to her husband in 1962 that she intended to obtain legal counsel to seek a formal separation. He was able to dissuade her, on the condition that he accept marital counseling and begin psychoanalysis. The latter led him to the unsurprising insight, recorded in a note to himself, that "as far back as I can remember, *hyperactivity*," in his emphasis, "has been my pattern of response to disappointment, deprivation, or failure." Yet he seemed not to have chosen to put into practice, or had an opportunity to practice, this new insight in the years immediately following.

Pike's energies as a church controversialist between 1962 and 1963 were occupied with a spiritual phenomenon for which neither he nor his critics within the Anglican Communion had much preparation: the sudden appearance of glossolalia, or "speaking in tongues," among Episcopal parishes within the state of California. "And they were all filled with the Holy Spirit and began to speak in other tongues, as the Spirit gave them utterance," recorded the author of Acts 2:4, describing how the disciples had gathered together on the day of Pentecost after the death of Jesus, a verse given little prominence in Episcopal thought. The Episcopal Church's usual exegesis had been that "to speak in other tongues" meant the sudden gift of multilingual or multicultural understanding. To interpret as a direct sign of the Holy Spirit a believer's explosive talking in an unrecognizable or previously unknown language had been the enthusiasm of only a few nonecclesiastical, "Pentecostal" denominations in the Appalachian South or in poor urban neighborhoods in Los Angeles. "We're Episcopalians, not a bunch of wild-eyed hillbillies!" an exasperated member of the affluent St. Mark's Church in Van Nuys exclaimed to a *Newsweek* reporter shortly after the phenomenon of glossolalia was first displayed by church members there in late 1959.

By the early 1960s, the Episcopal practice of glossolalia had become centered, against Pike's will, inside his diocese at the Holy Innocents Parish at Conte Madera, located just across the Golden Gate bridge in Marin County. Like many other Episcopalians, Pike had a doctrinal— and perhaps a socioeconomic—unease in accepting these vocal outbursts from his parishioners as a legitimate form of worship; but unlike Bishop Bloy of Los Angeles, who preemptively fired the rector at St. Mark's and forbade any further expression of speaking in tongues, he had a spiritual and intellectual curiosity about the extraordinary religious or psychological state of consciousness that produced glossolalia and its reputed consequences. He was intrigued by reports that (as he wrote in his subsequent description to the diocese) "a number of our clergy and hundreds of our laity have personally experienced this phenomenon" and that these Episcopalians later claimed "such beneficial results as physical cures, personal integration, marital reconciliation, the elimination of alcohol addiction, and greater devotion to the work of Christ in the world."

In studying this phenomenon, Pike consulted throughout 1962 and early 1963 with a theologian, a New Testament scholar, two psychiatrists, an anthropologist, a parapsychologist, two parish priests (including one who practiced glossolalia), a canon in residence at Grace Cathedral, and his personal canon advisor, Betts. On May 2, 1963, the bishop communicated his findings by having read throughout his diocesan churches a "Pastoral Letter Regarding 'Speaking in Tongues.'" Pike reminded his listeners that "the very rise of this movement within major churches in this country is a sign of a real need and hunger for a more vital, Spirit-filled Christian experience in life." He told his diocese that he was troubled by behavior he had observed among his diocesan congregations experiencing glossolalia, such as the laity laying on hands in apparent acts of apostolic succession, or the spontaneous use of incantatory phrases—such as "Jesus, Jesus, Jesus"—not countenanced by the Book of Common Prayer. Noting that "the religious categories and practices borrowed from Pentecostal denominations raise serious questions as to their consistency with the sacramental theology of the Holy Catholic Church," Pike ended his pastoral letter as prohibitively as the more conservative Bloy. Although not outrightly firing any of his rectors who had condoned or participated in this practice, Pike concluded, "I urge our clergy not to take part in the movement to nurture and spread the practice of speaking in tongues and not to invite preachers or speakers who have this purpose."

In writing this pastoral letter, Pike may have had the disturbing suspicion that, for the first time in his church career, he was slightly behind the curve of the coming spiritual movement. From his ordination as a deacon in 1944, his career had coincided with the remarkable postwar growth in membership among the mainstream U.S. churches. Episcopal, Methodist, Presbyterian, and Lutheran national headquarters all had reported historically high enrollment figures for their congregations within the decade and a half after 1945. However, by 1963, membership among these denominations had crested. A new plurality of Christian worshipers was emerging, variously described as the Pentecostals or the New Charismatics. In a prescient article written for *Life* magazine in 1958, Henry Van Dusen, a friend of Pike's and the president of Union Theological Seminary, had termed this emerging world church of believers in the United States, South America, and parts of Africa as the "third force"—being subsequent in appearance to Roman Catholicism and European-state Protestantism. This third force of Christianity, as described by Van Dusen, was distinguished from the first two historical forms of the Christian church by its non-ecclesiastical, nonnationalistic, relatively unsophisticated origins, and its emphasis upon Pentecostal worship and testimony, often including such activities as faith-healing, exorcisms, and speaking in tongues. In sum, liberal modernism had a growing rival within Protestantism in the rise of modern Pentecostalism, a movement that was usually scripturally conservative and emotionally demonstrative.

Although Pike had discouraged such activities within his diocese, his yearlong investigation of glossolalia indicates that he had something of a personal fascination with the Pentecostal, or at least the unusual religious experience, and that he recognized the significance of the third force in attracting new members to world Christianity. Even if he had not seen or recalled Van Dusen's article, Pike's observation of church parking lots throughout San Francisco on any Sunday morning would have led him to the same recognition of this rising Pentecostal wave, as worshipers who otherwise might have attended more mainstream services filled the Pentecostal churches. The same three Pentecostal denominations that Van Dusen had listed at the end of his article as most representative of the third force Christianity in the U.S.—the Assemblies of God, the Seventh-day Adventists, and the Church of the Nazarene—were the three fastest-growing groups in membership among U.S. Protestants in 1955–65. During this period, the Protestant Episcopal Church had grown at a respectable 20.2 percent, but the Assemblies of God, the Church of the Nazarene, and the Seventh-day Adventists had increased in membership by 43 percent, 27.9 percent, and 31.5 percent, respectively. Pike's possible intuition that he needed to participate personally in Pentecostalism or risk being left behind spiritually perhaps explains an otherwise perplexing incident. It occurred, in Darby Betts's description, "during his great battle with the tongue-speaking people." As Betts recollected this incident with the bishop: "One day he came into his office in the cathedral shaken. His face was the color of putty." When Betts inquired about his friend's distress, Pike told him "that he had waked up in the night reciting a psalm in a language he didn't understand. 'My God,' he said, 'I've been speaking in tongues!' "

Betts reacted in his professional role of the guardian against the bishop's enthusiasms. Upon questioning Pike, Betts ascertained that his friend had glanced at a Book of Psalms printed in an "archaic" Latin before he had retired for the night. Upon awakening, while speaking "a language he didn't understand," Pike simply was semiconsciously repeating, in Betts's assurances, an approximate memory of the low Latin that he had seen before having fallen asleep. He seemed to accept

Betts's rationalist explanation. The canon ordinary himself was not so sure. "Now, that incident took place well before he got involved with psychic phenomenon," Betts later mused. "Maybe later he would have interpreted the experience differently. I don't know." In fact, Pike wrote sympathetically about glossolalia in his 1967 book, *If This Be Heresy*, and by that time the bishop almost certainly would not have accepted his canon's empirical explanation.

These doctrinal and theological disputes had prompted Pike by the summer of 1962 "to write a book on what I *do* believe." He had begun composing such a manuscript, tentatively entitled *I Believe*, during a comparatively happy period of his relationship with his wife, when he and Esther were able to afford to travel to Cape Cod for a family vacation in the summer of that year. He was near to completion of his manuscript under contract to Harper & Row when in early 1963 he received in the mail a review copy of *Honest to God*, a slender book by a Church of England bishop previously unknown to him, John A. T. Robinson. Pike's response to this book was the most galvanic of his religious enthusiasms to date. He extensively revised and retitled the current manuscript of *I Believe*; he sought a personal introduction to Robinson; and he began in earnest throughout the remaining years of the decade of the 1960s to act at odds with the Christian establishment.

VI

A New Theology, a New Woman, and a New Heresy Charge

Here was a man who moved through life believing that he was entitled to forget it and start over, to shed women when they became difficult and allegiances when they became tedious and simply move on. . . . In a way, the Sixties were the years for which James Albert Pike was born.

—JOAN DIDION, *The White Album,* 1979

Honest to God, the advance copy of which so excited Pike, was the most *au courant* theological book for Protestants of the 1960s. At first glance, this short exposition on Bonhoeffer, Bultmann, and other radical theologians, written by Bishop John A. T. Robinson of Woolwich, England, and published by a small religious press in London, had not promised to be a literary event of great commercial success. But within twelve months of its U.K. publication in March 1963, *Honest to God* sold three hundred and fifty thousand copies, and international editions were being planned for Germany, Sweden, the Netherlands, Denmark, and the United States. The success of Robinson's book was not particularly due to the originality of its ideas. An existential interpretation of the Gospel had long been discussed at liberal Protestant seminaries in the twentieth century, and a demythologizing approach to scripture had been heard within the Anglican Communion since at least 1860, when Professor Benjamin Jowett of Oxford University emphatically insisted to his fellow churchmen that they should read the Bible with no more credulity than in reading *"any other book."* Robinson's genius was in his synthesis of these prior attitudes for readers in the 1960s and in his forthrightly telling the laity what their seminarians and clergy had been thinking for years. *Honest to God* touched a spiritual chord among Anglicans, and among liberal Protestants in general. Reading his copy in San Francisco, Pike at long last saw some vindication of his own public objections to Christian creeds he considered archaic. There was, in fact, a remarkable synchronicity of thought between him and this English prelate.

Robinson wrote in a jaunty, vernacular style, similar to Pike's, refreshingly free of academic obscurity. And, like Pike, he hoped to fashion a new theology for Christianity from the demythologizing of Bultmann, the depth-psychology definition of God by Tillich, and the call by Bonhoeffer for a more secular Christianity. To believers, Robinson suggested that the decade of the 1960s was a prime time for the church to sweep away such anachronisms as the Trinity, the Virgin Birth, and other accoutrements of an outdated concept of God. "If Christianity is to survive, let alone to recapture the 'secular' man," the bishop wrote, "there is no time to lose in detaching it from this scheme of thought, from this particular *logos* about *theos*, and thinking about what we should put in its place." Pike must have felt his intellectual pulses further excited in sympathy at finding himself mentioned approvingly by name. Early in the book's first chapter, Robinson declared that he had found "stimulating—and thoroughly constructive" the contents of Pike's article in the *Christian Century* declaring disbelief in the Virgin Birth. Robinson added, with forgivable hyperbole, that the article had "rocked the American church."

The two shared a further similarity beyond writing style. Both were celebrated by the media of their respective nations as the most culturally tolerant men of the cloth moving among what *Time*, somewhat after the fact in 1965, christened the "swinging London" of the sixties. Robinson had begun that decade by becoming known among London's tabloid newspapers as "the Lady Chatterley bishop" after he had testified with great success for the defense in the November 1960 trial on obscenity charges brought against the U.K. publishers of D. H. Lawrence's *Lady Chatterley's Lover.* The presence of a Church of England bishop in the dock at the Old Bailey was sufficiently unusual in 1960 to have provided good newspaper copy; but the subsequent testimony under oath by this handsome, forty-one-year-old, married bishop that sexual intercourse as described in Lawrence's novel was "an act of holy communion" had proved irresistibly quotable to journalists on both sides of the Atlantic. (Three years later, when the John Profumo–Christine Keeler scandal of illicit sex disturbed the Conservative government of Prime Minister Harold MacMillan, a Tory correspondent scathingly wrote in a letter to the Anglo-Catholic newspaper the *Church Times:* "Mr. Profumo can hardly be blamed if it should be found that in fact he had taken the bishop's advice.") The culturally relevant, socially sophisticated, and politically activist brand of religion practiced at Robinson's diocese south of the Thames River became known in city slang by the synecdoche "South Bank Religion."

The celebrity of Robinson and the favorable reviews of *Honest to God* were featured in the United States in 1963 by the larger metropolitan newspapers, including the *San Francisco Chronicle.* Within a few months, Pike wrote a friendly letter to Robinson praising his book, and inviting him to visit Grace Cathedral should he travel to America. The occasion arose in spring 1964, when Robinson's publishers sent him there to promote the U.S. edition of his book, with appearances scheduled in the San Francisco area. At Pike's invitation, the visiting bishop preached at the Sunday services at Grace Cathedral on the morning of May 24, delivering the message of what was now being called by academic journals and newspapers the New Theology. This pastoral message was summarized to San Franciscans by the *Chronicle:* "Mankind has outgrown the image of God as a mythical, physically supernatural being 'out there,' Dr. Robinson said, and must now conceive of him as 'ultimate reality.' " He spent the weekend as a guest of the California diocese, and he and Pike began an intellectual acquaintanceship.

There were reservations to a personal friendship, however, particularly on the part of Robinson. "Theologically, I've always been twinned by him by *Time* magazine and that sort of thing," he recalled after Pike's death. "I'm not quite sure I'm happy about that." He graciously described Pike as a "seeker and a contender for freedom and truth," and remembered him as having been "a warm person" and "absolutely disarming and very charming." But he also admitted that he had found "disconcerting" some aspects of his American acquaintance's behavior. "You always felt when he was talking to you that he was giving you a press interview," Robinson said. "You felt it was all for the tape."

Pike was less reserved in his estimation of Robinson. Partly this one-sidedness in their relationship was the result of his desire to emulate a role that the British bishop seemed effortlessly to fulfill, as he moved back and forth from pop figure in the U.K. media to seriously regarded scholar among theologians. (Robinson, prior to his ordination in the Church of England, had taken his degree in classics at Cambridge University, and before writing his best seller had been appointed there as a fellow and dean at Clare College.) In preparing a profile of Robinson and his theological associates in the mid-1960s for *The New Yorker*, Ved Mehta employed the felicitously apt phrase "don journalists" to describe those church and academic figures who were equally at home—and equally quotable—at their college's high table or in a newspaper interview. Pike was not among those whom Mehta interviewed, but he would have liked to have been. There is considerable suggestion that becoming known in the United States as the Episcopal Church's foremost don journalist had been the beau ideal of his mind ever since he attempted unsuccessfully to study at Oxford in 1944. Certainly he had had his share of celebrity, and his skills as a popularizer and a prolific writer were well known, but a nationally recognized academic reputation, desired by Pike since leaving California to study at an Ivy League university in the east, had eluded him.

A professional association with the bishop of Woolwich and his book was, therefore, a possible boost for Pike to become recognized as a substantial thinker within theological circles. After reading Robinson's book, he began to revise his earlier manuscript restating his own beliefs while serving as the guest rector of an English-speaking Anglican church in Mexico in the summer of 1963. He now frankly and enthusiastically described to Robinson during the San Francisco visit his plans to write a book complementary to *Honest to God*, but directed toward a uniquely American audience. His book would be written, as he described it, "for professionals and laymen who will read as they run." The new book, incorporating part of his uncompleted manuscript, *I Believe*, was now to be titled *A Time for Christian Candor.*

Throughout the summer and early autumn, Pike worked at his usual fervid pace in finishing his latest project. Characteristically, he also increased the pressures and risks within his private life. For example, he continued unsatiated in his extramarital affairs; according to his confidants Stringfellow and Towne, his infidelities to Esther Pike reached such a point that he installed a clandestine telephone line with a private number in the bishop's office, for his use with whatever woman with whom he happened to be having sexual relations. Women, at least these "other women," found the bishop an exciting conversationalist, and, as his future wife, Diane Kennedy, noted on meeting him, he never talked condescendingly to his female companions. There is little that can be said morally to justify his adulteries; but for whatever they might reveal about his character that can be constructed as positive, Pike seems to have been that rarest of male philanderers, one who is capable of post-coitally enjoying the company and thoughts of women.

More commendable than his adulteries was another of his actions, on June 30, 1964. Having recently joined Alcoholics Anonymous, Pike announced to his family, friends, and selected laity on that day his decision to become permanently "dry," renouncing his consumption of any alcoholic beverage—"not even communion wine," he declared enthusiastically. Despite his inevitable lapses, he usually was able to sustain his vow of abstinence for the rest of his life. In plain fact, his decision for sobriety that summer probably was both a lifesaver and a career saver. After decades of heavy drinking, Pike now appeared unhealthy to observers, including journalists, some of whom remarked so in print; his skin had a jaundiced hue, his face was deeply creased, and his neck and upper torso had thickened with excess flesh. He no longer resembled the irreverent cherub of his youth so much as a statue of a short, middle-aged ithyphallic god. He was unwilling at this time to also give up his chain-smoking of cigarettes and constant consumption of coffee, but his health and appearance improved somewhat after he stopped drinking. The decision also put the quietus to rumors that had been circulating in his diocese for months about supposed incidents of his drunken driving, condoned by the San Francisco police department. Herb Caen, the city's prominent gossip columnist, noted the change in an item printed in the *Chronicle* that summer: "It's much quieter on Nob Hill these days since one of its most distinguished residents joined Alcoholics Anonymous."

The second change was more destructive to his life and career. Pike had begun to consider his marriage "spiritually dead," in his phrase, and, in Esther Pike's later description in a complaint for divorce, long periods of time passed when she would neither hear from her husband nor have any idea of where he was staying overnight. He apparently welcomed an opportunity to spend two months away from his household that summer. His friend John Heuss, rector of Trinity Church in New York, invited him, apparently not aware of the bishop's domestic situation, to come to the city and be the guest preacher at Trinity through the months of July and August. Pike accepted, and traveled there alone, and as his marriage of twenty-two years and his direct oversight of their four children went unregarded on the West Coast, worked with an almost preternatural concentration at completing his new book and articulating his new theology on the East Coast.

Chapter by chapter, Pike weekly preached his first drafts of *A Time for Christian Candor* to increasingly numerous and receptive congregations that summer. The *New York Times*, sensing a remarkable news story occurring within the otherwise staid religion beat, began reporting Pike's sermons in its Monday editions following their delivery the previous day in the pulpit, allotting more space to Pike's pronouncements than to any other of the city's ministers or priests. Representative of his powerful rhetoric—when he seemed almost to be arguing face-to-face with his God and with the one he called his Savior—was the sermon Pike preached on August 30. "The Trinity is not necessary," he announced, somewhat incongruously, from the Trinity Church pulpit. "Our Lord never heard of it. The apostles knew nothing of it." He then further warmed to his subject, according to the *Times*, employing for his congregation a dramatically biblical metaphor: "Jesus warned us against putting new wine in old vessels, lest the vessels break. Let them burst," the bishop declared. "Why should we impose on new converts something which the apostles themselves would not have understood?"

The image of a sacred element contained within an impure or inadequate vessel appears to have been foremost in his mind as he was writing this book. In addition to Jesus' injunction against putting new wine into old wineskins, as told in Matthew 9:15 and to which Pike alluded in his sermon, the image was most fully and beautifully expressed by the apostle Paul in II Corinthians 4:7—"We have this treasure in earthen vessels, that the transcendent power belongs to God and not to us." Pike was fascinated by the implications of this biblical verse. He chose it as the frontispiece quote for his book manuscript (and it would later be inscribed upon his gravestone in Israel.) "We have a particularly interesting collection of earthen vessels," he wrote in the first pages, in regard to the Anglican Communion's beliefs concerning the Virgin Birth and the Trinity and its long tradition of elaborate liturgies. He then addressed himself in the following pages to answering the question of which of these "earthen vessels" to keep, and which to break or discard as having become incapable of holding truth.

But he wrote too frequently with an uncharacteristic heaviness and academicalism. He chose as a heading, for instance, to use the word *Historismus* simply to announce to his future readers his intentions to discuss the historical origins and circumstances of the doctrines he wished to discard; and he made too much out of a fairly easily understood distinction between what he called "two basic methodologies in the realm of philosophical and religious thinking," namely, "those whose system is primarily *ontological* and those whose system is primarily *existential*" (Pike's italics). In short, there are those who think metaphysically, and there are those who don't. The pretension underneath this prose may have been the result of Pike's authorial nervousness—and ambition—in considering that he might be writing a work equal in significance to the Anglican Communion's most notable book reconciling faith and reason, the once-famous *Essays and Reviews*.

Appearing in 1860 and authored by seven brilliant Anglican divines and dons, *Essays and Reviews* sought to reconcile to Christian believers in understandable terms such then-radical new ideas as the study of geological time, the theory of evolution, and the consequences of the German school of higher criticism of biblical exegesis. (It was in explaining the latter that Benjamin Jowett made his famous remark about how to intelligently read the Bible.) Although seldom mentioned or examined today, *Essays and Reviews* was the most acclaimed accomplishment of

Anglican scholarship in its century (as well as having returned a "handsome profit" for its essayists), and it was as famous in the 1860s as, say, a popularly written book on the New Theology might become in the 1960s.

John Robinson had already courted a comparison between his authorship and the venerable essayists in an understated, "British" way. Early in the pages of *Honest to God*, he had stated his regret at how his Church's refusal to accept the radical advancements in knowledge that the bishop had proffered had made all but impossible the effective presentation of the Gospel to an increasingly skeptical, twentieth-century audience. "I believe there are uncomfortable analogies to the ecclesiastical scene of a hundred years ago," he wrote, alluding to the opposition by his church's most conservative clergy to the publication of *Essays and Reviews* and the calls by some of them for ecclesiastical trials of its authors. Implicit was the understanding that if there existed uncomfortable analogies to the ecclesiastical reception of *Essays and Reviews*, there might also exist fortunate analogies between its now-revered essayists and the contemporary author of *Honest to God*. Pike's ambitions were at least equal to Robinson's. For example, the public relations writer of the California diocese, presumably with Pike's approval, described the New Theology, with no qualifying irony or sense of hyperbole, as "the New Reformation." The bishop of Woolwich himself used that phrase prominently. The possibility of writing a book as intellectually consequential as *Essays and Reviews*, or equal in historical importance to the documents of the first Reformation, was certainly considered as a possibility by both bishops, but the attempt seems to have fatally constrained Pike's prose style.

In fairness, there are occasional passages within *A Time for Christian Candor* in which Pike accomplished some of the best Christian apologetic writing of his life. A fine instance occurs well into the book when he compares the cataclysmic loss of religious faith to the sudden recognition that one is an alcoholic:

> He had not recognized the danger as such; he had been well equipped with the usual excuses, uttered the usual reassurances to those closest to him and concerned about the matter. But finally an emotional crisis occurs when he literally hits bottom.

The circumstances may have been that a public or semi-public scandal results in his losing everything. Or, by chance or Providence, there may have been more protective—and protecting—circumstances. But it is all the same as far as what has happened to him inside is concerned. Brushed away all at once are his excuses, the basis for his reassurances to others, his sense of security and surrounding supports—and, most of all, his sense of confidence in himself.

As his friend John Coburn had reminded him six years before during his installation ceremonies as a bishop, Pike was at his best when he personally embodied the causes for which he was the champion, or the darkness against which he struggled.

By October 11, 1964, six weeks after the delivery of the "burst wineskins" sermon at Trinity, Pike traveled to St. Louis, where the Episcopal Church was to open its sixty-first triennial general convention the following day. He brought the concerns expressed in his manuscript of *A Time for Christian Candor* with him. On the Sunday morning preceding the convention's Monday opening session, he preached the sermon "This Treasure in Earthen Vessels" to a congregation that filled St. Louis's Christ Church Cathedral to its capacity. Many of his listeners were convention delegates or bishops. Using his strongest language to date, Pike spoke of the "irrelevancy" of the concept of the Trinity, terming it "excess luggage," and called for his fellow Episcopalians to lead the way in putting an end to "outdated, incomprehensible, and nonessential doctrinal statements, traditions, and codes." There was an urgency in his words that went beyond his usual forensic energies. "The fact is," he told those in the cathedral, "we are in the midst of a theological revolution."

The word *revolution* was becoming overused even by Episcopalians in 1964, but Pike seemed sincerely to have been convinced that the movement for New Theology was, like the Reformation, an instance of *kairos*, or a Godly precipitated revolutionary time for a spiritual change in history, as had been described as experienced in 1919 by Paul Tillich. It was certainly tempting for the bishop to perceive a growing synchronicity and importance within the Christian church of the thoughts of Bonhoeffer, Tillich, Robinson, and, presumably, Pike. Others were

James Pike, his wife, and their children occasionally gathered for a conventional family portrait during his years in residence as the dean at the Cathedral of St. John the Divine in New York City. But more often Pike's family saw him at the deanery in the company of photographers for newsreels and television shows or on the move surrounded by a coterie of reporters and publicists. Seated on the sofa (*above left*) are, left to right, Catherine, aged twelve; Esther and James Pike; and James Jr., aged nine. Standing behind the sofa are the two younger children, Christopher, aged five, and Constance, aged seven.

Pike kneels upon his presentation to Bishop Horace W. B. Donegan, seated, during his installation as dean of the Cathedral of St. John the Divine on February 16, 1952.

Pike brought a new intellectual and liturgical vigor to his position as dean at the cathedral. Above, he and Bishop Donegan greet young arrivals at a presentation service for the children of the diocese. Below, Pike offers the host to worshipers at the communion rail of the cathedral.

The task awaiting Pike in 1958 as the new bishop of the diocese of California was monumental, as it was hoped he would successfully raise the money for the completion of Grace Cathedral, covered at its eastern end with unsightly metal sheeting since the Great Depression of the 1930s had curtailed fundraising for its exterior completion. Pike describes his building plans in a newsreel filmed while he stands underneath construction girding at the cathedral. The completed cathedral as it appeared in 1964, the year that construction was declared finished after Pike's successful, six-year fundraising campaign.

More than two thousand people attended Pike's consecration at Grace Cathedral as the Episcopal Church's fifth bishop coadjutor of the diocese of California on May 15, 1958. In an innovation appropriate to Pike's celebrity in the media, the ceremony was televised live from inside the cathedral. Following his consecration, Pike administered Holy Communion to three women of his family. Kneeling, from left to right, are Catherine Pike; his mother, Pearl Chambers; and Esther Pike. Back in California, Pike continued throughout the early 1960s to tape for the ABC network his weekly televised program, now called *The Bishop Pike Show*. He called these television appearances his making "a commercial for God."

Pike presented many different faces to the public. Above, an official photographic portrait commissioned by his church shortly after he left Christ Church, in Poughkeepsie, New York. He enthusiastically greets student visitors (*above right*), including those from the University of the South at Sewanee, Tennessee, to worship services at the cathedral. Below, a rare quiet and reflective moment at St. John's. Pike delivers a sermon from the pulpit of Grace Cathedral in San Francisco (*below right*). By 1965, he was complaining to friends that the political activism of his sermons and social ministry had alienated him from many of the generous financial donors to his diocese.

Pike in California as he appeared in August 1969, one month before his death in the desert near the Dead Sea.

In a dramatic incident at the memorial service for Pike at Grace Cathedral on September 12, 1969, his widow, Diane Pike, suddenly reached across her pew and grasped a startled Bishop Kilmer Myers. Myers, Pike's successor as diocesan bishop, had forbade Pike, shortly after his marriage to Diane Kennedy Pike, from performing any type of liturgical service in the diocese's churches or cathedral. Pike's first and second wives also were present at this memorial service. At right is Pike's mother.

not so persuaded. Pike was nothing more than "an angry, middle-aged rebel," the bishop of the diocese of West Missouri told the *New York Times* in an interview on the second day of the church's convention, who had "a deep-seated, psychological compulsion to become a martyr." Whatever the characterization of Pike, it was evident that the sixty-first general convention of the Episcopal Church, like the sixtieth general convention three years earlier in Detroit, again was to be dominated by the issues championed by him and by the advisability of bringing a presentment of heresy charges against him.

The twelve-day convocation of the House of Bishops and the House of Delegates at the Kiel Auditorium in St. Louis, which commenced October 12, soon became the type of fractious convention that distressed many of his fellow church members but Pike seemed to enjoy. The House of Bishops scarcely had finished its opening prayers that morning when Louttit of South Florida demanded that the House go into executive session to discuss a nontheological statement Pike had also made at Christ Church Cathedral. Preceding his remarks on the Trinity, he had asserted from the pulpit that southern Episcopal bishops had never disciplined a priest or deacon for the "large" sin of racism, but frequently had done so for lesser, "little" sins committed against fewer people. Louttit angrily demanded an apology, Pike flatly refused, and the more irenically minded bishops insisted that the House move on to other matters. But by Tuesday the other matters included the consequences from a statement by some of those attending the convention, released to the press that morning and printed nationally that afternoon, denouncing by name a prominent Episcopalian, Senator Barry Goldwater, and also U.S. congressman G. William Miller of New York. The two, who were the presidential and vice presidential candidates, respectively, on the Republican Party's ticket in the next month's presidential election, were rebuked by those Episcopalians signing the document for the "transparent exploitation of racism among white citizens" during their campaign. Among the twelve Episcopal bishops who had signed was Pike.

After the statement's release, the House of Bishops subsequently was "besieged," in the description of the *New York Times*, by "telegrams and telephone calls from persons who interpreted the statement as an official position of the church in favor of President Johnson." It was not, but its release at the convention seemed to imply that it was so, a situation that may have been intended by its author, William Stringfellow, the New York attorney known to Pike since the early 1950s. Their shared controversy at the convention over what became known as the Stringfellow Statement cemented the friendship between the bishop and its author, as well as with Stringfellow's domestic companion, Anthony Towne. Stringfellow and Towne were later to write the definitive account of the ecclesiastical charges of heresy brought against Pike, and, seven years after his death, wrote an idiosyncratic and highly anecdotal biography of their friend. But, for the moment, the bishops who did not share their views, or who thought that their church as a body should have no publicly expressed preference in the presidential election of 1964, were left holding the political bag. Two days after the statement's release, opposing bishops found it necessary to emphasize that those bishops who had signed the Stringfellow Statement did so as private individuals and to issue their own statement that "solemnly warned churchgoers from using the triennial convention as a sounding board for their personal views, political or religious."

There were other important issues debated or resolved in St. Louis—the House of Delegates, for example, refused for the second time within the decade to approve the ordination of women to the first clerical order of their Church as deacons; and the House of Bishops, voting on October 17, elected the Right Reverend John E. Hines to be their church's next presiding bishop, an election in which Louttit as a candidate had received a significant number of votes. But whatever the convention's agenda, the issue of Pike's possible presentment on charges of heresy continued to intrude itself. On the Sunday immediately following Hines's election, for instance, the most publicized news about the Episcopal Church, later printed in the *New York Times*, was not the selection of a new presiding bishop, but the sermon given in New York City by Rev. Charles Graf, in which the Episcopal rector suggested to his congregation that the time had come to take "steps" against Pike. The California bishop remained highly visible and voluble throughout that week on the convention floor, personifying the zeitgeist that would not go away, consulting with the advocates of women's ordination in the House of Delegates on future legal strategies, or urging a strong statement on the House of Bishops, contrary to Louttit's wishes, categorically approving nonviolent resistance by Episcopalians to racially discriminatory laws.

The newly elected presiding bishop, and many of his fellow prelates, believed with good reason that initiating "steps" against Pike—that is, allowing a formal complaint, or bill of particulars, of heresy charges against him to be introduced at this convention—would irrevocably tear their church apart over the doctrinal issues considered heretical before there was an opportunity for a mediated resolution of these new doctrines. Even Graf in his sermon had allowed that the repercussions of a possible heresy presentment "would be disastrous" for the national church, albeit adding, "If it has to be done, it has to be done." Clearly an application of the celebrated Anglican "middle way" was called for. On October 21, the House of Bishops issued by a safe majority what it termed "questions of good order." This pronouncement, although not mentioning Pike by name, obviously intended him as its object by stating, "This House is concerned that in the public presentation of the Faith, no Bishop or Priest, either in what he says or the manner in which he says it, denied the Catholic Faith, or implies that the Church does not mean the truth, which it expresses in worship."

Pike, to his credit, did not act exactly if he were motivated by "a deep-seated, psychological compulsion to become a martyr." He attempted a reconciliation with the bishop who had so described him, and apparently applied a liberal portion of his famous personal charm. After morning communion one day in the second week of the convention, he invited the Missouri bishop to his hotel room for a private breakfast. His critic accepted, and, over their shared meal, they agreed to propose that a special "Theological Committee" be appointed "to engage in continuing dialogue with contemporary theologians." Pike was to be a committee member. The House of Bishops approved their agreement and charged the new committee to report, in its diplomatic phrase, "from time to time" on what the bishops were willing to describe as "the crisis in the relationship between the language of theology and that of modern culture." Pending the future deliberations of the new committee, a bill of particulars alleging the bishop's heresy was thereby once more avoided—or unconscionably delayed, if one took the viewpoints of Louttit, Bloy, and others.

Pike returned to San Francisco in Episcopal pride that November, after an absence of four months, at the greatest height of his financial and political powers as a bishop, but also at the verge of the greatest chaos so far in his personal life. On November 20, before a large and triumphant congregation, he celebrated the consecration marking the physical completion of Grace Cathedral. It was an extraordinary feat of both construction and the bishop's fund-raising skills; within six years the diocese had raised the funds and pledges to remove the unsightly sheet metal and complete the cathedral. Like its bishop, the new building was an unusual combination of the traditional and the modern. Grace Cathedral had been designed in the usual neo-Gothic architecture, but in what was called a "revolutionary concept" of construction it had been built, not stone-by-stone, like the still-unfinished walls of the Cathedral of St. John the Divine, but in forms of reinforced concrete as it rose to its maximum height of 265 feet. Completion therefore had been much speedier than the laborious handiwork of stone-masonry. This unusual modernism was even more visible from the cathedral's interior. Pike had approved an extraordinary series of clerestory windows portraying "secular saints" in panels of stained glass. Portraits of John Glenn, Albert Einstein, Thurgood Marshall, Paul Tillich, and other contemporary notables were illuminated for their achievements for the betterment of humanity. All agreed that Grace Cathedral was different; many agreed joyfully that it was beautiful.

There was no joy, however, awaiting Pike at his Jackson Street residence. Preceding a constrained Christmas celebration together, Esther Pike announced to her husband her intention to seek a legal separation early the coming year. Her voice has not often been heard within this narrative, frequently because she was in public a much less voluble and self-dramatizing individual than her husband. But publicly undemonstrative people can feel pain and anger in private just as keenly as others, and, unlike as in 1962 when she had also declared intention to separate from Pike, this time she was adamant and retained legal counsel. Pike may not even have tried to dissuade her. In an admirable display of self-honesty, he admitted to her that, with a "clarity" resulting from his new sobriety, he saw now that his alcoholism and other behavior had degraded their marriage probably beyond repair.

Under these circumstances, he nevertheless had been able to complete the manuscript and proofs of *A Time for Christian Candor* for pub-

lication in November 1964. He was well aware that Robinson had dedicated *Honest to God* to his two oldest children "and their generation,"
and he followed the Englishman's suit, dedicating this book "To my son,
Jim." His elder son thereby became the first member of his family to
have received a book dedication. Not even his mother or wife had been
so honored. The dedication was most likely a sincere attempt by Pike to
bridge a gap of prior emotional neglect of his son and estrangement
between them. The younger Pike was, by many accounts, a likable, if
malleable, young man; but at the time of his father's return, he had
moved out of the Jackson Street home into an apartment with three
roommates in a neighborhood that was later described by newspapers as
"near a rundown section of Golden Gate Park," that is, the "Panhandle"
extension of the park, a few blocks from the intersection of Haight and
Ashbury streets. He had given up the plans his parents had for him to
attend San Francisco State University, and talked instead of his pleasur-
able experiments taking drafts of Romilar, an over-the-counter cough
medicine, and tablets of LSD. Perhaps a book dedication at this time
was the best Pike could do for his son.

Waiting for favorable reviews was presently the major hope in the
bishop's life. After the Christmas holidays, Esther Pike told her husband
that he would no longer be allowed to live at the bishop's house.
Although her lawyer had not yet obtained a separation decree, she was
able to enforce her decision with her threat that otherwise she would
move to new quarters accompanied by their children, a public removal
that had the potential of a career-ending scandal, even for Pike. They
agreed, for their shared professional, financial, and social benefit, that
he would have use of the house for official functions and that they would
attempt to keep notice of their de facto separation out of the city's newspapers as long as possible. But he would sleep elsewhere. Surprisingly,
he did not choose to stay at his mother's residence, as he, too, had come
to prefer keeping his distance from her maternal influence. Instead,
throughout the first winter months of 1965, Pike usually stayed at the
home of his friend Philip Adams, a prominent San Francisco adoption
lawyer and chancellor of the diocese; occasionally, he also stayed
overnight at the homes of his personal admirers. Among the latter was
Maren Bergrud, a middle-aged divorced woman who lived in San
Rafael, in Marin County. She had met the bishop earlier in 1964 when

she had arranged for him to address her local chapter of the American Civil Liberties Union. Later, he told Stringfellow and Towne, she had sent a "come-on" letter to him while he had been in residence at Trinity Church. Her home, and her bed, now became another of Pike's stops across San Francisco Bay as he lived "out of a suitcase," in Stringfellow's and Towne's euphemistic phrase.

In retrospect, probably due to the uncertainties of his domestic life, Pike had been uncharacteristically slow in anticipating the changing intellectual fashions in regard to his forthcoming book. *Honest to God* had been in print for nearly two years before *A Time for Christian Candor* appeared, and the New Theology had lost much of its shock value. Further, an even more radical theology explicitly denying the existence of God had been announced in the mid-1960s by academics at Emory University in Atlanta, and at universities elsewhere. Following *Honest to God* and the public's notice of the "Death of God" theologians, Pike's discourses on Bultmann and Bonhoeffer appeared merely imitative. He was in danger, despite writing as a theologian, of committing the original sin of the decade of the sixties: of no longer being *au courant*, of no longer being considered culturally *relevant.*

The first reviews were, at best, mixed. The *Christian Century*, usually editorially friendly to him, dismissed his book. "The theological modernism that is his cause Pike presents apologetically," the reviewer noted correctly, but "on the whole, the presentation is facile." The scholarly and British presses were even less responsive. The editors of the prestigious *Anglican Theological Review* ignored his book. (Their disregard was particularly disappointing to Pike. Early in his church career, he had ambitions to publish an article in this review, which he enthusiastically described to his mother as "sort of the *Harvard Law Review* in its field.") Abroad, the *Times Literary Supplement* damned his work with faint praise. "Bishop Pike writes persuasively and, perhaps taught by past controversial experiences, not ungently," the critic noted. Yet this same London review also noted that the Anglican theological debate into which the California bishop had recently entered "has been in progress for at least 100 years" and that "it is perhaps true that he is saying little that has not been said before."

Popular journalists in the United States also panned his book. Pike, as a general rule, was well liked by journalists; the habits of his personal life made him one of them, and he was always good for a story-making quote. But *Newsweek* picked up on the "superficial" criticism in its review, and *Time*, usually friendly to Pike, complained of the bishop's "Batmannerly" writing style. The harshest criticism, however, appeared on January 3, 1965, in the *New York Times*, also a publication usually favorable to him, written by John Macquarrie, a professor of theology at Union Seminary. Describing the book's author as one who "seems to have cast himself into the role of *enfant terrible* among the bishops of the American Episcopal Church [*sic*]," Macquarrie began his review with a flat statement: "This is a disappointing book." He continued:

> Bishop Pike seems to think that it might be an American coun-
> terpart to the book, *Honest to God*, by his English colleague,
> Bishop John Robinson. But in fact there is no comparison. The
> English bestseller, whatever its limitations, was on the whole a
> thoughtful, constructive piece of work by a man who is a first-
> rate scholar. Bishop Pike's book cannot be so described.

A Time for Christian Candor was riddled, in Macquarrie's opinion, by "careless misunderstandings," "snap judgments," and "vast oversimpli-fications." The theology proposed was described as no more than an "individualistic" reaction and "subjective preference." In fairness to Pike, it should be noted that Macquarrie was employed at Union as a professor of systematic theology with perhaps an intellectual disinclina-tion for Pike's elliptical style, and his criticism of the bishop's writings as individualistic and subjective could just as well have been leveled against the styles of such prominent Christian thinkers as Kierkegaard and Bonhoeffer.

Ironically, the review most sympathetic to Pike both as a person and as a theologian appeared in an issue of the *Saint Luke's Journal of Theol-ogy*, published by the divinity school at the University of the South. However much he personally may have bedeviled Sewanee in the past, the *Saint Luke's Journal* was willing to give Pike some sympathy. The review noted: "It is not necessary to agree with his opinions in order to see exactly what he is up to, to be a bishop whose task is theological crit-icism." Using the foremost spiritual metaphor of the book itself, the reviewer asserted that Pike was uniquely experienced to direct that criticism from the viewpoint of the secular, modernist nonbeliever: "Ever since he had been in clerical orders he was an apologist to the Gentiles [secular men and women] many of whom had never heard of the 'treasures' we have and who were not impressed when they were told or shown." Yet, surveying the hostility previously directed in print toward the bishop's apologetics and theology, written mainly by seminary professors and professors of religion, the reviewer doubted that the criticisms within *A Time for Christian Candor* ever would be taken seriously by his church's academic establishment. Pike had "somehow missed the charmed magic," in this reviewer's phrase, by not having studied at the Anglican Communion's most prestigious colleges in Cambridge, England, or at the Episcopal Theological School in Cambridge, Massachusetts. He was, therefore, easily dismissible as inadequately prepared for his subject by a transatlantic academic clique.

This discouraging appraisal of Pike's future successes as a theologian was also expressed later in 1965 by a publication of Pike's alma mater. The *Yale Alumni Magazine* ran an article analyzing the New Theologians for its readers:

> Traditional theologians assail men like Pike and Robinson because they "can't think straight" and suggest that preachers should stick to preaching. Preachers, of course, have a right to question the adequacy of traditional forms of expression, these men say, but they should not wander too far afield in theology itself—an area in which they are, self-admittedly, not professionals.

These "professionals" were quoted in this same article angrily criticizing Pike and addressing him directly. "You have ontologized your ignorance and called it theology," a Yale professor of philosophy upbraided him, while the university's professor who was director of religious studies dismissed the work in *A Time for Christian Candor* as no more than "a little bit of metaphysics, a little bit of common sense applied to words, a little bit of scientific outlook—stirred vigorously and applied promiscuously."

By the time these last two reviews appeared, Pike had been presented with a separation decree obtained by his wife's attorney. Although domestic use of the bishop's house was barred by this agreement, he was obliged to provide household expenses and financial support for his wife and their four children. His spirits certainly must have been depressed by this turn of events, but his energies apparently were irrepressible—as he had noted in 1962 in his private notes on self-analysis, as far back as he could remember, "*hyperactivity* has been my pattern of response to disappointment, deprivation or failure." Now, in the late winter of 1965, recognizing that he soon was not to be Esther Pike's husband and he was not to be a recognized theologian, he apparently redoubled his efforts—became *hyperactive* in his emphatic choice of word—to be a social prophet and activist, and to live with another woman outside of marriage.

He began by living openly with Maren Bergrud. By late March, he had arranged for her to move from San Rafael into a small apartment in San Francisco, for which he paid the rent. Their relationship does not give evidence of having been intended as a permanent match, at least on the part of the bishop, but the arrangement was mutually beneficial. Paying the rent for Bergrud relieved her from a serious financial crisis; she had accumulated a large number of medical bills from cancer surgery and unemployment; and, insofar as the bishop could claim an actual domicile in San Francisco that year, it was this apartment. He seems not to have introduced her to many of his acquaintances, but his new domestic companion was later remembered by those who knew her as a naturally dark-haired, intelligent woman, considered attractive on days that her chronic ailments or overuse of prescription painkillers had not sapped her vitality.

Despite the expenses and physical exertions of maintaining two separate households, Pike continued his peripatetic schedule. That same March, he traveled in an exhausting Louisiana-to-Alabama-to-Louisiana-to-California itinerary within one day in order to meet with Dr. Martin Luther King Jr. in Alabama. He had gone to Baton Rouge the second week of that month to address Episcopal students at Louisiana State University and there saw on television the events of "Bloody Sunday," March 7, when civil rights marchers were brutally beaten by state troopers at the Pettus Bridge in Selma, Alabama. He subsequently heard the appeal broadcast by King for the nation's clergy to come to Alabama and help resume the violently interrupted civil rights march from Selma to Montgomery. When, two days later, Pike telephoned his office long-distance, his wife told him of an earlier telephone call from Coretta Scott King, wife of the minister, who stated that both she and her husband were curious why the bishop had not yet come to Selma. (Despite their estranged lives, Esther Pike, with her husband's silent agreement, ran the diocesan office and made important administrative decisions during his absences. She had become known by some diocesan employees, not necessarily in admiration, as "Mrs. Bishop.") Pike immediately cut short his activities on campus and tried to book a commercial air flight to Alabama; frustrated by the paucity of flights into that state, he chartered a private plane in Baton Rouge on March 10 to fly him directly to Selma's tiny airfield. The Episcopal chaplain at the university, voluntarily accompanying him on the flight, saw four or five figures waiting at the edge of the tarmac for their plane to land. He assumed they were civil rights workers sent to provide the bishop an automobile ride to their church headquarters. In fact, they were news reporters, including a *Time* correspondent, waiting to interview Pike.

A ride into town was eventually arranged, and the two clergymen spent several hours that afternoon at Brown's Chapel AME Church, the gathering point of King and his supporters. Pike also experienced first-hand the intimidation the civil rights workers faced—the automobile in which the bishop and chaplain were riding was forced to the side of the road by town police a number of blocks away from the church, and the law officers insisted that the two approach the building on foot. Upon arriving at the church, Pike spoke personally with many of the demonstrators who had been beaten by Alabama state troopers the previous Sunday at the bridge. After learning from King that the next march likely would not begin for several days Pike decided to return to San Francisco until it was announced. He caught a ride back to Selma's airport, flew in his chartered plane to New Orleans, and later that same night boarded a commercial flight to San Francisco. Reporters waiting to meet him at the city's airport commented on his haggard appearance, he having spent at least twelve of the last twenty-four hours aboard airplanes traveling back and forth among three different time zones. His moral outrage, however, was not exhausted. Pike called for "wave upon wave" of clergymen to travel to Selma, and for the federal government to protect the safety of the marchers.

His presence at Selma, albeit brief, put the lie to a remark later made against him by Louttit. Speaking to a news reporter, the Florida bishop said condescendingly, "It's much easier to be in favor of Negroes in San Francisco than south of the Mason-Dixon line." Although he had not "marched with King" as is popularly believed and repeated, Pike at least had *been* in Selma, as Louttit had not, and he had traveled with the foreknowledge that his clerical collar or divinity degree was no protection against personal violence once he arrived there. On the day preceding Pike's visit, the Rev. James Reeb, a Unitarian minister from Massachusetts who had also answered King's call to come to Selma, had been savagely clubbed by a group of whites after he left a diner in a "colored" neighborhood; Reeb died of his head injuries within hours after Pike returned to California.

Nor, despite what Louttit and other critics suggested, was Pike's increased activism in 1965 on behalf of citizens of color an instance of a johnny-come-lately opportunism. In addition to his dispute with Sewanee in 1953, he had spoken out from the pulpit of St. John's as early as October 1955, exercising his church's "prophetic tradition," in his words, to denounce the acquittal of those charged in Mississippi with the murder of Emmett Till, a young black man who had been murdered after he whistled at a white woman. Later, as the chairman of the California Advisory Committee on Civil Rights, Pike used the occasion of a 1963 press conference to pick a satisfying fight with his old foe Bishop Bloy, and to irritate the police chief of Los Angeles over the issue of minority civil rights and representation. He criticized the police force of that city as having too few minority patrolmen and cultivating an indifference to civilian complaints, maintaining that the relations between racial minorities and the San Francisco police were much "healthier" than in Los Angeles. Both the Los Angeles mayor, Sam Yorty, and the Los Angeles police chief were incensed. Bloy felt compelled to answer publicly that Pike "did not speak for Southern California's Episcopalians."

Pike had also been an early spokesman for his state's low-income Spanish-speaking residents, appearing at several pro-union rallies in 1964–65 with the farm labor activist Cesar Chavez. Additionally, he had campaigned, inside the Grace Cathedral pulpit and out of it, for the defeat in 1964 of Proposition 14, a proposal to eliminate the state's fair housing law and return to the owners of real estate the "absolute discretion" of whether or not to rent or sell to a qualified minority applicant. When he learned that the state's association of real estate agents was financing passage of the proposition, Pike, in the fashion of the times, began sporting a jaunty lapel pin printed with a provocative message. His button asked, "Would you want your daughter to marry a realtor?" He decried the election results in November 1964, when this ballot proposition was approved by the state's voters by a majority of two to one.

In the midst of this possible "white backlash" in California, Pike invited King to worship and preach at Grace Cathedral on the Fourth Sunday of Lent, March 28, 1965. King had just completed the Selma-to-Montgomery march three days earlier, and his arrival at the cathedral was the first public appearance by the minister in a non-southern state since then. (Pike had not marched, having been frustrated again by bad weather trying to book an air flight to Alabama.) By ten thirty on that Lenten Sunday morning, the cathedral's interior pews were filled, and an outside congregation of several thousand, many of them people of color, was forming on the building's plaza and steps. Possibly never before had so many African Americans assembled at this Episcopal landmark. In his sermon that morning, King emphasized to the congregations inside and outside the building his convictions that "at this particular hour in history" he had been called by God to lead the nation in a civil rights campaign. "If physical death is the price," he said, "to save us and our white brothers from eternal death of the spirit, then no sacrifice could be more redemptive." Fearful for his security even among this largely adulatory crowd, the San Francisco police insisted that King enter at one of the cathedral's side doors and be accompanied by two armed plainclothes detectives, even while he prayed at the altar and spoke at the pulpit. After the conclusion of services, the cathedral's dean later recalled, "For security's sake, King had to be sort of spirited out of the cathedral"—but not before he had posed for a photograph with Pike and other cathedral officials. Pike was determined to align his diocese and his national church with what he believed to be the morally right side of the nation's civil rights struggle.

The next month, on April 8, the bishop initiated another struggle, this time for the ordination of women to the Episcopal diaconate. The national Episcopal Church, despite the support of many moderates, had twice refused at its triennial conventions during the 1960s to approve such an ordination. Certain laywomen distinguished by their Christian piety, learning, witness, and devotion could be appointed, or "set apart," according to their church's canon law, to the position of a deaconess; but this distinguished title for female laity was considered separate from the church's three canonically ordained orders of deacon, priest, and bishop. Reaffirming what he called "the great Reformation doctrine of the priesthood of all believers," Pike announced the first week of that month his intention to ordain a deaconess within his diocese as a member of the first order of clergy, a deacon. The consequences of this act were evident both to those who opposed it and those who welcomed it; once they were ordained into holy orders as deacons, there could be no canonical impediment to women eventually being ordained to the priesthood or the episcopacy.

His choice for the position of his diocese's first female deacon was excellent. Phyllis Edwards, a widowed mother of four grown children, had provided outstanding service during her time as a deaconess to the city's impoverished within the Mission District and had walked literally beside King day by day during the Selma-to-Montgomery march. In recognition of her witness to the poor and disenfranchised, the national Church had given her permission to teach the catechism to her charges, although it carefully withheld from her the authority to be the celebrant at communion services among the believers, or to administer sacraments to the sick, those actions being reserved for the clerical orders. Pike was willing to press this issue, even before the scheduled ordination of Edwards took place. On April 10, two days after he announced his intentions, it became known to newspapers that Edwards had already administered the Eucharist at the Church of the Holy Spirit in North Salinas, California, within Pike's diocese, in an "emergency situation." The emergency, which had justified prior approval of her actions by the bishop of California, was the absence of the church's vicar, Rev. C. Lester Kinsolving. He was in Washington, in the company of Pike, where the two had gone to lobby for passage of a federal civil rights bill. With a lawyer's nice attention to detail, Pike had provided that, even though Edwards's clerical status was unsettled, the validity of the communion service she administered could not be contested by her opponents.

Before he left for Washington, Kinsolving himself had consecrated the wafers and wine that Edwards subsequently distributed as holy sacraments.

Such a prearranged act, wonderfully presumptive and clever, galvanized the opposition to Pike's planned ordination of Edwards. Conservative Anglo-Catholics, both in the national Church and on his diocese's standing committee, applied considerable personal pressure to the bishop to withhold his ordination, at least until after a specially called meeting of the House of Bishops that September to consider the matter. Pike was amenable; he agreed to postpone the ordination. Most likely his lawyerly instincts persuaded him that he could win his argument for ordination before a hearing of the bishops. He had observed publicly that the Church had weakened its own reasoning against ordination by having seated deaconesses among the clerical orders at its conventions, and by having amended canon law at its sixty-first triennial convention to speak of deaconesses as "ordered" rather than appointed. He was content to wait for the fight until September.

Pike remained on the offensive throughout the summer of 1965, however, in other matters both large and small. On May 18, he addressed a convention of chemical engineers in the city, many of whom had brought their wives and children. Noticing that the San Francisco chief of police was also present as part of a welcoming committee, he decided in his speech to twit the chief regarding what the bishop called "the family bit." He ironically congratulated the chief for having made San Francisco safer for the conventioneers' families by his department's recent, highly publicized arrests of Carol Doda and other topless dancers in the city's North Beach bars. Apparently not noticing that the chief remained stonily unsmiling, or considering that his remarks might seem inappropriate for the audience, Pike jestingly expressed his regret that this police action had brought a halt to "interesting theological discussions of the glories of creation." The next day's newspaper headline of this event stated gleefully, with the inevitable pun, that the Episcopal bishop had a "view" on topless dancers.

The jokes were wearing thin. The provocative public behavior in contrast with the presumed ecclesiastical dignity of his position was beginning to uncomfortably resemble hoary jokes among Church of England parishioners that were considered stale even before Pike's first ordination. The jokes were the "as the bishop said to the actress" off-color remarks and double entendres introduced into conversations, as in, *Don't worry, my dear, it's just a job, as the bishop said to the actress.* The public shocks, the increasingly open secret of his cohabitation with a woman not his wife, the perennial heresy troubles, and his rushing from one crisis to another—all these self-created dramatics threatened to make Pike's professional life in San Francisco appear no more than a contemporary and tawdry variation of "as the bishop said to the actress." His personal standing was further exacerbated when, on July 4, he picked what can only be described as a stupidly pointless quarrel with Luci Johnson, the daughter of the president of the United States. In a sermon that day, later criticized by laity and some outside the church, the bishop described as "sacrilegious" and "a direct slap at our church" Johnson's decision to be rebaptized as an adult by a Catholic priest following her conversion to the Roman Church; she earlier had been baptized as an infant at an Episcopal church in Texas. To Pike, the decision by Johnson and the Roman Catholic priest for a second baptism implied that sacraments, including baptism, were spiritually null when administered by Anglican priests. The question of whether baptism is a spiritually unrepeatable, once and future act is an interesting theological exercise; less so is the verbal breaking upon a rhetorical wheel of an eighteen-year-old woman and her private act of conscience. Once, Pike had used his eloquence in Independence Day sermons to confront much more formidable opponents, such as Senator Joseph McCarthy, but he seemed not to have considered the falling off in substance of his public remarks.

Not so easily overlooked, however, was a decline in the money received at the diocesan offices that summer. Pike estimated by mid-1965 that tithes contributed by the diocesan churches to support the bishop's office and programs had fallen by at least 15 percent from what was given or pledged the previous year. He blamed the decline exclusively on the laity's anger resulting from his campaigns and sermons against Proposition 14 and his championing of King's civil rights march to Selma. There was some truth to this analysis, but he was not in fact the compulsive civil rights protestor as he was so characterized by his opponents. In 1963, for example, he chastised several diocesan priests who had organized illegal public demonstrations against what they

termed unfair employment practices along the "Auto Row" of car deal-
erships in the city. He reminded his priests that, unlike the civil rights
demonstrators in the South who protested statutory discrimination,
"the law of the state is on the side of the demonstrator" in San Francisco, that discrimination could be corrected by court order, and that
their demonstrations prior to litigation were, therefore, an instance of
moral grandstanding. The perception that the bishop was close to a
Jacobin in urging civil rights demonstrators to illegal, nonviolent
protests remained current, however. He was later to tell Stringfellow
and Towne that a group of unnamed, prominent Episcopalians had
approached him in 1965 and threatened "to cut him off at the pockets"
unless he tempered his civil rights zeal. But it never seemed to have
occurred to Pike that the decline in diocesan financial support was perhaps an expression of the laity's disapproval of his personal life, or that
the deficits increasingly threatening the diocese's operation that summer were the consequence of his financial decisions during the previous
two years.

In fact, the shortfall of 1965 at the Nob Hill diocesan office was a
repeat of the pattern that stretched back to all of the bishop's earlier
church stations—from his ministry at Christ Church, Poughkeepsie, to
his chaplaincy at Columbia University, to the deanship at the Cathedral
of St. John the Divine. At first, following his arrival at each of these
appointments, there had been the excitement of new programs and a
multiplication of salaried assistants to this innovative, intellectually fun,
and approachable new executive in a clerical collar. However, the number of programs soon would outgrow the available money, promises
would be unkept and staff laid off, and administration and financing
would be further complicated by Pike's weakness for polemics. Finally,
as the bills came due and the political situation was becoming unten-
able, Pike would leave voluntarily, usually to accept a promotion at a
different geographical locale.

The first warning that the diocese was heading for financial trouble
had been hesitantly articulated by Pike in his "Bishop's Address" to the
diocesan convention in 1963. His earlier decision to relieve the diocesan
churches from an annual assessment in exchange for a voluntary tithe to
support the bishop's office and activities certainly had won him popular-

ity, but it simply had not generated sufficient operating funds, particularly as Pike continued to expand the support of new missions under his controversial system of "presbyters." In cautioning the convention delegates to expect in 1963 "a year of austerity and stringency," he then attempted consolatory remarks that, even in the printed transcript of the convention, reveal his underlying nervousness about finances: "But we are basically in sound shape, we are really going, everything's fine, but there has been a turn-around necessary due to studies made by the Finance Department and due to certain special factors that will be explained to you later at the Convention." The next year, at the diocesan convention of 1964, Pike assured the delegates that "our books were balanced in all accounts." But a subsequent audit in early 1965 revealed that the budget for the previous year was $27,000 in arrears. By the end of his tenure as bishop, the operating budget was running $92,000 in the red. Even before this disclosure, there had begun to be heard bitter complaints in the diocese of Pike's style of ecclesiastical finances, which were later to be described by *Pacific Churchman* as "years of deficit spending in the vague hope of better times."

But the financial crisis in 1965 was soon set aside temporarily that summer for yet another heresy charge. At first, before he learned of it, Pike's attentions and public statements had been diverted on August 13 by the deadly Watts riots in Los Angeles, a frightening confirmation of his political "prophecy" two years earlier of the racial tensions in that city between the police and minorities. Only three days afterward, Pike learned that a bill of particulars for heresy charges had been planned during the last two weeks for presentation at the September meeting of the House of Bishops. Accusing the bishop of California of heresy—in 1961, in 1964, and now in 1965—was, like his personal life, accruing the repetitiveness of a stale joke. But this time, in an apparent spirit of "three strikes and you're out," the movement to force a heresy trial for Pike had picked up new advocates. The previous two calls had originated from offended clergy, with after-the-fact support for their complaints from some sympathetic bishops. But at this upcoming convocation of the bishops at Glacier National Park, Montana, he would face for the first time a formal accusation by one of his fellow prelates, Bishop Joseph M. Harte of Arizona. Pike was coming dangerously close to a career-ending presentment for his trial on heresy charges.

The new danger was that once Harte made his demand in August to introduce his complaint of heterodoxy, a disposition of the Arizona bishop's bill of particulars would become an official part of the House of Bishops' agenda the next month. Consequent to the bill's future discussion and disposition, the votes of any three bishops among the 142 planning to attend the convention in Montana would be sufficient to begin an examination by the House of Pike's sermons and publications for evidence of heresy to present at a trial. Harte had written his bill on July 28 at the express requests of fourteen priests serving within his diocese. They, in turn, first had been contacted and encouraged to take this action by a retired priest living in Phoenix, who was formerly a canon in Louttit's diocese of South Florida. (A group of Episcopal "concerned clergy" from Alabama also publicly expressed its support for Harte's action.) Here the Arizona bishop had taken a page from Pike's own history of polemics against Sewanee, when that school first had learned though journalists of Pike's declining an invitation to speak at graduation; Harte similarly had been remiss in sending a copy of the bill in a timely fashion either to the San Francisco diocese office or to the national church headquarters in New York. Pike first learned of his new heresy troubles by reading about them in newspapers two weeks later on August 16, leaving him little time to prepare an answer to the bill before the September meeting.

The bill, excerpts of which then appeared in the *San Francisco Chronicle*, complained of his plan to ordain women to the diaconate as "at variance with apostolic custom, Anglican tradition, and practical wisdom." More substantially for a heresy offense, it also charged that he "has been false to the vows he took at ordination." Specifically, it charged that he "has repudiated our Lord's Virgin Birth," that he "has denied the doctrine of the Blessed Trinity," that he "maintains that the Incarnation was not unique in Jesus, but has occurred in other great religious leaders before his time," and, for good measure, he "denies that the Creeds contain articles of faith at all." The bill had been privately forwarded on July 29, "with a request that it be placed on the agenda of the meeting of the House," to the chairman of the House of

Bishops' standing committee for the dispatch of business. That chairman was Henry Louttit.

Episcopal bishops from across the nation converged on Montana by the first week of September at the East Glacier Lodge, a rustically baroque hotel built at the turn of the century by western railroad barons. Although the lodge and adjacent national park were desired tourist destinations, Pike had the sense to arrive without either of the two women in his life. Once the House of Bishops convened on September 7, Louttit properly assigned the bill of heresy particulars to the Theological Committee, established at the church's triennial convention the previous year, rather than trying to manipulate the bill into an early discussion and vote on the House floor. He was a fierce opponent, but not a dishonorable one. Pike was a member of this committee, but without the opportunity for debate he was recused by Louttit while the five other members discussed Harte's complaint in his absence.

There are only Pike's words to support his description of eventually being called September 8 to come to a small basement room, supposedly the only space available at this large hotel, to read the committee's draft report to the House, while seated underneath an interrogation-style single bare lightbulb. According to his version of the events, the committee's intended report discredited the Arizona charges, and generally praised the principle of theological inquiry; but it also censured Pike for past actions that it characterized as "self-aggrandizement" and "publicity seeking." Pike balked, and threatened to gather support among his political allies to contest on the floor of the House both the committee's censure and Harte's bill of particulars. Overnight, a compromise was perfected between the bishops who were pro- and anti-Pike. The offending clause about Pike's self-aggrandizement was removed from the report, and in return Pike would reaffirm to the House his loyalty to Episcopal doctrine and discipline. The official records of the exchange the next day on the floor between Pike and the Theological Committee imply an almost paradisiacal comity existing at Glacier National Park. The committee asserted in its report that "the bishop of California is not on trial in the House, nor does the present accusation against one of our members have standing among us," nor did the committee wish to limit for their church "the necessary devout testing of the vessels of Christian belief." Pike immediately rose to speak to this report, and stated that he was "truly sorry" if he had offended any of his fellow bishops in his attempts "to distinguish the earthen vessels from the Treasure." In the exercise of that task, he said, "I reaffirm my loyalty to the Doctrine, Discipline, and Worship of the Episcopal Church." The House then "heartily approved" the bishop's statement. The remainder of the convention largely consisted of Pike and Louttit—who addressed one another as "Dear Jim" and "Dear Hank"—inconclusively sparring over the meaning of the word *ordination* as applied to deaconesses. Nothing was resolved in regard to this important issue. (Not until the church's 1970 triennial convention, a year after Pike's death, were Episcopal women formally admitted to the diaconate.)

Once more, the heresy complaint against Pike had been disposed of in committee, without fractious discussion or voting on the floor of the House of Bishops. However, the problem with this solution, which Pike seemed not to recognize, was that, after four years, his church was running out of peacemaking committees, and his fellow prelates and his parishioners were running out of patience. The day after the convention adjourned, the *San Francisco Examiner* ran a four-column headline above its news story of the convention: "Bishop Pike: 'I Reaffirm My Loyalty to the Church.'" Many diocesan readers may be forgiven for having silently wondered about the sincerity of a bishop who could occasion such news coverage simply by announcing that he really believed what he had been practicing for years at Grace Cathedral. The city's newspaper columnists probably reflected public opinion when they began to run derogatory opinions about Pike. Herb Caen began to refer to Pike in a seriocomic way as "The Thunderer of Nob Hill," and another *Chronicle* columnist with a less genial record toward the bishop, Charles McCabe, later wrote more brusquely, "A man of the cloth who is a mild public nuisance is not an attractive addition to any city, including San Francisco."

It was becoming increasingly undeniable by autumn of 1965 that both Pike and the diocesan laity of San Francisco could benefit from an extended absence from each other. Such had also been observed earlier by the bishop's cynical but steadfast friend Darby Betts. He had arranged for the expenses to be approved in late August by the diocesan standing committee for a "half sabbatical" for Pike, enabling him to study for six months in Cambridge, England. His stay abroad would begin almost immediately, on September 15, only a few days after his return from the convention. The bishop was highly gratified. At long last he would be able to enact his desired role of a "don journalist." Pike noted with pleasure that his sabbatical fellowship at the Cambridge college provided "high table," or faculty, privileges, and that funds were also provided for him to travel to London for further consultations with Robinson. (Despite the diocese's straitened financial circumstances that summer, Pike had made a brief trip earlier to visit with Robinson in the U.K. and preach in his diocese.)

The official press release from the San Francisco diocesan office announcing his departure noted pointedly that "Bishop and Mrs. Pike are hopeful that they may arrange their family schedule to permit her to spend a substantial portion of her husband's sabbatical with him in England." In fact, Esther Pike would never visit her husband while he was in Cambridge. Instead, much of the bishop's time within the small apartment awaiting him in England was to be spent with his son, Jim, Maren Bergrud, and a handful of other spiritually adrift individuals he had gathered around him by the mid-1960s.

His nightmare years were about to begin.

VII

The Years of Deception and Nightmare, 1966–1968

O the mind, mind has mountains; cliffs of fall
Frightful, sheer, no-man fathomed.

—GERARD MANLEY HOPKINS, S.J., "No Worse"

When informed of the death he covered his face with his hands,
bent forward, and said, hoarsely, "Oh, my God!"

—*San Francisco Chronicle*, February 5, 1966, describing Bishop Pike
after learning of his son's suicide

Pike's sabbatical commenced in discord. Maren Bergrud, who had been introduced as the bishop's "secretary" in public, insisted that she accompany him to Cambridge and remain there with him during his six-month residence. He balked at her desire. His twenty-year-old son had been persuaded to live in the Cambridge apartment with his father, and

Pike looked forward to spending unshared time with Jim, perhaps with a view toward repairing his earlier years of absence. Bergrud was persistent. An uneasy compromise eventually was accepted, whereby Pike and his son would arrive first in England by airplane, and she would come later, by sea. The bishop usually was unembarrassed by his relation with Bergrud, but the presence of the woman who was basically his common-law wife living in the same residence with his son apparently bothered him. In writing his account with his third wife, Diane Kennedy Pike, of the subsequent "psychic" incidents of that sabbatical, *The Other Side*, Pike deliberately manipulated dates, making it appear that Bergrud joined him—as a secretary—only after his son's death.

Initially, their arrival in Cambridge in late autumn 1965 and their first weeks thereafter went well. (They had a delayed start, having stopped for social reasons in New York, and the elder Pike had also made brief speaking engagements in Canada and New Haven.) Pike was an observant enough parent to know that his son had smuggled two packets of cigarettes containing marijuana through customs; he was indulgent enough to hope that these would satisfy Jim in place of Romilar and LSD. Until his son succeeded in finding dealers in hashish and psychedelic drugs in Cambridge and London later that fall, Pike was pleased by the absence of the usual depression and lack of academic confidence in Jim. His son had inherited his father's fondness for what that decade called "rap" sessions, and the two began staying up late in the apartment at 9 Carlton Court, debating and describing to each other the virtues of religion, hallucinogenic drugs, poetry, and higher education.

The bishop's reputation had preceded him to Cambridge, usually in a favorable way, and both the *Guardian* and *Observer* newspapers covered his arrival at the university. The *Observer* described him as "America's Bishop of Woolwich" and wrote of "his clear mind and gift of popular exposition." The *Guardian* wrote more expansively about Pike: "There is scarcely any point at which he coincides with the Englishman's image of a bishop. He truckles to fashion by wearing a purple stock, it is true, but his pectoral cross is parked in an inside pocket so that it looks as if he had merely arranged his watch chain eccentrically. . . . He very nearly chain-smokes. He speaks his mind without taking refuge in episcopal artfulness. And when he talks, the voice is the gravel pit grating of Edward G. Robinson in a dog collar, but the words are the prescriptions of the New Reformation."

Clare College, where Pike was to attend lectures and read independently during that Michaelmass term, was the academic center of the so-called New Reformation, seconded by the sermons and publications of priests within the Woolwich diocese. The subject that Pike intended to study in greater detail was, like so many others of the bishop's enthusiasms, prefaced by the word *new*. This time the object of his attention was the New Quest. This academic search for the historical origins of Christianity and Jesus himself had led some scholars to profess finding evidence of a proto-Christianity recorded in the Dead Sea Scrolls. In the elliptical style in which the bishop thought, New Quest equaled New Reformation. Pike "intuitively" came to believe, as Diane Pike was later to write, that a closer study of the disciplines and practices of the Essene community recorded in the scrolls found in Jordan at Wadi Qumran would justify his and Robinson's contention that first-century, "authentic" Christianity was much more minimalist in its creeds than was presently accepted. Although he knew no Hebrew, Pike was close at Cambridge to those who did, and he began accumulating a private library of, eventually, eight hundred books on the scrolls and the origins of Christianity. While he was beginning his latest intellectual quest, he also arranged for Jim to enroll at a local preparatory college with the understanding that he would enter San Francisco State when they returned home the next year.

Bergrud's arrival in Cambridge changed the situation inside their third-floor flat. Jim never seems to have been fond of Bergrud, petulantly criticizing her hairstyle, for instance. He resumed his Romilar and LSD habits, and smoking hashish became a chronic act. There is a certain frisson at reading Pike's later accounts in *The Other Side* of witnessing his son's drug addictions. Admittedly, a "parent can't be a policeman for a young man that age," Pike wrote, and his son certainly was safer, physically and legally, consuming his drugs inside the apartment than outside it. But, even without the foreknowledge that the younger Pike would die under the influence of narcotics within a few months, there is a chill at reading his father's self-consciously sophisticated warnings to his son. His desire to be unflappable and nonjudgmental appears almost equal to his fatherly concern for his son: " 'I think I'd cool it some, Jim,' I said, steadily looking him in the eye. 'I'm interested in your experiences; but they worry me.'" Such was the extent of paternal warnings. For her part, Bergrud apparently found a disturbing common ground with Jim, in their mutual need for illegal drugs. A later visitor to the flat was surprised that she knew the London address of the hashish dealer to the bishop's son and that she made unexplained trips to the district of that address in the city; the visitor inferred that she, too, had become a chronic smoker of hashish.

Pike's attempted resolution of these problems later in the year seems to have been, as often, more hyperactive movement. A sabbatical means, literally, a rest, but in the month between December 1965 and January 1966, this uneasy trio, or the bishop alone, traveled to West Germany, Israel, the nation then known as Rhodesia, Kenya, Iran, and Malawi. Beginning with a two-week lecture tour on religion and culture, at the invitation of the U.S. military to chaplains and dependents at Air Force bases in West Germany, Pike and his two companions spent the last week of Advent as tourists in Israel. Together, Jim and his father climbed the ancient path to the first-century mountaintop fortress at Masada, a shared experience that remained dear to the elder Pike. The bishop also talked with scholars of the Dead Sea Scrolls at Hebrew University in Jerusalem, where a decade earlier as a dean he had first been privileged to see the scroll of Isaiah. On Christmas Eve, Pike conducted services at the Anglican church in Nazareth. Later that same night, the indefatigable bishop also finished the manuscript of his thirteenth book, *What Is This Treasure?*

This small volume, fewer than one hundred pages, was simply a restatement, as Pike wrote in the introduction, "to my critics (and they were many—in fact, too many to name)" of the necessity for the church to be "reductive as to the number of *items* regarded as essential to authentic Christianity (italics in original)." He dedicated the book jointly to John Robinson, "good friend and companion spirit," and to the late Paul Tillich, "dear friend much missed." Tillich had died the previous October, and one observer of the two noted the similarities between the bishop and his former teacher, that "each lived on the boundary between the church and the world, between Christianity and secularity, between *eros* and *agape*, between theory and practice." Later the next year, Pike recalled having experienced "a crucial 'moment of truth,' " while reading Socrates following the death of Tillich, that had compelled him to compose *What Is This Treasure?* This experience apparently was further evidence that in promoting the New Reformation he was part of the *kairos* that his former teacher at Union Seminary had experienced and prophesied.

On December 29, Pike was thousands of miles south of Israel at the airport in Salisbury, Rhodesia. He had flown there to consult with Bishop Kenneth Skelton of the Anglican diocese of Matabeleland. This Rhodesian diocese, as it attempted to provide religious and social services to blacks, had been officially harassed and bullied by the white supremacist government of Ian Smith. Matabeleland had been selected in 1963 as a companion diocese to the diocese of California under the Anglican Church's Mutual Responsibility and Independence Program for dioceses in third world countries. Pike, after consulting on this program with Robinson in the U.K. and meeting with Skelton both in the United States and the U.K., characteristically decided to witness Matabeleland's difficulties himself.

Rhodesian police were determined that the bishop not enter the country. As soon as he arrived at the Salisbury airport, Pike was arrested, held for three hours, and then placed on the next airplane to London. This incident was particularly frightening for the next twenty-four hours for Jim and Bergrud, who had remained in Israel. They had heard on an English-language news broadcast only that the bishop had been arrested; there was no word on his physical safety, and Pike had been unable to telephone them. Finally able to return to Israel via a change of planes in Teheran, Iran, he rushed to the resort hotel where his son was staying, and the two emotionally embraced. "A beautiful embrace it was," Pike said, "and particularly because for all he knew, by then I was off in some remote part of Rhodesia in one of the detention centers. But here I was. And here he was. All was encompassed within two warm and loving smiles." He always considered this moment to have been his closest emotional intimacy with his son during the latter's short life.

"Pike Kicked Out of Rhodesia" ran the eight-column, above-the-masthead headline on the front page of the *San Francisco Examiner*, proving that, even though he was half a world away, he could still sell newspapers in his hometown. But despite his fortuitous avoidance of the

Smith government's notorious detention centers, Pike was convinced that he had been set up for his arrest by the actions of a retired canon, Rev. Frank Brunton, of Phoenix, Arizona, formerly of the diocese of South Florida. Brunton had been the instigator among the fourteen Arizona clergymen who subsequently petitioned their bishop to bring a bill of particulars for heresy against Pike, and he had a long history of writing and circulating scurrilous doggerel about the bishop, copies of which were sent almost weekly to his residence. The trip to Rhodesia had been well publicized even before his sabbatical, and it was known that Brunton had sent a letter to the Rhodesian government before the bishop's departure, advising that Pike was an agitator among people of color. The Smith government had a well-deserved reputation for physical brutality, particularly toward whites who opposed its supremacist policies. It is difficult to believe that Brunton did not at least momentarily consider that in mailing his letter to Rhodesia he was articulating to men of violent inclinations the type of provocation—"Who will free me from this turbulent priest?" as Henry II asked—that could lead to placing Pike's life in jeopardy.

But the bishop, ever turbulent, turned up two weeks later in the nation of Malawi. There he was able to meet freely on January 16 with church leaders from the Matabeleland diocese in neighboring Rhodesia and to promise his continual campaign in the United States to aid them financially and politically. Upon his return to England, Pike was unable, or unwilling, to remain at Clare College for more than a few weeks before traveling again. Partly, this impatience with continuing his studies was because the Matabeleland diocese was now his latest cause célèbre; more pointedly, he was prompted to return by a letter from his diocese, postmarked January 18, notifying him of the intention of certain clergy and laity there to establish a nine-member "Faith and Order Commission." The creation of this commission "could certainly be interpreted as a move to take away some of the authority in the diocese from the bishop," a diocesan spokesman told the *San Francisco Examiner,* as it proposed to study "doctrine, diocesan growth, and development."

Pike subsequently decided to travel briefly to San Francisco to address his diocese's annual convention on Friday, February 4, and then return to Cambridge perhaps as soon as the following Sunday. Jim also determined to go to the States on the same date as his father and remain there. He may have been serious about an announced intention to re-enroll at San Francisco State, or he may simply have been homesick, or he did not wish the time alone with Bergrud. Pike chose to travel non-stop on February 2 to San Francisco. His son booked a different flight the same day with a stopover in New York, in order "to see friends," he told his father. Before they left, over his father's objections, he bought additional Romilar pills, then legal in the U.K. though not the United States. On their arrival at Heathrow Airport the day of their flights, Jim discovered that he had forgotten his passport. A gate agent helpfully suggested to the father that his son could obtain a temporary passport in London from the U.S. Consulate General, rather than returning the greater distance to Cambridge to retrieve the forgotten document. Pike gave his son money for a taxi into the city and a return to Heathrow, said good-bye, and exacted a promise from him to telephone his parents in San Francisco later that week. He began to walk up the concourse stairway to the duty-free shops. Momentarily, he glanced back just as Jim looked up. Their eyes met, they both smiled, and father and son waved farewell.

The father soon was back to business in the United States. There, an "angry" Pike, according to a reporter's description, called a press conference the following day in San Francisco to denounce as "totally false" a story that had appeared earlier in the *Examiner* stating that the bishop was returning "to head off a move by some clergy and laity which he interprets as an attempt to lessen his power." The story was libelous, Pike declared. "Maybe I should sue," he said, dramatically waving a newspaper, "and use the money to help the struggling, censored Rhodesian newspapers." He insisted that his sole impulse in returning was to address the delegates at his diocese's 116th convention to emphasize the need for financial and spiritual aid to their Rhodesian companion diocese. Unmentioned by Pike or any of the reporters present was that the 1966 convention was to be a low-budget affair compared to earlier diocesan sessions, due to inadequate revenues. The majority of delegates would meet February 4 for that day and evening only at Grace Cathedral. Pike was to address the convention that evening.

He largely kept to his agenda Friday night, speaking from the pulpit on his "five-pronged project for the diocese of Matabeleland." Although he earlier had felt some unease that Jim had not yet contacted his parents, and that Esther Pike had left the convention in order to wait at the bishop's house in case her son telephoned in an emergency, Pike did not connect these events with the unusually large number of reporters he noticed gathered at the narthex, or lobby, of the cathedral. But while he had been seated in the cathedral prior to his speech and during his remarks, a frantic drama unseen and unheard by him had been taking place. Howard Freeman, the canon who was responsible for diocesan public relations, had rushed to the side of David Baar, who was the latest of Pike's many chaplains and executive assistants, and, in Baar's recollection, privately exclaimed "that Jimmy Pike was in New York and that he'd shot himself in his hotel room." Baar immediately went to the diocesan house, unlocked the bishop's office, and, using the "private line," telephoned Bergrud in England. "Is Jimmy there?" he asked. "My God, there are reporters here," Bergrud answered. "I don't know what to do. They say he shot himself." Freeman, meanwhile, confirmed the self-inflicted shooting death of Jim with the New York City police department and succeeded in persuading most of the local reporters from publicizing the story until the bishop and his wife could be told of their son's death.

At the pulpit, Pike appeared puzzled when, after his hour-long address, he was not ceremonially led by Baar toward his bishop's chair but instead was surrounded by canons and other diocesan clergy and officials, taken by his arm, and quickly led through a side door away from the reporters in the narthex. "You're needed outside now," he was told. There, in the darkness of the cathedral's parking lot, Baar haltingly told him the news: "It's Jim. . . . He's—dead." Pike reacted with a hoarse cry, covering his face, and was taken to the diocesan house and told further details. His son was a suicide, having shot himself in a New York City hotel room.

Later, from police and autopsy reports, the last three days of the life of Jim were reconstructed. Upon his arrival in New York, he had checked into the Hadson Hotel, a five-dollar-a-day residency located at the edge of what was then the city's garment district, on Wednesday, February 2. He prepaid the room through the hotel's afternoon checkout time on Friday. He received no visitors and made only two telephone calls, both to Pan American Airlines. At some time, probably on Thursday, he bought a Savage 30-30 hunting rifle and ammunition at a sports store, and returned with the weapon to his room. He then spent at least part of Friday writing and drawing a large number of messages in a school composition notebook, some addressed to his family and some to his friends, which police later characterized as having "rambled on and on"; one ended with the repetition of "Good-bye, good-bye . . ." and another was a drawing of a human figure with a rifle shooting dead a bird. The police, after examining his body, believed that, subsequent to leaving these notes, he had sat on the edge of the room's single bed, propped the rifle barrel in the direction of his right temple, and pulled the trigger with his thumb.

The first bullet missed. Police later recovered it from the room's ceiling. Remarkably, no other residents heard the shot, or had been willing to report it. Jim then chambered another round, readjusted the rifle's barrel, and again pulled the trigger; this time his attempt was successful and the bullet pierced his skull, killing him, as well as tearing away a large portion of his right jaw and face. Police were called after the body was found at about 3:30 p.m. Friday afternoon by a bellboy making a routine room check. The identity of Jim was confirmed by the temporary passport and an automobile insurance receipt found in a pocket of his clothing. An autopsy later reported the presence in his bloodstream of traces of illegal narcotics. The assertion by Stringfellow and Towne, based on anecdotes collected later, that the younger Pike killed himself as the result of unresolved homosexual longings can neither be proved nor disproved; no reason for his fatal action was specified in the notes he left, nor is this omission surprising. The whole point of suicide is to put one's private motives and circumstances beyond discussion and to reduce one's life to a pair of enigmatic dates—birth and death—with whatever is experienced in between rendered irretrievable. The following are the few certainties of what occurred in that hotel room: he had been depressed, which was experienced with an adolescent's intensity; illegal narcotics, taken either despite his parents' best efforts or with their oversight, had magnified his feelings; he had impulsively bought a firearm, at an age when its operator really did not believe the facts of what bullets can do to flesh or thought that death was simply another metaphoric "trip." And thus, the younger James Pike became a statistic of the 1960s. He was twenty years old, barely, when he killed himself; his birthday had been nine days earlier. His father would turn fifty-two on February 14, only a little more than a week after his elder son's death.

After being told the details, Pike exhibited a preternatural calmness to those assembled around him at the diocesan house. He remembered that his wife was at the bishop's residence and he spotted Philip Adams, the diocesan chancellor, in the small crowd. "Phil," he said, "will you call and tell Esther not to answer the phone till I get there?" He removed his vestments, and put on a suit coat and a topcoat. Baar drove him to the Jackson Street house, and Esther Pike met him at the door. "It's Jim," he said, and led her back inside to a sofa, and then told her that her son had taken his own life. She dropped her head into her hands. "Like me, she couldn't cry—not yet," he wrote. "I tried to be of some comfort."

That night, and for a few days and nights following, she allowed her husband to stay at the residence, although in a separate bedroom and in a partition of the house locked from entrance to her quarters. As Pike later recalled, when he retired to his bedroom that night, he saw a photograph of Jim on the top of a dresser, and began sobbing uncontrollably. His wife, also, "when the reality struck her with full force," he wrote, emotionally and physically collapsed into tears. There, each alone in a room within the bishop's house, Esther and James Pike wept separately for their dead son.

Friends did what they could. John Krumm officially identified the body, and, at the expressed wish of Pike, arranged for its cremation at a Brooklyn mortuary and the shipment of the ashes to San Francisco, where a memorial service was to be held. Meanwhile, condolences arrived in stacks of telegrams and letters at the bishop's house from throughout the world. (Among them was a note from Reverend Brunton in Phoenix. It read in its entirety: "Thank God for one less pike [*sic*].") John Coburn, who had preached the consecration sermon for Pike at Grace Cathedral in 1958, joined with the family in participating in the Requiem Eucharist held for the bishop's son at the cathedral on February 7. Jack Riley, rector of St. Paul's Church in Marin County and a close acquaintance of the bishop, arranged for a yacht owned by one of his parishioners to be made available to the Pike family, captained by the owner, in order to complete their wishes to cast Jim's ashes into San Francisco Bay.

The events on the morning the yacht set out, February 9, were nearly a disaster, exacerbated by Pike's macabre attempts at humor. The day brought "one of the biggest storms ever to hit San Francisco County," recalled Riley, who was aboard, and the voyage into the bay was "the roughest trip I've ever been on." The bishop and his wife, seated at the back of the yacht holding the container of their son's ashes, struggled in the heavy seas to keep from spilling the solicitously provided sandwiches and black coffee over each other. No one was quite sure if a legal requirement pertaining to distance from shore might prevent them from emptying the container so close to land, but then the captain declared his misgivings about proceeding more than a few hundred yards in the winter weather. Pike for his part began making jokes about "not wanting to empty the ashes into the wind and have Jim back in the boat all over the sandwiches." Finally, a decision was made to toss the ashes at the point in the water where the yacht was idling roughly near the shore, and the container was carefully opened to spill its ashes with the direction of the high winds. Pike suddenly broke from his bad joking into crying, and he was joined in his tears by his wife. Very little was said on the trip back to shore.

Pike did not return immediately to England. Instead, he sent David Baar to arrive ahead of him and stay at the flat at Cambridge. The official reason given was that Baar had "to collate all the necessary information for the Matabeleland project," although the bishop's "secretary," Bergrud, was already in place and supposedly competent for such a task. The actual reason appears to have been that Pike simply did not want a time of intimacy with Bergrud as "just the two of us," and with the presence of another young man in the space formerly occupied by Jim, there at least would be no grievously vacant second bedroom. In the days following the dispersal of his son's ashes, Pike returned to New York and to interviews with the usually friendly media of that city. He was not so much dealing with his grief as ignoring it.

His son's death had muted the discussion at the convention of two other issues in addition to Rhodesia. He had intended to bring before a larger audience his support for the escalating war in Vietnam, and his continued commitment to a reductionist, New Reformation theology. Pike in his earlier remarks to the convention that Friday night had described the United States as waging a "righteous conflict" in warring against Communism in Vietnam. His remarks certainly did "surprise my liberal friends," as Pike had promised that they would, and gave further evidence that he was not always the reflexive protestor his critics accused him of being. His support for the war remained, although increasingly conditional, throughout 1966. He also continued to be equally militant verbally against what he described as "meaningless" theological doctrines in a freewheeling interview he granted the *New York Times* on February 13, before departing for England the next day.

Once in Cambridge, Pike chose to deal with his grief by exhausting himself, particularly by traveling. Immediately after arriving at Heathrow, he insisted on conducting Baar and Bergrud on a tour of London cathedrals rather than returning to the flat. Three days later, he and Bergrud, again at his insistence, drove to Manchester to keep an appointment that he originally had arranged to also include Jim, a meeting with the remarkable Dead Sea Scrolls scholar then in residence at Manchester University, John Marco Allegro. An iconoclast who could match Pike in controversies, Allegro had been the sole secular member among the otherwise Christian team of translators first chosen to decipher the scrolls, and the only scholar of that group to have completed and publicized the translation of the scroll under his supervision, the "Copper Scroll." He had excited Pike's interest by his increasingly public criticisms of the other translators' dilatory progress and their refusal to share with other scholars or make public their partial translations. Allegro was willing to speak aloud what many nonacademic students of the scrolls, including Pike and the writer Edmund Wilson, privately were intimating: that a full disclosure of the contents of the scrolls might be an embarrassment to orthodox Christianity, and was therefore deliberately being delayed.

In 1956, Allegro announced in a BBC program that he had translated a portion from one of the scrolls, the *Commentary on Nahum*, a description of the crucifixion of a "Teacher of Righteousness" and his Essene followers in the first century B.C.E. Such a text confirmed to him that accounts of the later ministry and crucifixion of Jesus were more mythical traditions than historical facts, and that publication of other translations from the scrolls would refute much of Christian orthodoxy. He subsequently maintained this interpretation in letters and articles published in the London *Times* and in conversations with Pike. Pike also heard—and may have felt a vindication at hearing—Allegro's opinions that the proto-origins of the recorded Gospels that describe the Incarnation, Jesus' miracles, and the resurrection probably were far too unacceptable to the Christianity of the bishop's critics. The *ur*-versions of the Gospel stories, in Allegro's opinion, most certainly included early Christian beliefs that were later to be viewed as heretical. As he wrote four months later, in an article for *Harper's* magazine on the possible origins of the New Testament stories which greatly impressed Pike: "We are in the world of dark magic, and in particular that kind which deals with the calling up of the spirits of dead for necromancy."

After the visit with Allegro, Pike and Bergrud returned to the Cambridge flat. The following four weeks were to be among the strangest of Pike's life. He had found after his arrival that Baar and Bergrud were uneasy and argumentative in each other's company, a situation that Baar attributed to her attempt to seduce him during his first night's residence. Baar also said in his later descriptions of the bishop's common-law wife that "the quantity of drugs Maren was taking, for whatever reason," had led to his having "daily freaks," or confrontational scenes, with her. Pike himself was still "in shock," as Baar said, over his son's death, and as the bishop later made clear, was unable to find any solace or credibility in his professed religion's belief in life after death. There were also the personal effects of Jim, visibly scattered about the flat, which had not been put away during the previous week. This combination of drugs, covert sexuality, and grief within their shared quarters seems to have distorted their individual perceptions. Baar later attempted to describe how their presence together produced collectively "an altered state of consciousness. . . . I was able to look back at that and say, 'My God! There is no question about that being an altered state of consciousness. . . . [It was] like being on the approach curve to a really sound flu. It was very difficult to find the ground."

He went on to recount how the three began to stay inside the apartment "eight to sixteen hours a day," reading, writing, arguing, taking drugs, and, above all, omnivorously smoking cigarettes: "We must have consumed among the three of us ten packs of cigarettes a day, easily. We would smoke and smoke. . . . Eat butts, you know?" Correspondence to the bishop from the outside began to go unanswered, then disregarded, by both Bergrud and Pike; the apartment was filling up with cartons of half-eaten "take-away" food; laundry was sent out, when it was dealt with at all. It was, Baar later recalled, like living in an "isolation camp."

It also could be described by this time as a rat's nest of mutually suggested irrational perceptions, some as nightmarish as the vision of Jim's suicide itself. Psychokinetic events, which Pike and Bergrud claimed to witness inside the apartment and which they interpreted as signs of Jim's frustrated attempts to communicate with them, occurred frequently throughout the remainder of February. Baar hesitantly came to agree with them, and then he started to witness some of these apparent phenomena independently. The three maintained a log of these events, later expanded and published as *The Other Side*, although Bergrud would not live to see its publication. The supposed psychic events varied from the harmlessly subtle to the malignly overt: a childish scribble in yellow chalk noticed on the stairway to their apartment, at a time when no children lived in their building; books moved from bookcases inside a room where no one was remembered to have been; safety pins and other objects found in positions on the floor resembling the arms of a clock set at 8:19 p.m., the approximate time in the U.K. when Jim had killed himself in New York; and, most dramatically, two incidents centering on Bergrud. The first was her awakening to find that her hair, previously styled in the bangs that Jim had disliked, had been partially burned in her sleep, supposedly without her awareness. On a second morning, she awoke semiconscious, groaning in pain, bringing Pike and Baar to her bedside. There the two men observed on her face an expression "clearly of horror and fear," in Pike's description. Upon examination, her fingernail was discovered to have been broken, and the skin underneath other nails to have been punctured by a needle-like instrument. She denied doing this damage to herself. A search of the room found no pins or needles. Pike discussed these events privately with John Pearce-Higgins, a canon he had met at a clerical gathering who was a member of the Society for Psychical Research. Pearce-Higgins in turn recommended that Pike apply for a séance with Ena Twigg, a London medium of considerable repute among spiritualist circles. He did so and, accompanied by Pearce-Higgins and Bergrud, met with Twigg on March 2.

She was, to Pike's pleasant surprise, a tea-cozy medium. A diminutive, cheerful woman with dark hair, and with the traditional "penetrating eyes" set in an otherwise kindly face, she and her husband, a retired military officer, lived in East Acton in a respectable middle-class house. There the séance took place. Twigg, when she entered mediumistic trances, did not speak in the voice of a deceased "control," as did the most celebrated nineteenth-century mediums, but all agreed that she was a gifted monologuist. After taking in her hand Jim's passport (which Pike had found in the Cambridge flat after his son's death), she began her trance, speaking intermittently in the first and third persons: "I was worried about you, Dad, because they were kicking you around," she first spoke. "I came to your room, I moved books, I knocked on the door—came to your bedside—you dreamt about me and spoke to me." Twigg then spoke as herself: "He is saying something about a gate—golden . . . a golden gate. Does that mean anything to you?"

Perhaps no more open-ended a question could be asked of one who had been a resident near San Francisco Bay and its bridge for the last eight years, but Pike immediately, and joyfully, took her words as confirmation that his deceased son approved of the dispersal of his ashes. The séance drew to a close, but not before Twigg briefly contacted what seemed to be the spirit of the recently deceased Paul Tillich: "Someone with a foreign accent—German, I think—is speaking. Wait . . . *Paul*, there is a Paul here. . . . He says, 'Thank you for dedicating your new book to me.' " (Hannah Tillich, learning of this pronouncement after Pike publicized this séance, was furious with him, and sent him an indignant letter.) Pike was impressed, since the book was not yet published in the United Kingdom and by the apparent fact that the book's dedication therefore could not have been known beforehand. Jim then apparently spoke through the medium, employing the fustian vocabulary so often heard among the dead speaking at spiritualist circles: "I want to thank the scribe [Pearce-Higgins] for acting as an intermediary and helping me find the path."

Pike believed. One should not jeer too much at the bishop's credulity within a month of his son's death, or the public embarrassments into which it later led him. Credulity and death are the common lot of humanity, and, sooner or later, one or the other will leave us all in embarrassing positions. It is also pointless at this late date to try to determine whether Twigg or the other mediums with whom Pike later consulted were shams, or actually possessed of some unclassified psychic powers, or, as William James thought about most mediums of his acquaintance, a combination of the two. Spiritualism itself has a plentitude of defenders and detractors and needs no space here for either. The theological and personal circumstances of the bishop's belief in spiritualism will be considered in the next chapter, but, for the moment, it is sufficient for this biography that Pike *believed*. "Jim and Maren came back from that with a whole new attitude," Baar said of their successful séance with Twigg. The psychokinetic incidents inside the apartment also stopped, perhaps as a consequence of its occupants having become psychically, or psychologically, at peace with the death of Jim. Most important, Pike became able psychologically to leave his self-imposed isolation and deal with professional issues, one in particular needing his urgent attention.

The first was a highly irregular meeting of the Episcopal Church's metropolitan bishops, or those charged with speaking for regional areas of the church, called for March 5 at the O'Hare Airport Inn in Chicago by the Church's presiding bishop. The subject was Pike himself and his most recently published statements. Presiding Bishop John Hines urged Pike by letter to meet with the metropolitans personally, advising that it would be much in Pike's interest to do so. Pike was able to attend and keep to his schedule at Cambridge only by completing a grueling, one-day London-to-Chicago-to-London itinerary. The bishops had been distressed by the contents of an article, "An American Bishop's Search for a Space Age God," that had appeared two weeks earlier in *Look* magazine. Although the article was highly favorable to Pike personally (it was written by Christopher Wren, a senior editor at *Look* who as a Yale undergraduate had been one of the numerous collegiate admirers of Pike), there were inconsistencies embarrassing and infuriating to some of the bishops. For instance, Pike had not been "acquitted" of heresy at Glacier National Park, as described, because the church prelates had maneuvered energetically to avoid bringing him to a heresy trial. More troubling, his statements quoted in the article—"I've abandoned ship on the Trinity"—put the lie to his earlier, public action at Glacier National Park reaffirming the creeds of his church. The meeting with the metropolitans was terse. Pike promised to write a lengthy letter to the magazine's editor, pointing out what he considered to be the article's important factual or theological inaccuracies, and he promptly returned to England.

After closing out the tenancy of the Cambridge flat and donating some of his dead son's clothing to charity, Pike and Bergrud returned to the United States at the end of his sabbatical on March 15. The couple did manage to schedule an additional séance with Twigg before they left. Jim, purportedly speaking through the medium, promised to be "in touch" by August.

Pike did not tarry in San Francisco. By the first week of April, he was in New York, as the invited preacher for Holy Week at St. Thomas Episcopal Church on Fifth Avenue. (The clergy and congregation had a reputation as intellectually adventurous, and until his practice of spiritualism became known, Pike had always found a receptive audience there for his sermons.) It was in his sermon on April 7 that Pike made what was probably the most succinct and uncompromising public statement of his clerical career on the New Reformation. "What we need," he told his fellow Episcopalians, "are fewer beliefs and more belief." This phrase was the working title of the book he was presently completing. Pike wittily compared the orthodoxy of the present Christian church to the situation of owners of a new restaurant opening in a Jewish neighborhood who observe fewer and fewer customers arriving to eat, until the owners realize their food is not kosher. "The old forms are gone," he told the worshipers, "they can no longer make sense today. The question is whether we can come up with the new ones—the kosher kitchen—fast enough."

The following week he again spoke his mind, or witnessed, as perhaps Pike would have preferred, when he gave the closing address to the annual meeting in the city of the National Council on Alcoholism. Candid about his own alcoholism, the bishop praised the organization of Alcoholics Anonymous as a model for his church to emulate in its nonjudgmental acceptance of those who seek its services. In the type of spiritual segue that infuriated his critics, Pike then continued his analogy to urge his church to nonjudgmentally accept professed homosexuals into its communion. "There are eighty thousand homosexuals in San Francisco," he said. "We can't ignore eighty thousand people."

Pike may have spoken his mind so bluntly at pulpits and podiums in New York because he knew he would not long be occupying his diocesan bishop's chair in San Francisco. The Chicago interview was proof that factions desiring his presentment on heresy charges were still keeping a watchdog vigilance on him. The financial troubles in the diocese also were accelerating; two motions for a public discussion of his administration of diocesan finances had been introduced at the last convention, later withdrawn as "inappropriate" after the news of his son's suicide, but there was a certainty of future struggles to maintain his administrative powers over money. On May 9, Pike submitted to his church's presiding bishop his resignation as the bishop in ordinary, or foremost bishop, of the diocese of California. "Back on the job, I am all the more aware of how difficult it will be for me to continue in a role of scholar-teacher and administrator-leader," he wrote to John Hines. The same date as his letter of resignation, he appeared at one of his diocesan churches to debate before the congregation charges by the church's rector that the bishop was encouraging heresy.

Pike's resignation was first to be approved by his diocesan standing committee, and then, by canon law, submitted for approval by Hines to the church's other bishops. The standing committee accepted his offered resignation "with regret" but with an almost embarrassingly quick response. No difficulty was perceived by Hines in obtaining the consents of Pike's fellow bishops. By no means was he was no longer to be a bishop, however; Pike was to retain the title of his ecclesiastical office. One advantage of an episcopacy is that there is a bishop for all occasions, and he was now a "supply" bishop, or, officially, an auxiliary bishop, expected to serve the diocese part-time "wherever his assistance was sought and needed." His resignation was to be effective September 15; until that date, he claimed unused leave and vacation.

Pike chose well to keep out of the public eye during this period. On July 21, Esther Pike and her attorney filed for divorce in the Superior Court of San Francisco County on the grounds of extreme cruelty. In a statement released to newspapers and signed by both of them, James and Esther Pike mutually expressed regret that "outside factors beyond the control of either of us have contributed for some time to our drifting apart." They added that neither of them had plans to remarry, and that this statement would be their final public comment on the divorce. An interlocutory decree, its terms to become final within a year unless contested, was granted to Esther Pike. Given his infidelities over the decades, the divorce was conducted in a dignified manner as these things go, but its terms cost Pike dearly. He was obligated to pay maintenance and support to his wife, who had moved from the bishop's residence to her own house on Webster Street. He further was responsible for paying the educational, medical, or psychiatric bills for his two minor children, Christopher and Constance Ann. (Catherine Pike was of legal age in 1966.) Additionally, Pike was to maintain large life insurance policies on himself with his children as beneficiaries, and, after paying literary agents' fees, he was to share 50 percent of his royalties with his former wife on all books he had partially written or researched during the last years of their union. Some undeveloped land was to be owned jointly until a buyer could be found, but, basically, what Pike got to keep from his marriage of twenty-four years was his personal library of scholarly books and a used car.

Characteristically, he overworked his way through anxiety and depression. He accepted two part-time teaching appointments, at the University of California, Berkeley, and at the Graduate Theological Union, encompassing the same campus. He planned two future books with Harper & Row. He also accepted a full-time position, which would occasion a permanent move in mid-July to Southern California, at the Center for the Study of Democratic Institutions, a left-of-center think tank located in Santa Barbara. He was to serve there, as he liked to say, as the worker-priest in residence, and he delighted in the headline announcing his move—"Mind Over Miter"—that appeared in the New York *Daily News*. Pike initially fit well into the organization at the center. Directed by the former "boy wonder" president of the University of Chicago, Robert Hutchins, the center occupied a mansion on Eucalyptus Hill in Santa Barbara where Hutchins had assembled an eclectic "fellowship" of cross-disciplinary scholars and writers.

In an interview one year after his appointment, seated in his office "dominated by a small, dark painting of Christ," Pike explained, while "lighting one cigarette after another," how he had been appointed to the center. "I needed advice last summer so I came to Bob Hutchins," he said, apparently in reference to his decision to resign his bishopric. "He said, 'Why don't you come here?' I told him I didn't come looking for a job, but when I thought about it I knew this was where I wanted to be." He added, "There is more theological dialogue here than in any House of Bishops meeting I've attended." Pike apparently was to fulfill his long-held ambition to be a "don journalist" not within the confined colleges of Cambridge University but, more appropriately, at a mid-twentieth-century institution in California overlooking the Pacific Ocean. Before moving to Southern California, while he was fulfilling his teaching contracts at Berkeley, he also found himself becoming attracted, sexually and emotionally, to a twenty-eight-year-old, intelligent, blond woman, Diane Kennedy, who was a student in one of the two classes he taught there, "The New Morality." She got into the habit of giving him automobile rides back to San Francisco after classes.

It was Maren Bergrud, however, who accompanied Pike to Santa Barbara. This move initially presented a problem in the person of his widowed mother, who was now known as Pearl Chambers. Refusing to stay in San Francisco after her son's removal, she convinced, or coerced, him into sharing his newly rented apartment, number 307, on the Coast Village Road in Santa Barbara. Bergrud rented an adjacent flat. These two emotionally possessive women temporarily satisfied, Pike found that his duties at the center, which began in August, were easily accomplished. The primary responsibilities of the staff were to have interdisciplinary conversations among themselves and to publish judiciously. During one of the conversations, Pike mentioned his interest in spiritualism. A visitor present at the conversation, John McConnell, suggested that he might wish to contact George Daisley, an English-born medium with a large clientele in Southern California. A few days later, in the first days of August, when his dead son had promised, in Twigg's voice, to be "in touch," the bishop and Bergrud had their first séance at Daisley's house. Jim was believed by the two to be heard speaking in Daisley's voice. "Hello, Dad," he said, according to them.

Pike eventually was to have five séances with Daisley in the twelve-month period from August 1966 to August 1967. The results were mixed, even by the standards of a spiritualist believer, and, although Pike remained a true adherent, he extracted from his American friends who knew of his attending séances their firm promises not to make this practice known to the public. Daisley himself, apparently unembarrassed by his producing more psychic "misses" than "hits" in divining details of the life of Jim, appears to have been a medium who would not have been out of place among the dubious expatriates from England described by Evelyn Waugh in his novel of Southern California, *The Loved One*. Yet this strange man and self-proclaimed psychic medium served as the partial intermediary in Pike's meeting an even stranger individual, the science-fiction writer Philip K. Dick. Posthumously to become vastly popular, Dick in 1966 was a Bay Area cult figure, a darkly pessimistic and paranoiac believer in alternate universes, an enthusiastic consumer of illegal drugs, and, surprisingly, an Episcopalian. He had married Bergrud's stepdaughter in July, and Pike had attended the ceremony and blessed the union. The couple occasionally traveled from their San Rafael home to visit Pike and Bergrud in Santa Barbara. According to the recollections of those also present, Dick joined with Pike and Bergrud's séances with Daisley, and the science-fiction writer's supportive belief in contacting Jim led to a close friendship with the bishop. The two began having long "rap" sessions together, which on Dick's part were fueled partially by his use of amphetamines and his proselytizing beliefs that they all were under government surveillance and also liable to alien "divine invasions." Pike, for his part, took his friends as he found them in the mid-1960s. He remembered the couple in his foreword when writing *The Other Side*, thanking "especially my good friends, Mr. and Mrs. Phil Dick," for contributing to the experiences described in the book.

In early September, Pike returned to Grace Cathedral to deliver his last sermon as diocesan bishop. His career there ended with an unusual goodwill on both sides. Casper Weinberger organized a farewell dinner for him at the Fairmont Hotel, and tactfully presented Pike with a check of donations from those present, supposedly to help with his scholarly activities; in fact, it was a personal gift for the cash-strapped bishop. The congregation for Pike's subsequent farewell sermon overflowed the pews and was seated as well in the choir stalls, at the bishop's request. Commenting that his past crowds of worshipers "was never like this on Christmas or Easter," he playfully noted that "I should have resigned once a month." Avoiding speaking of his current interest in spiritualism or John Allegro's scholarship, he satisfied himself with a recount of his "quest" for a twentieth-century belief, and wittily predicted that, given the success of the New Theology, he would be remembered as "the conservative bishop you had here once."

Pike then returned to his new home in Santa Barbara, and to what passed for domestic peace. His mother had moved out of his apartment, in apparent protest of Bergrud's proximity and frequent visits. Never particularly friendly to any of the women with whom her son became involved, Pearl Chambers was particularly hostile to Bergrud. She remained nearby, however, at a separate apartment building. After her departure, Bergrud promptly moved many of her clothes and personal effects into Pike's apartment. He seems to have silently acquiesced to her decision, but he also continued to pay rent for her former apartment, which, for the present, he used as an office for part-time secretaries who fulfilled work for Bergrud.

He was away from the shared Santa Barbara apartment for most of September and October fulfilling speaking engagements at colleges in Florida and at Duke University in North Carolina. Speaking to what again was described in the press as an "overflow crowd" at the Duke School of Law, Pike called for the revision of all the states' laws regarding both homosexual relations between adults and clinical abortions for women of legal age. Both acts, he told his audience, were "nobody's business but the individuals involved." The controversies over this speech would outlive Pike, but what was consequential for the time was that in having preached and held a chapel service at a college in the Episcopal diocese of South Florida without notifying the diocesan bishop, Pike had offended—knowingly or not—his old bête noire, Henry Louttit.

Stories vary. Some Episcopalians privy to the quarrel maintain that, after this perceived insult, Louttit began a late-night habit of telephoning other bishops, often with a bottle of the premium scotch he was known to enjoy within easy reach, declaring that the prelates "make an honest man" out of Pike, through forcing him to choose either a heresy trial or leaving the church. Others maintain that Louttit happened to meet Presiding Bishop John Hines while both were vacationing at the Grove Park Inn, a resort for the moneyed outside Asheville, North Carolina, and hectored Hines "to do something about Pike." In any case, the tiresome ecclesiastical quarrel over whether to try Pike for heresy was once more resumed at Louttit's insistence in late October 1966, at that year's meeting of the House of Bishops. This time, the dispute was expressed with all the bitterness and unforgiving repetitions of an unhappy marriage.

Louttit solicited the support of twenty-eight other bishops in urging that a bill of particulars for heresy be approved against Pike; the grounds were, again, Pike's disbelief in the Incarnation, the Virgin Birth, and the Trinity. Having learned of Louttit's intent, Pike arrived at the convocation at Wheeling, West Virginia, on October 22, in the company of the "Association of Episcopal Clergy, Inc.," a group of priests and bishops mainly from California who had been organized to protect his interests. This group in turn submitted a petition to the House of Bishops for a formal investigation "into the activities of Bishop Louttit and a priest, the Rev. Frank Brunton of Phoenix, Arizona, who was formerly connected with the South Florida diocese." Louttit was a fighting bishop. "Let them investigate and be damned," he declared when he learned of the petition.

However, a majority of the bishops at Wheeling "were weary" of this perennial conflict, as they were described by the *New York Times*, and perhaps the prelates also were weary of Pike personally. Under the direction of Hines, the proposed bill of particulars was sent to an ad hoc committee, the Special Committee of Advice, as had been done in the past, in order to allow Pike to make his defense in private before the committee members and to mediate a public compromise to be announced on the floor of the House. This time, however, Pike was refused the opportunity to argue before the committee, and Louttit was assigned as a committee member. So was Angus Dun, the now elderly bishop who had ordained Pike with such high hopes both as a deacon and a priest in the 1940s. The report of what was called the Dun Committee was harsh. Once again, as with past committees, this committee declined to accept the bill as actionable; but, in a change from the past, the report did not even faintly praise Pike. "His writing and speaking on profound realities with which Christian faith and worship are concerned are, too often, marred by caricatures of treasured symbols," the six-member committee unanimously wrote, "and, at the worse, by cheap vulgarizations of great expressions of faith." The report continued, "This is a hard thing to say," revealing perhaps the rue expressed to them by Angus Dun, but, after hoping that Pike's reaffirmation of creeds the previous year "would strengthen" his authority as a bishop, the committee found "this hope was in vain." In short, there was the strong implication that Pike had lied.

In a tumultuous late-night session on October 25, the House of Bishops approved this censorious report. All attempts to ameliorate its wording for Pike's benefit were voted down. The final count was 103 to 36. Some voted their approval with zeal, such as the bishops of the dioceses of Los Angeles and North California; others, such as Horace Donegan, the New York bishop who had overseen Pike's deanship at St. John the Divine, voted in the affirmative with visible distress. Louttit apparently had been persuaded in committee that this censure was sufficiently punitive so as to make unnecessary his call for a heresy trial; the convention apparently hoped that Pike would accept the rebuke as at least more palatable than a trial. If so, they had misjudged their man. After the report was approved, shortly before midnight, Pike angrily stepped to the microphone at the meeting hall and announced to the surprised bishops that he was invoking Section 56:4 of the Episcopal Church's canons. That section guaranteed to a bishop, upon the support of two others, the right to call for a full and open investigation should there be "rumors, reports, or allegations" affecting his fitness to serve. Two other bishops favorable to Pike promptly seconded his call. "I may be leading myself into formal heresy charges," he declared, "but I am in an ambiguous position now, and I want it settled." His intent apparently was to determine on record the limits of theological inquiry within his church, even if such a determination was to be made by means of his trial for heresy.

Pike's action therefore meant that an investigation must proceed; and, in order to have time to assign bishops to an ecclesiastical court should a trial follow, the affair would carry over to the Church's next triennial convention, scheduled for September of the following year. However weary his fellow bishops might be of their brother in Christ, they were not shut of him yet. His action also negated the final sentence of the final paragraph of the Dun report, which had urged that no more time or energy be spent on presentments or investigations of Pike: "The

Church has more important things to get on with." Perhaps it was this last sentence that most angered Pike.

The malign year of 1966 ended with no further nightmarish suffering for Pike or any of his intimates, and the new year began without any extraordinary events, other than continued séances with Daisley and, purportedly, the spirit of Jim. After what Hines described as a "cooling off" period following Pike's demand for a heresy investigation, he agreed in January not to contest the presiding bishop's motion to appoint a committee to advise the church on the meanings and usages of heresy trials. As a result of the controversy of the October censure, Pike had been featured in a cover story in the November 11 issue of *Time*. The article was noticeably favorable to him, and the brief discussion of the bishop's personal life was as circumspect as he possibly could have wished. After a short mention of his control of his alcoholism, printed above a photograph of a smiling Esther and James Pike, the anonymous writer noted, "He also had to overcome some marriage problems; now, while he lives and works in Santa Barbara, his wife maintains the family house in San Francisco. Jim comes up on weekends to teach a class at the University of California at Berkeley and to see the children." The same month as the article appeared, Pike and Diane Kennedy had become physical lovers. She remained in the San Francisco area, and he saw her intermittently.

Pike occupied himself during the first five months of 1967 in attempting to balance his increasingly inadequate income against his domestic expenses. His former diocesan salary of $17,000 yearly was almost matched by his salary at the Center for the Study of Democratic Institutions, but he no longer had the benefits of discounted housing at the bishop's residence, a travel fund, or a discretionary fund available to him. Additionally, he was, in effect, supporting three households—his own with Bergrud in Santa Barbara; the apartment he also maintained in her name and used as an office; and Esther Pike's household, including their two children, in San Francisco. The lawyer representing Pike in his divorce suit and other personal matters warned him of "the serious financial problems which you face," and advised him to transfer as much cash and other assets as possible to the New Focus Literary and Lecture Agency, a private corporation established by Pike to provide nominal employment to Bergrud as an editor, literary agent, and travel manager. "For the asset account designated as 'furniture and fixtures,' New Focus should buy as much as possible. If a list can be roughed indicating $10,000 worth, I will be very pleased," the lawyer advised him. "Any expenses which can be considered to be business expenses should be so treated; for example, the purchase of liquor or of groceries may often be for business entertainment, whereas medical expenses are clearly personal." These practices, although sharp, were legal; but Esther Pike and her attorney became angered when they learned that Pike had also reduced the financial burden upon himself by having New Focus pay Bergrud an extraordinary 25 percent commission for sales of his manuscripts to Harper & Row. (Ten to 15 percent was the usual business norm, with this amount deducted before issuing payment to the author.) This generous commission for his domestic partner of course reduced the money available to Esther Pike's 50 percent share in the sale of the bishop's manuscripts. It was also perceived by her to be a personal insult. The resultant maneuvering between their attorneys over the commission delayed, and exacerbated, the final resolution of their divorce.

In April, Pike appeared before the committee of eleven bishops, priests, and laymen who were considering his church's policies regarding heresy investigations and trials. As if in deliberate confirmation of what his critics so frequently had said of him, he seemed to be flirting for a heresy trial by urging its members not to consider such an event anachronistic or to automatically dismiss its possible use to the general assembly in September. Either a flame of conviction, or of self-destruction, was brightly burning in his mind.

In May, Pike had intended to travel singly to Switzerland for the Pacem in Terris II conference, an international peace gathering of prominent individuals invited by the center to discuss ways of improving political and religious relations between Western and non-Western countries. The conference was prestigious—Pope Paul VI sent his blessings—and its location at Geneva in the springtime was appealing. Bergrud also wanted to go. A replay of the Cambridge sabbatical threatened, with Pike's relenting and allowing Bergrud to travel with him; but, as in England, unhappiness followed. According to later accounts by his friends, her drug addictions left Bergrud near comatose on several occasions during their trip, and she once almost set her hotel room on fire, apparently unintentionally. The couple returned to Santa Barbara by the second week in June with Bergrud more depressed than ever.

She seems to have been suspicious of the bishop's infidelities (actually, both to her and to his wife, as his divorce was not yet final), but apparently she did not know of Diane Kennedy, at least by name. On June 14, Bergrud and Pike had a bitter quarrel after midnight, when he returned to their shared apartment later than expected with an excuse that did not satisfy her. According to Pike's version of the subsequent events, she ended their argument by threatening to kill herself. As a precaution, Pike then took from her the large bottle of sleeping pills she habitually used and went to bed alone in one of the apartment's two bedrooms. He was awakened about 3:00 a.m. when Bergrud entered the room, turned on the light, and resumed their quarrel. Angry, he handed her the bottle of sedatives and said, "Take your pills and go." She did, and he returned to sleep. She came back into the bedroom about 5:00 a.m., barely conscious, and told the startled bishop that she had taken at least fifty-five of the pills.

Pike's initial three reactions were panic for his own social and religious positions, apparent callousness toward a dying woman, and, possibly, committing the serious crime of misprision in deliberately concealing the circumstances of a death from a police officer. He later insisted privately that Bergrud had said to him, before falling unconscious, that he should "get me back to my apartment before anything happens. And use your head when the police come." He apparently took this statement as a caution not to be involved with the police. Whether she said so or not, Pike dragged the now-comatose Bergrud from their shared apartment, number 307, down the hall of the building, to the apartment that was nominally her residence. There, according to his later account, he telephoned her physician, who in turn promptly called for an ambulance and a police car to rush to the Coast Village Road address. Apparently not taking time to try to resuscitate Bergrud himself, Pike frantically used the moments before the arrival of the police and the ambulance to move some of her personal belongings to the office apartment; and, in what must have been a grotesque struggle, ran with bedsheets from his apartment and made the bed at the second apartment, wrapping Bergrud, with her loosely falling arms, head, and legs, into the sheets, as if she had overdosed in her bed. He placed the almost empty bottle of pills, which he had found in their shared apartment, on the bedside table next to her. Again, by the bishop's private, later account, he also discovered two suicide notes in their shared apartment, one addressed to him and the other to her three stepchildren from her prior marriage, toward whom she was very affectionate. The note to the stepchildren ended with some lines about him, the specifics of which Pike never provided. He tore off the bottom half of this note containing these sentences, apparently to destroy it later, and placed the top half by the pill bottle. The note addressed to him was placed innocuously among other papers on the bishop's desk in his apartment. He may have had time to give it at least a hurried read; it would be more than a year before he could bear to show or discuss its contents with others.

Bergrud had stopped breathing by the time the ambulance arrived, and she did not respond to the administration of oxygen. She was pronounced dead shortly after the arrival of the ambulance carrying her body to the Cottage Hospital in Santa Barbara. "Secretary of Pike Dies—Maren Bergrud" was the headline in the June 15 edition of the *San Francisco Chronicle.* Even in death, she received second billing to the bishop. (In a further grotesquerie, it was Pike who was reported to have died early in the morning of June 15 in an announcement made to a convocation of Methodist ministers gathered for their annual convention at Stockton, California. A convention attendee apparently misunderstood a radio news report. Pike's successor as the Episcopal bishop of California, C. Kilmer Myers, was onstage waiting to address the Methodists when the announcement was made, followed by official expressions of grief.) Meanwhile, the police had become suspicious. Pike had stated to them that Bergrud had telephoned him from her apartment shortly before lapsing into unconsciousness. But both the sergeant and the detective investigating her death observed that the apartment where she was found was furnished more like an office than a residence. There were few undergarments or other personal clothing in the furniture's drawers and shelves, and Bergrud's purse was also missing. (It was later found by the police in Pike's apartment, where he told a police officer he had taken it after receiving her call in order to find the telephone number of her physician.) There was also the question of what the police assumed was a missing portion torn from the suicide note found beside her body. "Mystery on Pike Aide's Suicide Note" was the headline in the next day's *Chronicle*, and the story began with an almost California *noir* style: "Bishop James A. Pike told authorities that he had no idea what might have happened to the lower half of a suicide note scrawled by Maren Bergrud, 48."

But with the county coroner's office returning an official judgment of suicide, the police were willing to accept Pike's speculation about the torn note, that "she had apparently changed her mind and decided that the last part was something she did not want others to see." Pike at least made certain that no one saw it. Unmentioned by him to the police was the existence of the *second* suicide note that had been addressed to him. The other matters about the discrepancies in his account of the two apartments and his actions were dropped. On June 16, he conducted Bergrud's funeral service before a gathering of about twenty people. Her body was then returned to San Rafael for burial. On June 24, a week and a day after the suicide, police questionings, and the funeral in Santa Barbara, the bishop remarkably kept his composure at the wedding of his elder daughter, Catherine. The previous days may have been a personal harrowing of hell, but, either by self-control or cold-bloodedness, he remained good company during the small ceremony at Grace Cathedral attended by his family. The *Chronicle* tactfully noted in its coverage of the wedding that the reception was to be held "at the house the Pikes took here when he resigned as Episcopal bishop to California."

His divorce was declared final in August. That same month, Diane Kennedy moved into the bishop's apartment in Santa Barbara. He was fifty-four; she was twenty-nine. Kennedy assumed the management of the New Focus Agency with a greater competence than her predecessor, and visitors began to remark how "cheerful" their apartment had become. She accompanied Pike to his church's triennial convention the week of September 17 in Seattle, where he wanted to settle his self-described "ambiguous situation" by either being investigated for heresy or not.

The Episcopal Church did not want to oblige him, except for some die-hard Anglo-Catholics supporting Louttit. Strangely, they and Pike were now in the same political bed, the Anglo-Catholics wanting to reaffirm authority over heresy, and Pike wanting a heresy investigation to clear his "ambiguous" situation and force a declaration of what was and was not acceptable theological deviance in his church. The committee assembled by John Hines to advise the church on heresy policies—the Committee on Theological Freedom and Social Responsibilities—had disappointed Pike by reporting officially to Hines before the convention that heresy trials, in their collective opinion, were "anachronistic." A further discouragement from taking any further action against Pike came from on high, when the archbishop of Canterbury, the most Reverend and Right Honorable Arthur Ramsey, made a stop while traveling in a donated Learjet at the San Francisco airport on his way to address the convention in Seattle. Ramsey's primary purpose in speaking at the convention was to urge the American church to further support his call for the U.S. government to seek a negotiated settlement with the government of North Vietnam in the ongoing war; however, he found time to deliver himself of a few opinions about Pike in an impromptu news conference. Resembling in his physical appearance and his blunt manner of speaking the archetypal John Bull of England, Ramsey discouraged further attempts to prosecute the California bishop for heresy as "it advertises the man and his work and gives it an importance that it doesn't deserve." Asked by reporters whether he had read any of Pike's books, the archbishop responded that he had read "most" of them, and had found them to be "superficial stuff."

Pike was at his most dramatic in Seattle. Seeing a group who were protesting his continued status as a bishop outside the convention hall by unfurling a banner that equated his theological opinions with the perniciousness of LSD, he exclaimed, "I'll overcome them with flower power!" He then uprooted some bachelor's buttons growing in a nearby window box and gave them to the protestors in exchange for their gift of a Bible. Later, he made it a point of irony to present Archbishop Ramsey, with elaborate courtesy, a copy of his latest book. Despite these antics, Pike's last call for a heresy trial ended anticlimactically. On September 25, 1967, the House of Bishops "affirmed," but not officially "accepted," the report of the Committee on Theological Freedom and Social Responsibilities. Pike, angrily noting that the committee had not addressed his censure, then demanded that "the proceedings be initiated forthwith" to try him for heresy.

He was mollified, however, after other delegates pointed out to him—and after he held conversations while he drank coffee with Stringfellow, Towne, and Kennedy in a bar with a view of the Seattle Space Needle—that the committee had also called for a revision of national canon law in order to investigate heresy. Rather than a heresy presentment being initiated by a bill signed by three bishops, the committee proposed to raise the minimum numbers of required prelatic assents to ten. Pike took their proposal as an implied criticism of his censure since the legal barrier would now be much higher for official disciplinary action. (Thankfully, no one pointed out that Louttit in 1966 had obtained many more than the proposed number of ten bishops to support his charges against Pike.) Both houses at the convention approved this canon change. Claiming he had been "vindicated," Pike agreed to withdraw his demand for a trial.

Thus the six-year campaign to prosecute Pike for heresy ended with a statutory whimper, not a judicial bang. Ironically, this was the resolution desired by Pike's critics, made weary by his maneuvering. It was a remarkable reversal of the original roles begun in 1961 when he had opposed the attempts of the Georgia clericus to bring him to trial. Also ironically, and sadly, his church lost in all this maneuvering the opportunity for thoughtful debate over the New Theology, which had occasioned the controversy in the first place. The arguments in conventions had become centered upon Pike's personality—the censure concentrated totally upon his manner of writing and his personal truthfulness—rather than the theological ideas he advocated. In Pike's terms, the Church had spent too much time discussing the inadequacies of the vessel and not enough discussing the possible treasure.

In fairness, it must be observed that the actions of the Seattle convention also were obscured because of a bizarre act by Pike himself. On September 17, the same Sunday as the triennial convention opened its first session, a previously taped program was broadcast on Canadian television. It recorded a séance held before a studio audience between Pike and a professional American medium, Arthur Ford. Pike had agreed to this public "experiment" after it had been suggested to him by Allen Spraggett, the religion editor of the *Toronto Star*, with whom he had discussed spiritualism at the Pacem in Terris conference. Spraggett also regularly hosted the television program for which the séance was filmed. The transcript of this forty-minute séance contains little that is extraordinary by spiritualist standards. Ford was an elderly and traditional medium, and, after blindfolding himself with a large black cloth and beginning what he called his "yoga breathing," he contacted spirits through the intermediary of a control, "Fletcher." This latter was said to be the spirit of a soldier known to Ford in his Florida childhood and subsequently killed in the First World War. At the bidding of Fletcher, there was heard supposedly the spirit of Jim talking in a friendly manner with his father. Another deceased, one of the ubiquitous Kinsolvings of that Episcopal family, also was called up by Fletcher.

News of the program, although not yet broadcast in the United States, let the spiritualist cat out of the bag for Pike. His motives and timing in taping this show are difficult to understand, at a time when he supposedly was concentrating upon winning his quarrel with his church's prelates. Perhaps he desired to publicize spiritualism while he was still a bishop; if so, he certainly succeeded. Marshall McLuhan, the celebrated scholar of pop culture and communication, was widely quoted in both Canadian and U.S. newspapers as joking that the notoriety of Pike's televised séance had vindicated McLuhan's epigram that "the medium is the message." Reporters in both nations, following up rumors of previous séances, published lengthy articles quoting both Daisley and Twigg as confirming the bishop's participation, and Pike himself gave a relevant interview to the *New York Times* the week following the adjournment of the Seattle convention. He described for the first time publicly the psychic phenomena he believed he had witnessed the previous year at the Cambridge flat, and on September 28 the usually staid *Times* ran an uncharacteristic headline over the story: "Bishop Pike Tells of Eerie Events." That same evening, an excerpt from the taped séance was shown nationally on Walter Cronkite's *CBS Evening News*. In October, a New York television station, WNEW, broadcast a longer excerpt.

Revelations of these séances cost Pike a previously extended invitation to preach at St. Thomas' Episcopal Church in New York. After reading descriptions of the séances, Rev. Frederick Morris, an advocate of the New Theology, wrote to Pike withdrawing his invitation. Pike's appearance, the rector wrote, "would not be in the best interest of the cause we both believe in." By this time, the bishop was back on the West

Coast, and he had reduced himself there to promoting his belief in spiritualism on such novelty venues as *The Joe Pyne Show*. Pyne, an early personification of the "shock jocks" of later television and radio broadcasting, gained attention by such boorish behavior as deliberately blowing cigarette smoke into his guests' faces, or urging the studio audience to join with him in noisily heckling them off the stage. Pike was treated no differently when he appeared on this program in October.

Describing himself as surprised by the public criticism of his séances, he spent the winter of 1967–68 in the continued domestic company of Kennedy while he researched at the Center the subject he now considered to be his foremost interest: the origins of Christianity and the possible anticipation of this religion in the texts of the Dead Sea Scrolls. Christmas of 1967 arrived and brought him the memory, as it did for the remainder of his life, of how he and his son Jim had climbed Masada in late December two years earlier. The approaching anniversary of Jim's death was ameliorated by messages he believed his son frequently sent absolving him of any guilt or responsibility for his death. At a séance held in December at the Philadelphia apartment of Ford, the medium's psychic control, Fletcher, had allowed Pike to have the following exchange with his son: "I just wanted to be close with you," the bishop said, explaining why he had invited Jim to share his time at Cambridge. "I know that," his son responded in the control's voice. "I never knew it until six months before I came here, and I am sorry that my actions have caused the thing that happened since then that made you unhappy." Diane Kennedy, who was present at this séance, tried with less success to engage in talk with Maren Bergrud through Fletcher.

Pike turned fifty-five on February 14, 1968. His daughter Constance, who was seventeen, visited with him and Kennedy throughout that week. On his birthday, while he was at his office at the center late in the afternoon, Connie telephoned and asked him to return to his apartment and talk with her immediately. Instead, he telephoned Kennedy, who was at the office apartment formerly used by Bergrud, and asked her to check on his daughter.

In a subsequent statement to police, Pike told how, before lapsing into unconsciousness, Connie had informed Kennedy that she had experienced "a nightmare" and had taken a large number of sleeping pills. She then became comatose. Kennedy immediately called Pike, who frantically telephoned for an ambulance and rushed to his apartment. He arrived when the ambulance did, and watched as his unconscious daughter was carried out of his apartment, just as he once had carried Bergrud, and placed into an ambulance. Her survival was precarious for a night. The following day, February 15, she was reported by St. Francis Hospital in Santa Barbara to have "responded satisfactorily" to treatment for an overdose of sedatives. By this time, Esther Pike had arrived from San Francisco to bring her daughter back home.

The near death of his daughter was the final incident for a while in the succession of events of self-destruction and cruelty experienced by Pike and inflicted by him during the preceding years. The events of his life from 1966 to 1968—the suicide of a son and near suicide of a daughter, sexual infidelities, the suicide of a former lover and the mistreatment of her body, personal animosities between bishops expressed in ecclesiastical disputes, bitter quarrels over diminishing money, and questionable attempts to raise the spirits of the dead—all confirm what the Roman emperor Julian the Apostate in the fourth century C.E. is said to have observed of a convocation of bishops and their followers: no wild beasts are such enemies to mankind as these Christians are in their acts toward one another.

VIII

A God-Shaped Blank: Pike as Spiritualist, Heretic, and Iconoclast

And I don't belong anywhere, do I?

—Alleged voice of Bishop James Pike, deceased,
spoken by Ena Twigg at a séance, September 4, 1969

Pike reinvented himself so rapidly from 1966 to 1968 with new ideas and beliefs that it might be stabilizing to look steadily at his last three enthusiasms in those years. Among those enthusiasms, the most perplexing to observers was his practice of spiritualism and its reconciliation with his intellectual reputation and his church's traditions. The difficulties raised in attempting to present equitably Pike's belief in spiritualism were well expressed in 1936 by Archbishop William Temple. "The trouble with the whole question," Temple wrote privately, "is that people either despise the subject and therefore cannot attend to the alleged evidence, or else become enthusiastic and lose their critical balance." Pike of course was among the enthusiasts, and he always approached his new enthusiasms with the additional naïveté of assum-

ing that he was among the first discoverers. What he called the "psi factor" of paranormal phenomena, including spiritualism, he described as
"new areas of empirical investigation" in his 1967 book, *If This Be
Heresy.*

Yet, as the observation by Archbishop Temple evinces, the practice
and investigation of spiritualism were noticeably present among some
Church of England communicants at least three decades before Pike
participated in a séance on television. Temple's remark had prefaced his
work on an ecclesiastical committee established in 1937 "to discuss the
relationship, if any, between spiritualism and the traditional teachings of
the Anglican Church." The committee's majority report, which was not
made public until 1979, recommended that "representatives of the
church should keep in touch with groups of intelligent persons who
believe in spiritualism." There was, therefore, a tacit—although not
officially announced, and at best tepidly encouraged—tolerance of
those communicants who also considered spiritualism as confirmation
of their Christian faith. After all, Pike had been introduced to his first
medium, Ena Twigg, by a Church of England canon of good standing.
So it was that, long before Pike briefly succeeded in repopularizing
séances in American culture in 1967, twentieth-century spiritualism had
established itself within the Anglican Church as a type of minor gnosticism. It was not so widespread as to be considered a competing faith,
but, at the same time, it possessed an apparatus of mediums and prose-
lytizers within his Church ready to welcome Pike when he felt the need
for explanations of the events he had witnessed in his Cambridge flat.

The initial cause of this remarkable popularity of spiritualism
among Anglicans in the early twentieth century was, like Pike's own
later interest, the result of a grieving father convinced of his dead son's
communications. Remarkably, one particular medium was known to
both this father, Sir Oliver Lodge, and Pike. A noted physicist and
member of the Society for Psychical Research, Lodge had been notified
in September 1915 of the death of his son, Raymond, on the western
front only a few months after he volunteered for military service in the
First World War. There followed for Lodge and his wife in the months
afterward the usual phenomena of displaced objects, childish pranks,
and visual puns convincing them that the spirit of Raymond Lodge was
attempting to communicate with his parents. Lodge in 1916 published

his account of these events, together with selected letters received from his son in the months preceding his death by shell-burst, as *Raymond, or Life and Death*. The book proved immensely popular for the duration of the war. *Raymond* went through twelve editions between 1916 and 1919, and tens of thousands of grieving families, including many devout Church of England members, found solace in its message that the English war dead were happy and eager to talk with their surviving relatives. The popularity of *Raymond* prompted a discussion of spiritualism at the first Lambeth Conference of Anglican bishops after the war, and led eventually to the appointment of Archbishop Temple's committee on spiritualism in 1937. Lodge himself was visited throughout the 1920s by many spiritualist admirers from both sides of the Atlantic. Among them was a young Arthur Ford, who forty years later would demonstrate his own mediumistic skills with Pike on television, speaking through his psychic control, "Fletcher."

Ford successfully practiced psychic readings for years based on his associations with Lodge and, later, with Harry Houdini, but by the time he came to conduct his first séance with Pike, there was at least one duplicity practiced on his part. This was revealed in 1973 by two biographers of Ford: he had had an extensive file of press clippings and notes about Pike compiled before the first séance with the bishop, and apparently used by Ford to supply "Fletcher" with the tellingly dramatic details provided by this control during the televised séance. When this disclosure was reported in the *New York Times*, both Pike and Ford themselves were dead; but during the bishop's lifetime numerous friends of his, including Stringfellow and Towne, were chary of such figures as George Daisley or Ford and had urged the bishop to be less credulous in dealing with them.

Not all of those who gave Pike this advice fell automatically within the group Temple had characterized as despising spiritualism whatever its evidences. Diane Kennedy, for example, was intellectually and emotionally sympathetic toward a belief in paranormal phenomena during the years she was Pike's companion and wife; but she seems to have asked the mediums empirically "tougher" questions during séances than did Pike. The unspoken disappointment among Pike's friends and later biographers was not that he had become fascinated with spiritualism, but that he applied none of his considerable forensic and rationalist strengths to his new interest, as did, say, more reputable twentieth-century investigators of the paranormal such as William James, Gardner Murphy, or Antony Flew. Why did Pike, after his grief for his son was assuaged by his first séances, remain such an easy mark for these "Sludge, the Medium" type of frauds?

Pike so easily lost his "critical balance" over spiritualism, in Temple's description, not because he needed its continual reassurances that his son's personality had been able to exist after death; indeed, after mid-1968, his attendance at séances seems to have fallen off, and his recorded conversations with Jim are much less frequent. Having participated in at least four séances in 1967, Pike apparently attended only one in 1968, when he returned for a single sitting with Ena Twigg on his way back from Israel that summer. Rather, he uncritically welcomed spiritualism and other paranormal phenomena of any kind—or authenticity—because they were supportive evidence for his other great interest, the belief that the late-twentieth-century Church was entering into a time of great spiritual change, the *kairos* described by Tillich.

This conviction, rather than the critical examination of spiritualism, occupied most of his time and energies from 1968 onward at the Center for the Study of Democratic Institutions and on research trips to Israel. The possibility of the Dead Sea Scrolls being a Gnostic precursor of early Christianity, the acceleration of reports of paranormal experiences, and the increased usage of psychedelic drugs all were described by Pike without qualification as "discernible signs of religious quest" unique to the twentieth century and proof that he was living in a new Axial Age or awakening of world religions. It was in arguing this point to the public that he somehow lost his balance and became an easy mark for charlatans and cultists. The uncritically compiled instances of spiritual questing that he enthusiastically described in *If This Be Heresy* are practically an inventory of all the subjective and unprovable exuberances of the 1960s: astral projection, ESP, Timothy Leary's League for Spiritual Discovery (Pike, with touching naïveté, pointed out to his readers that Leary's organization could be "abbreviated LSD!"), reincarnation, and glossolalia, which he now described with great sympathy. Metaphorically and spiritually, the bishop was so eager to see the New Jerusalem that he was willing to run to the top of any prominence, no matter how slight.

His uncritical acceptance of spiritualism also gave Pike the opportunity to master a new jargon and to use it forensically, two activities in which he delighted. To the objections raised, for example, that the phenomena at Cambridge of psychokinesis—burned hair bangs, moved books—occurred only when Maren Bergrud was present and ceased completely after her suicide, it could be answered by Pike that she had been a *percipient*, the spiritualist term for one who is not the actor of psychic events but who, perhaps unconsciously, allows others to release their psychic energy. Or the similarity of open safety pins found at the Cambridge flat to the arms of a clock stopping at the time Jim died could be called *veridical*, a term first popularized by William James to describe psychic events with some empirical evidence and used by Pike in *The Other Side*.

That book, published in late 1968, was his fullest accounting of the events before and after the suicide of Jim and the subsequent contacts with his deceased son at séances. The manuscript was completed with the assistance of Diane Kennedy, and there was no mention of Maren Bergrud in the acknowledgments. The reviews were mixed. "Perhaps ESP and postmortem communication are possible, but this account is too highly colored by Pike's own absorption with himself and his own responses to trust," *Newsweek* concluded in its review. Troubling also to some readers was Pike's offering of these psychic "facts" in his book in support of Christianity by the application of an axiom he now called "facts + faith." This apologetic axiom was, according to one reviewer, simply "a bit of popular philosophy masquerading as truth."

Pike's initial interest in spiritualism eventually was displaced by another enthusiasm, a characteristic frequently seen within the events of his lifetime. By 1969 he was absorbed completely in his study of the Dead Sea Scrolls and the possible connections of these Jewish Essene documents to the origins of Christianity, an enthusiasm that was fatal to Pike. But his death was not necessarily the end of his involvement with spiritualism, at least in regard to evocations of his name and voice. Ena Twigg supposedly contacted the spirit of the deceased Pike even while searches for him were still under way in Israel and his wife assumed he was still alive. In defense of Twigg, the bishop likely *was* dead at the time she claimed to have spoken to his spirit. Also, for several years after the death, his friend Philip K. Dick believed sincerely that the spirit of the deceased bishop was attempting to take over Dick's personality and was giving him peremptory advice. One advisory message from Pike's spirit recorded by Dick was the instruction that the writer drink more wine and less beer, and spend his publishing advances more wisely.

Pike's advocacy of spiritualism during his lifetime at least bound him closer in 1968 to the new family he was assembling around him. His domestic companion and future wife, Diane Kennedy, and her brother, Scott Kennedy, were both sympathizers with his belief, and both accompanied him to his séance with Twigg in midsummer of that year. However, his spiritualism alienated him from his former family. He had sent a copy of *The Other Side* to Esther Pike without any prior notice and with "no sensitive or empathetic letter enclosed," in the diplomatic words of one family member. She found it painful to open this book and read transcripts of supposed conversations with her dead son. There was also the unpleasant knowledge that this book about her son had been coauthored by the bishop's present consort. Connie Pike, who celebrated her twentieth birthday within months of the book's publication, wrote a letter composed with a remarkable maturity in early 1969 to her father reproaching him for his actions. She reminded him that "Jim was not your only son," in a pointed suggestion that the bishop might spend more time with his surviving son, Christopher, and that, although she did "believe you had to write the book, some consideration for her [Esther] should have been taken." Connie closed her letter by adding the news that a casual former girlfriend of her deceased brother "has been having visits from Jim, evidently." She then observed, with the irony for which her father sometimes could be noted in debating his opponents: "He really shouldn't be visiting after three years. It's getting a bit absurd."

Pike's two-year enthusiasm for practicing spiritualism, although regrettable to some who knew him well, was not a heretical action within his church. However, a separate issue is whether his expressed skepticism toward beliefs such as the Trinity could be considered heretical by the catholic creeds of the Anglican Communion. The mundane answer is no. The Episcopal Church on four separate occasions declined to investigate his public statements on the Trinity or the Virgin Birth on grounds of heresy because of a lack of political support for such action.

On at least one of these occasions, the meeting of the House of Bishops at Wheeling, West Virginia, in 1966, Pike had been just as disappointed as his opponents that he was not going to trial. He appeared at that time to be confident that he could defend himself against a heresy presentment (or indictment), and he anticipated that such an action would be taken against him. In assuming the latter, his judgment of the theological situation was correct. From a transmundane point of view, Pike was indictable as hell.

He unquestionably had declared himself an advocate of theological Unitarianism in his sermons and books, such as *A Time for Christian Candor* and *What Is This Treasure?*, in which he frequently asserted that belief in the Trinity "is not essential to the Christian faith." Louttit's bill of presentment in 1966 had dedicated three-quarters of its length to cataloguing Pike's alleged offenses against belief in the Trinity of the Father, the Son, and the Holy Spirit. To a secular reader, or to a member of a very modernist communion, all this concern over Pike's not accepting the Nicene Creed of the fourth century C.E. may seem puzzling. But the denial of the reality of what Pike liked to call a "committee God" was correctly seen with alarm by Louttit and others as leading to a denial of Christ's co-divinity with God, and, ultimately, to the Arian heresy of the assertion of Jesus Christ as a highly enlightened but merely mortal individual. Such was where Pike's theological thinking seemed to be headed, with his calls from the pulpit for a new redefinition of Christ as "the man for others." His expressed views on the Trinity were, therefore, his most heretical act, but it must also be remembered, constituted his only true heresy throughout the 1960s.

In his other writings, Pike was also not the *enfant sauvage* of unfettered morality and free love as he is sometimes remembered. He did publicly enter the discussion of situational ethics with two books, *Teenagers and Sex* and *You and the New Morality*, published in 1965 and 1967 respectively. He forthrightly wrote in both that the public perception of the "new morality" he was defending was popularly considered simply another term "for a 'free' sexual ethic which is becoming increasingly articulate." However, he buttressed his arguments for adopting situational ethics by demonstrating that in many cases the "new morality" brought its practitioners to the same conclusions as reached by believers of natural law and authoritarian codes of behavior.

In his private life Pike certainly had been practicing a moral relativism for decades, but at least in print throughout the 1960s he seemed unable to totally disassociate himself from the concept of a natural law applicable to all situations. A contemporary Anglican theologian, Joseph Fletcher of the Episcopal Theological School in Cambridge, Massachusetts, accurately got Pike's number in his review of *You and the New Morality*:

> Although he seems to assume that some norms are intrinsically and inherently right (a questionable notion, given his working relativism), he nevertheless holds that normative principles about monogamy, non-divorce, extra-marital sexuality, usury, and so forth are morally suspendable when to suspend them is the lesser evil or the greater good.

In short, Pike kept a foot in both camps. Although his fellow Anglican ethicist spoke of his "working relativism," and although, of the four situations listed by Fletcher as likely to be "morally suspendable" by Pike, three happened to deal with carnal relations, the bishop was by no means a total practitioner during the 1960s of a "New Morality."

He also did not argue any further beyond a qualified denial of natural law to call for a denial of the existence of a religious impulse or a denial of the existence of God. Pike was an iconoclast, but he liked breaking other people's icons, not his own. He took no supportive part in the most radical theology of the 1960s, the Death of God movement. He apparently had not even heard of Death of God theology or of its two most prominent explicators, William Hamilton and Thomas Altizer, until a visiting *Look* reporter at Cambridge in early 1966 happened to mention to Pike the increasingly popular interest in—and outrage over—the movement in the United States. His oversight must have appeared more glaring upon his return to the States, where he saw in the first week of April 1966 the cover story of *Time*, "Is God Dead?" On April 6, Pike preached at St. Thomas's in New York, where he waved a copy of the magazine from the pulpit. "I agree with those who say God is dead, if by that you mean that belief in Him figures less and less in Western culture," he told the congregation. "What I don't understand, though, is the statement that God once existed and then died." (His puzzlement apparently was in response to Altizer's statement that God willed his own death as a transcendent being, and that only in the last two hundred years has humanity accepted the finality of this death.) "I know they're trying to say something significant," Pike spoke, almost in frustration, about Altizer's and Hamilton's theologies, "but I don't know what it is."

He had been more blunt earlier that week in an interview with the *Washington Post*. "I don't dig it," he said, as the reporter also noted how "he stabbed out a cigarette and reached for his pack to light another." Pike amplified his view. "If Altizer means what he seems to be saying—that there once was a God and now there isn't any more—that is nonsense, in the strict meaning of the term. It just doesn't make any sense. Either God has never existed or He is eternally existent."

Pike never debated his terms publicly with the proponents of this radical new theology. The sole exception was an exchange of letters—arranged, paid for, and published in 1967 by *Playboy* magazine—between Pike and Hamilton. Neither engaged the other's argument in this correspondence, and each simply repeated his terms. (The bishop's letter was one of the last documents Maren Bergrud helped him write.) Pike simply shared no conceptual language with the Death of God theologians. He was convinced that everyone had a religion in a Tillichian sense that even an atheist has "ultimate concerns" of reason and materialism. He also believed in H. G. Wells's assertion that there exists "a God-shaped blank in man's heart." The bishop believed so intently in this assertion, as a matter of fact, that he used Wells's phrase twice in the titles of two of his early apologetic works in 1950, once in a speech at Wellesley College and again as the title for an article written for *Vogue* magazine. Altizer and Hamilton maintained that such language with its religious and metaphysical referents had lost meaning by the late twentieth century. Hamilton in particular, in a later exposition of his Death of God theology, seems to have chosen by synchronicity Pike's favorite expression of faith only in order to flatly negate it. "There is no God-shaped blank within man," Hamilton wrote in 2002.

Pike, once-born spiritually, had never really considered that there might not be. A generation much more "tough-minded," in William James's phrase, was now taking its place as teachers in Protestant seminaries, and there were intimations, even by Pike's early fifties, that he was becoming old hat theologically. *Time* magazine, in its 1966 cover story on him, had quoted, apropos of the bishop's troubles with his church's creeds, from a divinity professor at the University of Chicago: "The younger men don't even raise the issue of the Virgin Birth or Original Sin. They're discussing the existence of God. And, if there's no God, you don't have to worry about the other doctrines." By the mid- to late 1960s, he had been superseded both in the popular news and the religious press by younger men who were more radical, more reductionist, and much more iconoclastic than he.

Pike's third reinvention of himself from 1966 to 1968 was his emergence as a public critic of the Vietnam War. The bishop's political route to opposing that war had been circuitous, since first having declared it a "righteous conflict" in 1966. Early the next year, while maintaining that any immediate withdrawal of U.S. troops from South Vietnam would be "very irresponsible," he also had asserted in a speech at Dallas that the North Vietnamese leader, Ho Chi Minh, would be elected the leader of all Vietnamese if free elections were held in both countries. "I'd bet on it," he said.

Qualified misgivings about the American military mission in Vietnam were becoming more frequently expressed in 1967, but in the following months he moved even further politically to an unqualified opposition. By the end of 1967, Pike had joined a diverse group of 250 other clergy and public figures, including Rev. William Sloan Coffin, the Yale chaplain; Dr. Benjamin Spock, the noted pediatrician; and Allen Ginsberg, the bohemian poet, pledging financial and legal aid to young men who resisted conscription into the U.S. military on the grounds of conscience. A month later, he added his name to a declaration pledging those who signed it to risk fines or imprisonment in order to give such assistance. Among the other eighteen signatories were Harvey Cox, the Harvard theologian; Rev. Kilmer Myers, Pike's successor as bishop of the California diocese; and Rev. Daniel Berrigan, a Jesuit chaplain and poet at Cornell University.

Pike's reversal of his position on Vietnam in 1967 was likely the result both of his private studies of early Christianity and his attendance at the Pacem in Terris conference at Geneva in the spring of that year. He had heard the most prominent guest speakers, including the Nobel

Prize–winning scientist Linus Pauling and U.S. senator William Ful-
bright, decry the American involvement in Vietnam as leading "to the
murder of tens of thousands, hundreds of thousands of men, women,
and children," in Pauling's impassioned speech to the delegates. Robert
Hutchins, supervisor of the conference under the aegis of the Center
for the Study of Democratic Institutions, presumably had included Pike
in his statement to the press at the close of the Pacem in Terris conference that "the more than 300 participants had agreed that the war in
Vietnam was at best a mistake." Pike's concurrent readings in New
Quest studies of the historical Jesus had also convinced him on religious
reasons to oppose the state and its powers to make war. Two scholarly
works frequently mentioned by him throughout late 1968 and 1969,
The Passover Plot by Hugh Schonfield and *Jesus and Zealots* by S. G.
Brandon, emphasized the political activism of early Christianity and left
no doubt in the bishop's mind that the first-century Jesus would have
considered the U.S. military in Vietnam as waging an unjust, imperial
war. "Jesus was a revolutionary like the Vietcong and a freedom fighter
like Martin Luther King Jr.," he asserted in a Sunday sermon delivered
in New York on April 8, 1968, at Central Presbyterian Church on Park
Avenue. Pike entitled this address "The God of Law and Order Is
Dead," and he made unambiguously clear his belief in a Christology of
revolutionary protest against those who have "made an ideal out of law
and order," and who were willing to acquiesce to the Vietnam War.

This was a serious argument, seriously expressed. Pike seems not to
have realized, however, that his effectiveness for the antiwar movement
came as the result of speaking from his position as a high-ranking
prelate of one the nation's most "establishment" churches and as an
honorably discharged veteran of the Second World War. When, for
instance, he told his audience in a speech at Gettysburg College that he
had "faked an eye test to get into World War Two" but that he "would
not in good conscience go to Vietnam," his words carried a historical
and moral authority that simply were unavailable to any undergraduate
protestor of the war. (Given his lifelong need for thick eyeglasses, Pike
likely had not rhetorically exaggerated in telling the college students he
had bluffed his way through a military eye exam.) But he was far less
effective when he relied upon his penchant for self-dramatization and
his media celebrity in order to popularize opposition to the war. A

regrettable instance of this was Pike's public actions when he traveled to Baltimore on October 6, 1968, at the encouragement of William Stringfellow, to attend the opening arguments at the trial of the Catonsville Nine as a self-styled "celebrity counsel." The Catonsville Nine included Frs. Philip Berrigan and his brother, Daniel Berrigan. The previous year, the Berrigan brothers and seven others had seized the draft records of the Selective Service board at Catonsville, Maryland, and burned them with homemade napalm. For this destruction of federal property, the nine now faced charges that could bring them individually fines of $22,000 and sentences of eighteen years in prison.

Pike had arrived at the Baltimore airport the night before the trial wearing a large lapel button reading "Defrock Cardinal Spellman," in an apparent reaction to the cardinal's declared support of the war. The next day, on encountering the more than 1,500 demonstrators who had gathered in the city streets in support of the defendants, he became almost ecstatically happy. "Oh, yes! Oh, yes! This is where it's at! This is where the action is!" he exclaimed. Spotting some pro-war demonstrators gathered around a monument to the War of 1812 and separated from the pro-Catonsville demonstrators by the police, Pike saw a chance to reprise his performance of a year earlier at Seattle during his heresy controversies. Quickly darting across the street to the pro-war crowd, as television cameras and newspaper reporters recorded the scene, he picked flowers planted near a fountain and presented one to each of his opponents. His gesture delighted the antiwar assembly.

Earlier in the day Pike had talked his way into the capacity-filled federal courthouse and invited himself to sit at the defense attorneys' table during the opening proceedings. He does not seem to have made a perceptible contribution to the strategy of the defense team led by William Kunstler, nor did this lawyer mention him in his subsequent six-page description of the trial in his memoirs. That night Pike spoke at the rally of about a thousand supporters held at St. Ignatius Roman Catholic Church. Appearing at the door of the church with a new button pinned to his coat, "Support the Nine," he was handed an armband reading "Support the Milwaukee Fourteen," which he also promptly put on. "Who the hell are the Milwaukee Fourteen?" he then whispered to a friend. (The Milwaukee Fourteen were the group of war protestors in that city, including seven clergymen, who were also facing state and federal charges for having destroyed draft records there.) Walking up to the microphone on a stage without waiting for an introduction, Pike evoked roars of approval from the audience by repeatedly raising his right hand in the two-fingered "Peace" gesture. He then began speaking in an apparent spirit of improvisational comedy, verbally composing for his audience his own possible indictment on charges of inciting draft resistance. "I don't trust the Justice Department to do it," Pike told his laughing audience, "I can do it better myself." Skilled in forensics and homiletics as he was, he quickly turned his audience's goodwill toward him into a righteous indignation against others, excoriating "my good friend, Patrick O'Boyle," the Roman Catholic archbishop of Washington, D.C. To shouts of approval and applause, he rhetorically addressed the archbishop to "tell me, sir, where you stand on that war, where you stand on the trial of these priests?" Somewhat gratuitously, he returned to his old quarrel with the Roman Church over the use of contraceptives, and shouted to the absent archbishop over the applause: "Don't you dare *try* to tell me what pill I can give my wife!"

After a few more turns at the microphone and once more arousing the crowd, Pike left for the airport. He did not return for the conclusion of the trial, at which all of the Catonsville Nine were found guilty and received prison sentences. Nor did Pike seem to consider that in acting his part in a "celebrity" appearance, he was losing his gravitas as a morally principled opponent of the war and was becoming the type of stereotyped "middle-aged rebel" his critics long had accused him of being.

Pike was not taken seriously as a radical theologian or politician, was distrusted for his faith in spiritualism, and was frustrated in his attempts to provoke a heresy trial and determine the limits of theological questioning within his Church. The unavoidable question is what, if any, importance these searches for a personal spiritual identity by Pike had upon his fellow Episcopalians. He was seen as an influence upon his church only by having demonstrated that the Episcopal Church would no longer pursue heresy trials of its bishops as a means of enforcing discipline and practices. Even that significance was negated by the 1996 Episcopal trial of the retired Bishop Walter Righter on the heresy presentment of having assisted at the ordination of noncelibate homosexuals. Righter was acquitted, after a legal fight Pike likely would have enjoyed, but what remains of the California bishop's influence upon the church which he both loved and, eventually, left a few months before his death in 1969? His theology and that of the Death of God movement both have dated badly, and are of interest more to their readers as artifacts from the decade of the sixties than as any ongoing intellectual engagement with the idea of God. In the area of spiritualism, despite Pike's enthusiasms, the paranormal and the normal worlds remained unmoved by each other.

In attempting to fill the God-shaped blank he felt existing within himself, Pike did accomplish one great effect upon his church, by introducing the colloquial and the secular into Episcopal liturgy. Few were so devoted as he to reclaiming humanity's secular activities within the purview of the Christian Church and to attempt that Christians see all the created world as sacramental. He was one of the first bishops of either the Episcopal or Roman Catholic Churches to stage a "jazz mass," for instance, and other Episcopalian clergy followed his example for a more colloquial and celebratory worship. Consider, for instance, an informal worship arranged at a coffeehouse for college students in 1959 by Malcolm Boyd, an Episcopal chaplain at Colorado State University who as a student at Union Seminary had been intensely affected by hearing the Sunday sermons delivered on Cathedral Heights by then-Dean Pike:

Seated alone on a stage under a spotlight, Boyd read "some lines of Tennessee Williams's *The Glass Menagerie* and *Sweet Bird of Youth*," followed by "that part of Truman Capote's *Breakfast at Tiffany's* where Holly Golightly leaves her cat behind in Spanish Harlem." He then read from Camus's *The Plague* and Eliot's "The Hollow Men," and ended "by reading, without music, the lyrics of Cole Porter's 'Love for Sale'—very immediate, threatening, close to contemporary man's questioning of the meaning of love and sex." Such "worldly Christianity" certainly would have been practiced without the influence of Pike, but it is unlikely that it would have been practiced so early and with such enthusiasm in the Episcopal Church without his career.

Of course, such an insistence upon contemporariness and a constant bowing of acknowledgment to secularism in liturgical practices as promoted by Pike runs a risk—particularly when seen from the historical perspective of nearly half a century later—of having been no more than what his acquaintance Bishop John Robinson called with a nice irony "old-fashioned modernism." Pike as the practitioner of a High Church, trendier-than-thou liberal Christianity is an easy target; yet the California bishop also can be seen as trying to reinvigorate, as best he knew how, the threatened existence of prelatic and doctrinal Protestantism. His personal experience of the "third force" of Christianity, as when he struggled in 1963 against the popularity of glossolalia within his own see, seems to have been a convincing experience for Pike that the conventional Church *must* become more culturally relevant and emotionally immediate in its liturgies and theologies; otherwise its communicants would be lost, some to secularism, but many more to the nonecclesiastical, nondenominational, dramatic Pentecostalism of the third-force churches. These were, to Pike, largely outside the Christian Catholic belief and represented a newly appearing form of Gnostic Christianity, against which he also struggled personally with limited success within his own spiritual thoughts. In fact, it can be argued that Pike spent the last year of his life in 1969 as an iconoclastic and wandering Gnostic, seeking in the Dead Sea wilderness the spiritual insights he felt conventional Christianity had denied him.

The word *gnostic* in the last decade of the twentieth century and the first decade of the twenty-first, like the word *revolutionary* in the last decade of Pike's life in the 1960s, has been used loosely. Pike defined it well in his 1967 book, *If This Be Heresy*. "Until recently, gnosticism has been seen as a Christian heresy," he wrote, "a later departure from the pristine message borne by the authentic New Testament books and original teachings of the primitive Church." He then further amplified in this book what he believed to be the heretical difference between "the gnostic school" and "the predominately eschatological bent of the canonical books":

> A rough and ready distinction between these outlooks is this: Proponents of the *eschatological* school, while differing widely among themselves as to what precisely is ahead, see the fulfillment of men, or more especially of the Elect, as yet to come through divine intervention into human history—and soon. Proponents of the *gnostic* school regard the consummation as

already accomplished; it can be appropriated for present fulfillment by those individuals who *know* the realities [italics as in
original].

In writing of this "gnostic party," Pike meant primarily the historic
Gnostic Christians whose writings were included among other Gnostic
codices in the Nag Hammadi "library" of papyrus books placed inside a
clay jar and buried in the fourth century C.E. and discovered in Egypt in
1945. (*Gnosticism* customarily is capitalized, despite Pike's usage, when
describing that particular philosophical school of late classicism or the
Christian heresy based upon it; *gnostic* is commonly an adjective meaning an occult or hidden knowledge. Nag Hammadi is the proper name
for the spot along the Nile riverbank where the Gnostic jar was acci-
dentally uncovered.) As with the jars containing the Dead Sea Scrolls
hidden inside caves three centuries earlier, this jar had been concealed
presumably to protect the writings inside from depredators, apparently
in this instance orthodox Christians. From the second century C.E.
onward, the powerful bishops and other leaders who would establish the
canonical books of the New Testament, and later would become known
as the Church Fathers, considered Gnostic Christianity with its philosophical emphasis upon secret knowledge about God subjectively
obtainable by an elect to be the "root" of all heresies, to be extirpated
whenever it was encountered. Both in regard to the Essenes and the
Gnostics, the concealed clay jars served their purposes almost too well,
ensuring that the hidden writings of each group of believers would not
be revealed to the light of day until the mid-1940s.

Before the Nag Hammadi discovery, Gnostic Christian texts had
been known to interested twentieth-century readers such as Pike only
by a few disapproving excerpts or paraphrases in the writings of the
Church Fathers from the second to the fourth century. But, by the time
Pike began his fellowship to study the origins of Christianity at the
Center for the Study of Democratic Institutions in 1966, a project to
translate the Nag Hammadi codices from their ancient Coptic language
into English had been organized at another scholarly consortium in
California. This was the Institute for Antiquity and Christianity, located
at Claremont University and directed by a noted philologist and New
Quest scholar, James M. Robinson. By 1967, when he published *If This*

Be Heresy, Pike had read at least two of Robinson's early scholarly publications on the Gnostics and cited these studies approvingly within that book.

On the one hand, Pike apparently had a distrust of what he considered the most modern reappearances of Gnostic Christianity, such as glossolalia and the phenomenon of a "born again" evangelism or of "having a personal relation with Jesus" replacing a communally celebrated formal liturgy or the Church's organized engagement with history and politics. Yet, four years after his pastoral letter in 1963 denouncing glossolalia, Pike evidentially was becoming much more open-minded spiritually to other forms of Gnosticism. In contrasting the contents of the canonical books of the Church Fathers with the Gnostic Christian writings found at Nag Hammadi, Pike asserted in *If This Be Heresy* that "there is no longer a clear basis on which to attribute authenticity to either one of these radically different outlooks as against the other." The bishop then wrote a remarkably even-minded and politically realistic observation about these non-canonical documents of early Christianity, including such Nag Hammadi codices as the hidden Gospel of Thomas: "It was touch and go: had the gnostic party won we would have by and large a different set of books in the New Testament, and the canonical books thus excluded would be regarded as variant heretical writings."

Pike did not go so far as to assert, as did John Allegro, that the Gnostic Christians were both the religious and physical descendants of the Essene Jews after their forced dispersal from their Judean communes, but, within *If This Be Heresy*, he did emphatically state that, alongside the myths of the Essenes, Gnosticism was "widely held by various groups and individuals among the Jews who were focusing their religious responses around the image of Jesus." Pike's own focus from 1968 to 1969 on the texts of the Essene Jews seems to have become increasingly Gnostic in that he displayed a belief that if he personally studied these scrolls and then experienced the Dead Sea landscape in which they were written, he would received a *gnosis*, or knowledge, that would reform established Christianity. After his death by misadventure in Israel in 1969, more scholarly examiners of early Christianity, such as James Robinson and Elaine Pagels, published their own works from the mid-1970s onward emphasizing in more documented form the importance of Gnosticism to the theologies of the early Church. Pagels in particular later vindicated in detail Pike's assertion that only the exigencies of political "touch and go" had prevented the Gnostic codex of the Gospel of Thomas from being accepted as a canonical book of the New Testament. An iconoclast even to the end of his life in challenging the Church Fathers' historical rejection of Gnosticism, Pike characteristically anticipated what would become, in the years after his death, an absorbing interest to the next generation of scholars and practitioners of Christianity.

Before his death, Pike performed a useful and good service to his church. As the Christian Church frequently is symbolized as a lamb, he can be pictured as the brass bell hung around the lamb's neck, its clapper giving evidence of where the lamb has wandered, where it is advancing, or where it has found new pastures. The brass vessel itself, however, took a beating.

IX

Leaving the Church, a Fascination with the Dead Sea Scrolls, and Death

On such a pilgrimage, one can only wish the pilgrim well.

—PRESIDING BISHOP JOHN E. HINES, on hearing of Pike's intention
to leave the Episcopal Church, April 14, 1969

"Do we have a decent map?" Lucas said.
"Just this," said Sonia. She handed him the rental car company's map.
It was not very detailed.
"This is the kind of map that killed Bishop Pike," Lucas said.
"The one for us," said Sonia.

—ROBERT STONE, *Damascus Gate*, 1998

By James Pike's fifty-fifth birthday and the near-suicide of his daughter, in early 1968, until his death, a year later in Israel, the bishop approached—if he did not actually cross the line—becoming what the contemporary author Graham Greene called "a burnt-out case." Such a marked individual, in Greene's description in the 1960 novel of the same name, was cured of a spiritual malady only after the sufferer had lost much of his life in extremis. Pike in 1968 had lost his marriage, his son, his diocese, and many of his Episcopal friends. One former acquaintance and lover, Maren Bergrud, had spent her final moments accusing him of having lost, or never having possessed, the capacity to love. Nearly a year had passed after Bergrud's suicide before he could bear in 1968 to show her suicide note—the existence of which he had concealed from the police—to his current companion, Diane Kennedy. His eventual disclosure of the note evinces the trust in which he held Kennedy, but his reluctance to disclose it earlier reveals that the contents had struck hard:

> Jim—the ease (five minutes of psychology?) with which you consented to this makes it obvious that it will be a basic relief to you. Sorry about the extra twinges it will produce—to explain the reasons for my death are tiresome and would be out of your depth anyway. Let's just say that I have finally accepted the fact that you do not love me. For a long time now that's all that has been important to me. Both of our inadequacies (a) I am unloveable and (b) you are unloving. Anyway, the one you really want is Esther (the Roman Catholic in you?) and a blood sacrifice will probably effect reconciliation. Now to business: 1. Use your head about the coroner and the publicity 2. My last wish is that even though my will which is in the safe deposit box leaves all to you, please see that the kids (*mine*) get something. They have loved me unreservedly. I've loved you in a way you haven't wanted or understood. I needed hope. You never offered it— never once offered it—Maren [italics in original].

One way of dealing with such painful words and personal losses in the past is to deny feeling them, to allow a spreading burnt-out space inside one self, and to concentrate interests and affections solely upon the present and future. Such explains Pike's apparent declining interest in his former family and friends, and his determination in 1968 to begin his long-anticipated book on the Dead Sea Scrolls and to marry Diane Kennedy. As to the first, the bishop's fascination with the scrolls as having exercised a great, but previously unknown, intertestamental influence upon the canonical books of Christianity had continued since he first talked with John Allegro in 1966. This belief had also been affirmed in his mind by his continual study of the New Quest biographers of Jesus. He invested a good deal of theological energy in establishing this connection. If the earliest creeds of Christianity could be shown to have been practiced within the Essene community, it could be proven where "the trolley went off the track," in Pike's lively words; that is, such later doctrines as the Trinity or the Virgin Birth would simply be seen as historical incrustations and not central to Christian belief or practices. He was not such a radically Gnostic reader of the scrolls as Allegro, who by the time he met Pike was asserting in his conversations and in an article published in *Harper's* in 1966 that the gospels were actually Essene documents, that the names of Jesus and the disciples were, in effect, pseudonyms for Essene figures, and that the gospel narrative was an Essene myth. But in maintaining with Allegro the importance of the Dead Sea Scrolls in redacting the Christian creeds, Pike was where he enjoyed being intellectually and spiritually, at the extreme of a controversy. By no means did all of his church's authorities or historians regard the scrolls as having major significance for religions other than Judaism. (Pike did not live to read Allegro's 1970 book, *The Cross and the Sacred Mushroom*, which argued that the gospel and the Dead Sea Scrolls were symbolic retellings of an earlier phallic and hallucinogenic drug cult.) "I think he bought into Allegro a little too much," Darby Betts later remarked.

Looked at with more askance by clergy and laity in his church was Pike's marriage in late December 1968 to Diane Kennedy, "a woman half his age," as she was described unkindly that month by the *New York Times*. Actually, Pike's age, as previously stated, was fifty-five that year, and Kennedy was thirty; she had completed a graduate degree at Columbia University and worked for three years in South America as a missionary before she met Pike while attending his Berkeley class on the New Morality. She was, in sum, a mature woman with accomplishments in her own life. But the public perception remained that the bishop had robbed the cradle in making his third marriage to a woman who was only four years older than his eldest daughter. Anthony Towne made much of the fact that Kennedy was a virgin before she met Pike, and, after talking with her in Seattle during the bishop's heresy controversies, referred thereafter to her as a "milk maid," perhaps in complimentary observance of her blond, light-eyed appearance, her girlhood in a Nebraska farming town, and her adolescent-appearing female physique; but also, perhaps, Towne chose the word as patronizing toward one whom he considered naive and not at the bishop's intellectual or cultural level. It should be noted, however, that from 1967 onward she had shared discussions with the bishop on his research of the Dead Sea Scrolls and first-century Judea, a degree of involvement with his scholarly work that he had not allowed Esther Pike. And it was, perhaps, that same presumed naïveté in the year following their marriage that convinced Diane Pike to refuse to accept herself and her husband dying in a biblical wilderness and motivated her to walk ten hours through the Judean Desert in an attempt to save both their lives.

She later recorded her thoughts and emotions after first meeting Pike in a memoir. These passages provide a vicarious understanding of how the bishop, even when burdened in 1966 with considerable cares and in the thick of middle age, could exercise a charismatic—and erotic—appeal to women. She initially had considered her teacher at Berkeley as simply "too old" to be a potential social or sexual companion, and it was her understanding that he was securely married; the bishop and his wife had not publicly announced their separation. She also had expected considerable inhibition from an Episcopal bishop. However, after volunteering after class to drive Pike across San Francisco Bay back to his temporary living quarters in the city, she discovered his willingness to talk volubly and apparently on equal terms with someone much younger than he; further, Pike's wit and demonstrable liking of verbal play—his "Little Self," or inner child, in her description, "was almost always at home when someone knocked"—convinced her that Pike was a desirable physical and intellectual companion. He soon told her of his marital estrangement. As she confided in her memoir: "Very early in my relationship with Jim—perhaps the third time we talked—I had a very strong intuitive feeling that there were two things I had to do with Jim, and that one of them had to do with sex." The other, presumably, was to share her life with him.

In the sixteen months they lived together, from her moving into the Santa Barbara apartment in August 1967 to their marriage on December 20, 1968, she successfully accepted the bishop's domestic crochets: finding both front seats of her automobile "literally covered" with cigarette ashes, in her description, the result of Pike's incessant chain-smoking while traveling; bringing a book or magazine to the table and reading during meals, rather than conversing with her; and forgetting to telephone on nights when he was away from home and staying late with those who had requested his pastoral counseling. (This habit, particularly when Pike was counseling single females, had led to the argument with Bergrud the night of her suicide.)

For his part in their relationship, Pike eventually gave up smoking when he noticed it bothered her. The bishop also changed himself and was rejuvenated in other ways. Kennedy was much more an up-to-date believer in paranormal phenomena than he, and, in addition to attending traditional séances and experiencing what she believed was ESP communication with her future husband, she was a practitioner of what would begin to be called by the early 1970s "New Age" practices, such as "channeling" prior lives and experiencing out-of-body visions. She later wrote that she had experienced her first mystical vision when she was only twelve, shortly before her family moved from Nebraska to California. And, to those who asked, she was frank in answering that she found sexual activity with her older partner to be very satisfying.

Pike in different terms paid her the highest compliment he possibly could have given any of his domestic companions. Kennedy recalled being told by him that "their love had made it possible for his mother to be restored to him. For the first time, he reported, he looked forward to seeing her and thoroughly enjoyed the time spent with her." This was, generally speaking, an Oedipal, and double-edged, compliment. Not every man would praise his younger lover by telling her she had enabled him to love his mother more. Pearl Chambers may also have underestimated Kennedy as being young and malleable to her will, and therefore welcomed her and her son back to her Santa Barbara home. She had evidently been keeping her emotional distance for a number of years while her son had been married or living with the more formidable, and older, Esther Pike or Maren Bergrud.

Kennedy, having previously been a devout Methodist, received instruction and was confirmed by Pike himself into the Anglican Communion on October 13, 1968. Her conversion was taken preparatory to her and Pike's plans to marry in a month in an Episcopal ceremony in a chapel at Grace Cathedral. According to the couple's version of subsequent events, they had been assured in a September meeting in San Francisco with Bishop C. Kilmer Myers that he consented to their marriage within the Episcopal Church, and that he himself would officiate at the ceremony. The only caveats the couple recalled was Myers specifying that before formally granting his assent to the marriage, he would take counsel from the diocesan Marriage Committee, and that at least two members of that committee must concur with him that Pike's second marriage was "spiritually dead." Following a second meeting in October with Myers the day after Kennedy's confirmation, the couple said they were told to proceed with plans for their wedding. A chapel was reserved for November 14, and, in an uncharacteristic effort by Pike to avoid publicity, or in an act of prudence by the cathedral dean to prevent the clamor that seemed inseparable from Pike's presence, a pseudonym was used; the nuptials in the cathedral were to be known as the "Smith wedding."

Pike apparently assumed that a dispensation by the Marriage Committee was his for the asking, spiritually invalidating his second marriage of twenty-four years and enabling the bishop to wed anew within his church for the third time. He frequently had spoken to his friends of his marriage to Esther Pike as being "spiritually dead" since at least the early 1960s, but this phrase had a canonically specific meaning to Myers and the committeemen as they examined the ecclesiastical law texts of canon 17, "Of the Solemnization of Holy Matrimony," and canon 18, "Of Regulations Respecting Holy Matrimony." By the latter's instruction, the impossibility of any future reconciliation between a divorced couple could justify a bishop finding that the prior marriage is "so completely destroyed as to be the equivalent to the dissolution of the marriage band by death." Pike's second marriage could plausibly be so presented, thereby enabling him to remarry within his church. But having determined that he was canonically eligible for marriage, the bishop and his advisors now felt obliged to consider the proposed union of Kennedy and Pike under the strictures of canon 17. Here the twice-divorced Pike was a much less plausible candidate for church nuptials. Section 2 (b) of that canon listing the impediments to a marriage being recognized by the church—the same section that Pike had cited in arguing for the annulment of his first marriage to Jane Alvies—includes the impediment of a potential couple maintaining a "concurrent contract" between themselves. An accepted commentary upon this section further defines the meaning of such a concurrent agreement:

> For example, if a priest preparing to solemnize a marriage learned that the couple was entering into the anticipated marriage on a temporary or "trial" basis—anticipating an easy resort to divorce if "things didn't work out"—he would have reason for not proceeding.

As this commentary on canons 17 and 18 continues: "Should the bishop, despite his every good wish for the couple, perhaps find it not possible to give a favorable judgment, the couple cannot be married by a minister of the Church."

Myers sent Pike and Kennedy his judgment by telegram to Santa Barbara on October 28. His answer to their application to marry within the Episcopal Church was no. In a subsequent telephone conversation among the three of them, Myers stated that, although with the assent of the Marriage Committee he had found Pike's second marriage to be spiritually dead, neither he nor the committee was convinced that the proposed new marriage was undertaken with sufficient intent that it be a permanent union. Pike reacted as he had in 1958 when the canonical legality of the annulment of his first marriage had been challenged during the canvass for his nomination to be a bishop: he launched an extensive letter-writing campaign to change legal opinion. He asked for a reconsideration of his case after the diocesan bishop read letters from friends of his and Kennedy's attesting to their intent for a permanent marriage. Myers agreed. There followed in the next days what Stringfellow and Towne described as a "deluge" of letters to the San Francisco diocesan offices, all urging Myers to reverse his canonical judgment.

Unmentioned by the two biographers was that Pike also called upon his children to join the campaign. Connie Pike declined, in a letter to her father that showed a political maturity beyond her twenty years: "Kim Myers will get hell if he marries you," she wrote. She then graciously and evenhandedly added, "I obviously believe in your marriage [to Kennedy]. I literally have never seen two people more compatible or happier together, *etc.*, and it is a really beautiful thing. I can appreciate it and feel gladness and warmth about it, but I can also feel great ties and emotion towards my mother and I don't feel it was really right to be asked to write a letter for you when mom has been pretty much disregarded by you."

Two days before the scheduled November wedding, Myers sent a second telegram to Kennedy and Pike in which he "regretfully" stated his unwillingness, supported again by the Marriage Committee, to marry the couple within the Episcopal Church. He did suggest, however, that after eighteen months they should reapply to the bishop for a reconsideration of their request. Myers seemingly considered, in a pragmatic and situationalist way that might have appealed to the like-thinking Pike, that a further, successful year-and-a-half cohabitation by the couple would be convincing evidence of their permanent intent to share their lives. Pike, however, was not to be delayed. He requested, and Myers provided on December 10, a letter in which the diocesan bishop formally stated his finding that Pike's second marriage was spiritually dead. Myers apparently did not anticipate any public use of this letter.

But then Pike employed the same presumptive strategy he had used two decades earlier when the questionable annulment of his first marriage had frustrated his desire for a second church wedding to Esther Pike. At that time, he had represented Bishop Stevens's letter to him in 1942 that he was a communicant "in good standing" as an a posteriori approval of the annulment of his 1938 marriage to Jane Alvies. Three decades and another marriage later, Pike now represented Myers's letter stating his second marriage was spiritually dead as an implicit approval for Pike to be married within the Episcopal Church by a priest at a future time, even if the diocesan bishop personally chose not to do so himself for the next eighteen months. Pike presented this letter and made this argument to his friend Philip Adams, who had remained as the chancellor of the California diocese. Adams, to his later regret, gave his approval to Pike's argument.

Kennedy and Pike were married during the third week of Advent, December 20, 1968, by an Episcopal priest at a Methodist church in San Jose. Christopher Pike, the bishop's son, was the best man. About seventy-five to one hundred people witnessed the marriage, which was widely publicized in the San Francisco and New York newspapers. The Episcopal ceremony was generally followed, with the highly notable exceptions of an electric guitar playing as the guests sang the Lord's Prayer and the couple composing their own vows. "Diane, you are the one I want to be with, to share all that matters and, come what may, to be beside you," Pike said. Kennedy replied, "firmly and cheerfully," according to news reporters: "You're that for me too, Jim. And you're the one with whom I want to explore more deeply our own possibilities and those of others, to fulfill our particular roles in what the All shall become." About an hour and a half before the beginning of this ceremony, Pike released to the press the letter from Myers affirming the spiritual death of Pike's second marriage and told reporters that he had invited his successor to officiate at his third marriage ceremony, but he had declined. (This statement seems to have been a deliberate conflation by Pike of Myers declining to officiate at the wedding in November and subsequently sending this letter at Pike's request in December.)

Myers's anger was fierce. Pike married on a Friday; on the following Monday, Myers apparently first learned of Adams's canonical approval of the marriage and fired the chancellor early the following night, on Christmas Eve. The bishop "meant no reflection on Mr. Adams's competence as an attorney," a press release from the cathedral coolly stated, "but since he had been Bishop Pike's attorney, the [diocesan] bishop felt it only fair to relieve him from what might be considered a conflict of interest." Also on Christmas Eve day, Myers distributed a mimeographed sheet to reporters throughout the Bay Area, reiterating what he insisted were the facts regarding Pike's most recent marriage:

> He made application for permission to remarry, and asked me to give my blessing to the marriage. I declined to grant the application and advised him of my reasons. He then asked for a declaration of his marital status, and I wrote a letter dated December 10, which he interpreted as a "judgment" which left him free to marry. However, this letter has NO relation to his proposed marriage to Diane Kennedy and was not intended to be an approval or blessing of that marriage in any way [capitalization in original].

Myers had also taken direct action against Pike. Announcing a "personal request" on December 23 to all clergy under his jurisdiction, he asked that Pike be banned from appearing in the diocese's pulpits or from performing any priestly duties, such as "preaching, ministering the sacraments, or holding any public service in this diocese until further notice from me to the contrary." Pike, answering from the San Francisco hotel where he was spending the next few days with his new wife, issued a statement declaring that Myers had "absolutely no canonical authority to suspend me from functioning in our diocese." He further ironically compared Myers's ban on performing churchly duties with the supposed tolerance of one of Pike's most ardent political enemies, Bishop Eric Bloy of Los Angeles. Pike noted that his marriage ceremony had been performed by a priest from the Episcopal diocese of Los Angeles and with the knowledge of Bloy. Pike failed to note, however, that he was already banned from preaching or administering the sacraments at any churches in the Los Angeles diocese, an action taken by Bloy after the general convocation's censure of Pike in 1967.

The newly married bishop, by an earlier invitation, administered Holy Communion at St. Aidan's Church at San Francisco on the evening of December 24 without further incident or reproach from Myers, but apparently the time was drawing near when he would no longer speak, as he did in his public rebuttal to Myers, of "our diocese." Pike sought a meeting with Myers to discuss their differing interpretations of the letter, but the request was refused. He then circulated his own chronology of the events throughout the diocesan churches and made it clear that he intended to oppose the canonical legitimacy of Myers's ban when the diocese met in convention early in 1969. Pike was convinced he and his wife had been done an injustice. As he later wrote in *Look* magazine: "The irony and the injustice was that not only had I *not* committed any canonical offense (and the bishop cited none), but also that Diane and I had gone to great lengths to be married *according* to canon law and had in fact been freed to do so by Bishop Myers's own clear written judgment" (italics in original).

Pike attended the opening day of the diocesan convention symbolically carrying a large copy of canon law, and his allies later attempted to force a vote requiring Myers to withdraw his prohibition. His estrangement from the will of his church and his political defeat, however, was total. Not only did a majority of the delegates refuse to consider lifting the ban, voting instead to send the matter on to Presiding Bishop John Hines to resolve, but they also gave Myers a standing ovation at the end of that vote. Diane Pike later wrote that, on tearfully hearing the news with her husband, Pike had said aloud, "Lord, now lettest thy servant depart in peace."

Although Hines offered to dispatch three bishops to mediate the dispute between Myers and Pike, Pike had made up his mind to officially leave the Episcopal Church; his wife, a convert to the Anglican Communion for less than half a year, joined him in his decision. Having acted peremptorily in marrying, Pike now seemed genuinely and profoundly shocked at his church's reaction, and he took his bishop's objections as personal insults to himself and his wife. In explaining their departure from the Episcopal Church to a friend, Bishop William Campbell of West Virginia, Pike wrote in a private letter on March 17 that "Diane and I have reached the point that it really doesn't matter anymore. You can only hurt so long about something." A month later, in an interview with the *New York Times*, he would explain, "I'm still a Christian in that I have been shaped by the Christian heritage, and I still believe in God and Jesus' resurrection and life after death." But, in regard to the Episcopal Church and organized religion, the bishop was a burnt-out case.

The occasion for his separation from the Episcopal Church may have been personal, but Pike chose to frame his reasons in terms of his decade-long dissatisfaction with its theologies and policies. He publicly announced his decision in an article for the April 29, 1969, issue of *Look*, "Why I Am Leaving the Church." He asserted that the Episcopal Church was failing its communicants due to its three shortcomings of a "credibility gap" in theology, a "relevance gap" in political commitment, and a "performance gap" in the quality of its new seminarians and clergy. He also announced his intention to formally forsake his ecclesiastical title as a bishop. "Although 'bishop' has almost become part of my name, I simply go back to my earned doctorate at Yale: 'Dr.' Pike will do. ('Jim Pike' is all right too.)" Describing the organized Christian church as a "sick—even dying—institution," he stated that he and his wife did not intend to join another church, but soon would undertake a new ministry outside of sectarian or ecclesiastical boundaries.

But the canonical requirements that had so often entangled him in the past prevented once again any quick action on leaving his church, however much it may have been desired by Pike or his opponents. Nor was his ecclesiastical title so easily renounced, as it was considered given by Anglican authority in an unbroken act of apostolic succession; in the eyes of his church, at least, Pike would die a bishop. Canon 61 of the Episcopal Church did allow for a bishop by his own volition to "abandon the communion," but such an action in Pike's case promised to take a year and a half. First, he was required to declare his intention to leave the Church to his diocesan bishop and standing committee, who would then notify Presiding Bishop Hines. The latter, with the concurrent advice of three other senior bishops, would then temporarily suspend Pike from his office for six months. This suspension would become permanent upon a majority of the House of Bishops approving Hines's action in general convention. However, the bishops were next scheduled to meet in convention in September, a month before the requisite six months were to expire; the prelates were not to assemble again until October 1970. Pike therefore would have to wait until autumn of the following year in order to be found to have abandoned the communion, or he would have to be willing to waive the six-month temporary suspension, or be the occasion for a specially called meeting of the House of Bishops to vote on his abandonment. Some of his fellow bishops might gladly have granted Pike the gift of a special convention in order to remove him from their communion, but Hines suggested to Pike that he consider waiving the six months' waiting period in order to speed his exit. However much the presiding bishop may have wanted to end the Californian's tenure as bishop, he spoke gracefully and generously about Pike when contacted by the *New York Times* for comment on the article in *Look*.

"The claims of individual integrity are more important in the church's eyes than any published description of the church," he said, in apparent acknowledgment that Pike felt he was "doing the truth" by continuing his ministry outside of the institutional church. "The church will miss the constructive use of the talents God bestowed upon Bishop Pike," Hines added, with a notable choice of adjective to describe Pike's use of his talents, "but on such a pilgrimage, one can only wish the pilgrim well."

The same month as that article, Pike incorporated the Foundation for Religious Transition as part of what he considered his ministry for those who were considering, in his phrase, becoming "church alumni." The foundation was to provide opportunities for discussion, study, and mutual encouragement among former clergy and laity. He and his wife also organized the Professional Refocus Operation to help clergy leaving the Church to find other jobs. The idea may have been suggested to him the previous year by the extensive and favorable coverage given in the press to The Next Step, a San Francisco group that had been organized in 1968 by an Episcopal priest and two women formerly of a Roman Catholic religious order and college, in order to aid in the transition of former clergy to secular employment. Pike was not connected in any way to The Next Step, but by the last day of June 1969, he himself was unemployed. The Center for the Study of Democratic Institutions had eliminated his position, along with several others, as part of an ideological restructuring and the result of an endowment shortfall. The director, Robert Hutchins, apparently wanted to steer the center's activities away from direct political activism and more toward an exclusively academic community, and the highly speculative financial investments that had paid for the Center's operations during the 1960s were losing their value as the decade came to an end. Pike knew that the reason for his dismissal was not personal, but friends described him as emotionally depressed, and the loss of his yearly salary, by then over $20,000, put a greatly increased pressure upon him to give many more public lectures and quickly write additional books.

The loss of his job at the Center that summer accelerated the personal decision by the couple to live as "urban nomads," a style of life, as Pike described to *Look*, "far more suitable for today's post-rural, post-urban people for whom the city never really becomes home and who are more and more on the move." Such a nomadic life would begin with a trip to Israel the couple had planned for early September, and Pike expanded the number of books he expected to write on the move in order to finance their lives. In addition to his much-discussed manuscript on Christianity and the Dead Sea Scrolls, he now planned books on some of the disciples and the apostle Paul in light of the Essene tradition and what he called the "varied psychic phenomena" experienced by those contemporary to Jesus. He also expressed his interest in writing or promoting a motion picture about the historical Jesus that accurately portrayed first-century political and messianic movements.

He was still "the bishop." In late August, Pike declined to cooperate with Hines by waiving his right to a six-month suspension prior to the House of Bishops meeting that September. Very likely, his reason for this refusal was to prevent action being taken on his status until after he returned from Israel and could be present at a future convention to comment on leaving the communion. Hines was left in the uncomfortable position either of calling a special convocation of the House of Bishops as soon as practical after their adjournment or of holding over for another year a vote on the bishop's presence in their communion.

Meanwhile, the metaphoric pilgrimage on which the presiding bishop had wished Pike a good journey was now a real one. The Pikes departed the United States on August 24 for Israel and an anticipated visit to the desert wasteland around the Qumran archaeological site near the Dead Sea. Ever since studying the Essene and early Christian movements together at Berkeley in 1967, the Pikes had found a personal significance in the line translated from one of the earliest discovered Dead Sea Scrolls, the document known as *The Rule of the Community*. Within this line, the Essenes had proclaimed their dedication to a spiritual quest by separating themselves from the mainstream of first-century Judaic observance: "This is the time for the clearing of the way into the wilderness." This declaration by 1969 had become a personal rallying cry for the couple as they disassociated themselves from institutional religion and a conventional livelihood, and proposed to study in Israel a historical Jesus far different from the accepted view of most of Christianity. "We cleared the way, and went," Diane Pike later wrote in 1970, describing their commitment and their trip. Her husband also had quoted this line from *The Rule of the Community* in his 1969 article for *Look*, declaring his departure from the Episcopal Church as "clearing a way into the wilderness," presumably toward a more spiritually and historically truthful Christianity.

After a stopover of several days in Paris as a delayed honeymoon, the Pikes arrived in Israel on Friday, August 29, a few hours before the commencement of the Jewish Sabbath. They subsequently checked into the Intercontinental Hotel in Jerusalem. A photograph of the couple shows

Pike wearing a florid necktie in the fashion of the decade, decorated with a large pattern of the peace symbol. He had publicly announced that so long as he remained a bishop he would wear some version of the peace symbol beside his pectoral cross as a protest of the Vietnam War. On September 1, they left their hotel for what they planned as a day trip to the caves and ruins around Qumran. Pike wore a yellow shirt with black pants and leather shoes, and his wife had on a light dress and sandals. Anticipating an early return that afternoon, they made a 7:30 p.m. dinner engagement in the city with Professor David Flusser, a scholar at Hebrew University who had written on messianic figures in the Dead Sea Scrolls.

Neither of the Pikes had the linguistic or archaeological skills of Flusser or the bishop's acquaintance John Allegro, nor were they making this trip to the Qumran vicinity for scholarly reasons. "We only wanted to get a feeling for the area—to drink it all in, as Jim said so many times," Diane Pike later wrote. They had visited the Qumran site together during a visit in the summer of 1968, but this year they wished to drive up into the Judean hills overlooking the Dead Sea and the ancient commune, in order, in her words, to "see the wilderness in which the Qumran covenanters had spent their time meditating and fasting. That same wilderness, our research suggested, was where Jesus went after his baptism."

Pike seems to have come to the belief, at about the time he was experiencing the events recorded in *The Other Side*, that certain geographic areas themselves are numinous, and that he could obtain a spiritually intuitive understanding of those who had been there earlier by visiting the sites himself. He had written passionately of such an experience in *The Other Side*, when he recalled his strongly affective response in 1965 after climbing to the ruins of the first-century fortress of the Jewish defenders at Masada in the company of his son Jim.

> Standing at the top of the plateau and looking out over the vast, barren desert, I somehow felt caught up in the courage which must have enabled those 960 to stand to the very end against 10,000 Roman soldiers. So much so that I felt I too could almost believe—as they did to the end (as a recently discovered fragmentary farewell note shows)—that God *would* break into his-

tory, through the Son of Man and his angels, to bring victory to his people Israel if I would wait there long enough. I felt transported onto a plane of hope where time is no longer significant and courage is the motivating force. It was a kind of psychedelic experience without drugs [italics in original].

The Pikes' day trip by automobile into the Judean hills apparently was thus made in a similar hope by the bishop and his wife that "God *would* break" through and that it was possible that they would experience there insights into first-century Christianity in a geographic area "where time is no longer significant."

Before they drove their rented Ford Cortina out of Jerusalem at about twelve o'clock, no one, including the Pikes, had thought to check the contents of the automobile's trunk or the accuracy of the oil company map they took with them. This map showed a tertiary dirt road branching off from the Bethlehem highway and leading eastward across the Judean Desert to Qumran. The distance indicated on the map by this route was about an hour's driving time. The apparent simplicity of this way to Qumran convinced the Pikes not to hire a guide to lead them in a Jeep, and the couple set out southward from Jerusalem toward Bethlehem. Diane Kennedy, as was their custom, was at the steering wheel. Pike studied the map.

About an hour later, at approximately one o'clock, they were approaching the outskirts of Bethlehem, and it was obvious to the couple that they had missed the turn-off eastward onto the dirt road. After stopping at Nativity Square to buy two bottles of Coca-Cola to drink later, they determined a new route to follow that would lead out of Bethlehem and then turn northeast to intersect with the tertiary road they originally had sought. Once having driven out of Bethlehem, however, the Pikes soon found that all the roads were dirt, and most were not marked; a wrong turn taken a few miles outside of Bethlehem meant that they unknowingly began to drive south once more, away from Qumran. Their situation best can be visualized by the fatal clock imagery that the bishop in *The Other Side* so often had associated with Jim Jr.'s death: Jerusalem was located at ten o'clock; Bethlehem was at nine o'clock; Qumran was at two o'clock; and the Pikes now were traveling in the direction of four or five o'clock across the Judean Desert, where the dirt roads simply end, or turn into the dry, rocky streambeds known as wadis.

The road they were driving became rockier and the heat more enervating as the afternoon progressed. The temperature was well above one hundred degrees. As far as they knew, the nearest drinking water available to them was at Qumran. Twice, Diane Pike expressed her opinion that they should turn back. The first time, not having recognized any landmarks from her previous visit to Qumran, she said, "Sweetheart, it looks like endless desert, just endless desert." Pike, sitting beside her with the map, implacably rejoined, "It can't be endless desert. The map doesn't show endless desert." On a second occasion, when she worried aloud that the road ahead was looking increasingly impassable, he curtly replied, "If the Israelis can drive it, so can we." However, he obviously was sharing her worry, at least in his own way, and several times he cautioned his wife to slow down driving over rocks in order not to do damage to the rented automobile. Once, vexed, he exclaimed, "I don't know why they would mark this as a road on the map!"

Frequently the road descended into a wadi, followed the dry bed for a distance, and then ascended the opposite bank to continue into the distance. At one such juncture, the heat and the emotional stresses of driving under these conditions suddenly made Diane Pike sick. She had stopped their automobile in a wadi and gotten out in order to help her husband find where the road resumed when she unexpectedly vomited on her hands, legs, and dress. Pike insisted that she use the contents of one of their two bottles of Coca-Cola to wash herself.

Continuing to travel on what they thought was the tertiary road to Qumran, at about 3:00 p.m. the right rear wheel of the Ford Cortina slid into a deep rut in the middle of a wadi. The tire began to spin uselessly without gaining traction, and they were unable to free their automobile by pushing from behind. The couple then opened the trunk, planning on jacking up the right rear of the automobile, pushing the car off the jack, and thus freeing the wheel from the rut; but, upon examining the tool, they found the jack assembly incomplete. Without a metal base, the jack could not be used. After about an hour of vainly trying to use the jack and pushing the automobile by simple strength, they were dehydrated, tired, and dizzy. "We're really into trouble," Pike said to his wife. "I know," she said. Plainly, they would have to leave the automobile and walk out of the dry canyon for help. The couple then made a fatal decision. Several miles earlier, they had encountered two Bedouin herdsmen, with whom the bishop had tried unsuccessfully to communicate. "Qumran?" he had asked. The two herdsmen had shown no signs of having comprehended the place name or his question, and continued on their way. Now, the couple considered walking back that way, where they knew there was the possibility of finding the Bedouins again; but, convinced that they were within a mile or so of the Dead Sea, they decided to continue walking down the wadi toward what they believed was Qumran, "where we know there is water," they told each other.

The temperature was now at least one hundred and twenty degrees. The Pikes shared part of their remaining bottle of cola, and then began walking. The bishop stripped to his undershirt, carrying his trousers, and used his shirt as a head covering. Diane used their map to cover her head. Their differences in physical endurance soon became apparent. She was younger, and athletic; her husband was a former heavy drinker and smoker, unaccustomed to exercise. Pike soon seemed to become mentally distracted as they walked, and unable or unwilling to maintain a conversation. Commenting on the barren landscape, Diane attempted small talk: "This reminds me of the movie *Lawrence of Arabia*," she said. "What?" Pike asked, in a tone of voice that seemed "puzzled" to her. "Did you ever see it?" she asked. "Yes," he said, and then said no more for a long period of their walking.

They finished the remainder of the bottle of cola. At about 5:00 p.m., the bishop complained of heart pains, and insisted that they stop. Twice they rested in the shade of small fissure caves in the side of the wadi. Pike's pains subsided, but he spoke of being so light-headed that his condition reminded him, after six years of sobriety, of being drunk. Both were so enervated by the heat and their bodies' lack of water that they could not summon the energy even to raise their arms and brush away the flies that were immediately attracted to their faces as soon as they lay prone inside the shade of the caves. At their second resting place, Diane felt the bishop raise his hand to her lips, carefully cupping some liquid for her to drink, and she realized that he had urinated into his hand in order to provide her some relief from her thirst. Gratefully, she licked the liquid; he did the same, and then together they

spread the remaining urine over their legs, arms, and faces for its evap-
orative, cooling effect.

Inter faeces et urinam nascimur, Saint Augustine wrote in his *Confessions.* Both Pikes were now in danger of dying in the same excretory circumstances, at least partly as a consequence of Pike's decision, despite
having traveled to Israel on six earlier occasions, to proceed unguided
into the desert with no more liquid than two bottles of Coca-Cola.
Given the bishop's lifelong history of self-destructive behavior, the
question must be addressed of whether Pike consciously or unconsciously manipulated their trip to a suicidal ending for himself, and,
incidentally, a death for his younger wife. The considered answer is no.
In fact, Diane Pike later wrote that among her motivations in trying to
save herself and her husband was that if their bodies were found in the
desert, their detractors would claim, mistakenly or malignly, that the
couple had committed suicide. Pike's self-destructive actions appear to
have been the consequences not of suicidal impulses but of a profound
recklessness. He had always been reckless—of canonical law, of other
peoples' careers, of diocesan budgets, and, in the case of Maren
Bergrud, of another person's life. But this recklessness never assumed
that it would be his life in danger. That he had not planned this trip with
the idea of its becoming a final reckoning is supported by the facts of the
dinner engagement with a scholar arranged for that evening and Pike's
voluble discussions with Diane prior to this trip of the books he planned
to write after their return from Israel. Included in his future literary
projects was a memoir, he had told his wife, in which he intended to
reveal publicly his actions on the night of Maren Bergrud's death. He
was planning to title the book *Nothing to Hide.*

The bishop now insisted that he needed to sleep before walking any
further, and they agreed that Diane would walk ahead, and that he
would follow after he rested. She would return with help when she
reached Qumran, and, with hope, reunite with him before he had to
travel very far. At about 6:00 p.m., as the wadi suddenly darkened as the
sun went down behind the canyon walls, she left a torn portion of the
map with him and started out alone. "Tell them to bring lots of water,"
he told her in final instructions. "Tell them I'm feeling faint—to bring
something for that. Tell them to bring whisky; I'd even try whisky."
Diane later wrote that she was moved to tears by this last remark of his

willingness to drink liquor after years of abstinence. He added, apropos of both their fears of dying in the desert, "If I die here, I die in peace." They expressed their love for each other. Neither thought, or wished, to say the word *good-bye* before she left.

For the next ten hours, Diane Pike walked down the rocky path of the wadi under the partial light of a half-moon, frequently twisting her feet, falling down, and cutting her legs. "Every now and then," she told a *Jerusalem Post* reporter three days later, "I called into the night— 'Help, help, Shalom, Salaam Aleikum, Israel Army, help'—but I could only hear my own echo." In place of the one or two miles the couple had assumed they were from Qumran and the Dead Sea, the distance she had to walk to the end of the wadi was about eight miles; and rather than heading directly for Qumran, she was actually twelve miles south of the archaeological site. Early on, her left ankle twisted badly in her thong sandal; she ignored the pain of the injury, concentrated on keeping her weight on her right foot, and persevered. "I kept thinking, I've got to get help for Jim," she later told a reporter. Shortly after dawn, she literally stumbled into a group of Arab watchmen at a construction site on the Ein Feshka-Ein Gedi road along the Dead Sea coastline.

Given tea and treated kindly by the Arabs, Diane Pike was taken to Nahal Kallia, later to become Kibbutz Kalia in 1974, where her ankle was taped and her cuts cleaned and bandaged; the exhausted woman was then driven in a military vehicle to the Bethlehem police station. From there, at about 12:45 p.m. on September 2, the five-day search for the bishop began, involving at its height about three hundred military personnel and border police climbing over and walking through the Wadi ed Daraja, where the Pikes had become stranded. Their Ford Cortina was found just as they had left it in the wadi, and Diane, accompanying the searchers on their first day, was able to locate the cave where she and her husband had last rested. But there was no sign of the bishop.

The London *Times* had been the first to report the news, in a dispatch from its Tel Aviv correspondent dated September 2, of Pike reported as lost in the desert. By the following day, the *New York Times*, the *Jerusalem Post*, and the international wire services had all provided major stories on the search for Pike. Diane met with reporters and a battery of television cameramen in a press conference on September 4 in the Intercontinental Hotel. She was supported in walking by one of the hotel personnel, her legs bandaged and bright red with Mercurochrome spots. "She described the efforts of the search for the last two days and answered questions in a composed manner," the reporter from the *Jerusalem Post* wrote, "once or twice breaking into sobs."

She was interrupted during the conference in order to take a telephone call at the hotel desk, and she returned to the room full of journalists in a much more ebullient mood. "I have just received a call from my family in California," she told them, "who had word from Arthur Ford—a medium, a seer—that he has seen a vision of my husband alive in a cave not very far from where I left him." She also said she had received telephoned "readings" from two mediums, one in Tel Aviv, who had swung a small pendulum over a map of the Wadi ed Daraja and determined where the bishop was resting.

Nor was the first medium whom Pike had consulted in the U.K. remaining idle during his publicized disappearance. Ena Twigg produced what was certainly the most detailed paranormal contact with the missing bishop, purportedly summoning up the spirit of a deceased James Pike in a London séance on the evening of the same day as the news conference in Jerusalem. In an attempt at psychic veridicality, this séance was tape-recorded, and the transcription of Pike's purported remarks speaking through Twigg to Canon John Pearce-Higgins, who was also present, runs to nine printed pages. A sample from the transcript gives evidence, if nothing else, of Twigg's talent as an energetic impersonator (ellipses appear in the original text):

TWIGG/PIKE: Help me. . . . Oh, God, help me. . . . Help me, please help me. . . .

PEARCE-HIGGINS: We're trying to help you. . . . God bless you. . . . Who are you?

TWIGG/PIKE: Oh, you know who I am.

PEARCE-HIGGINS: You're Jim. . . . Are you dead?

TWIGG/PIKE: Yes, I'm nowhere. . . . And I don't belong anywhere, do I? . . .

PEARCE-HIGGINS: Yes, you weren't killed, were you? . . . You died naturally, didn't you? . . . Your heart?

TWIGG/PIKE: Choked. . . .

PEARCE-HIGGINS: Yes, choked. . . . What with?

TWIGG/PIKE: With the throat, you fool. . . .

The day following her press conference and a telephone call from Twigg telling her not to be hopeful for her husband's safety, Diane Pike returned on Friday to the Bethlehem police station in the company of her brother, Scott Kennedy, who had just arrived from the United States. There the two were told by the police chief, A Ben Schmauel, that the Israeli military, the town's police, and the border police no longer would be assisting the search. The reason officially given was that the troops and police were needed elsewhere. (The military was also not pleased that one of its soldiers had suffered a broken leg in a truck accident during the search.) The quest would continue, the police chief told them, using Bedouin tribesmen and some civilian trackers. In unspoken fact, both the military and the police had concluded that, after three days, the search no longer had the urgency of a rescue but was, rather, an attempt to find the bishop's body. A police official who chose to remain anonymous gave his opinion to a *New York Times* reporter: "A man without water and without shelter in the unbelievable conditions of the Judean wilderness—I don't think he can hold out."

The trackers found nothing. That night, Diane Pike telephoned Major Enosh Givati of the border police at his home and literally pleaded with this official to resume the search the next day based upon information she had received from mediums. Givati, perhaps reluctantly, agreed. "The search for the missing churchman has posed something of a dilemma for police and Israeli officials," the *New York Times* continued to report that week from its unnamed sources. "They are torn between the desire to help Mrs. Pike and to respond to any new information and their skepticism of the data being produced by seers and mediums." Scott Kennedy accompanied the small group of border police who set out for the desert early Saturday morning. They were joined by six volunteers from the Nature Preservation Society, an organization of hikers and naturalists familiar with the wadi. Late that afternoon, the searchers came across an extraordinary find: a deep pool of rainwater had collected in the wadi and been protected from evaporation by the overshadowing walls of the canyon. Floating in the water was a pair of men's undershorts. On their return to Jerusalem, they showed the garment to Diane, who excitedly identified the shorts as her husband's. Cheered by this evidence that the bishop might still be alive, she insisted on joining the trek the next day.

She was in radio contact with the searchers from a Jeep parked atop the wadi when, about 9:40 a.m. on September 7, they reported finding other articles belonging to the bishop. A pair of his sunglasses was found on the ground pointing to the left where the wadi bifurcated into two smaller canyons. When they entered the leftward wadi, into the area of connected canyons known as the Wadi Mashash, they came upon a plastic contact lens case, left with the bishop by his wife, floating in a smaller pool of water. Clearly, Pike had been attempting to mark a trail. Then, about 10:30 a.m., after they had advanced approximately one-quarter of a mile farther into the Wadi Mashash, they radioed another message: the bishop's body had been spotted, swollen and decomposing in the desert heat, lying in a kneeling position on a rocky ledge above the wadi floor. The bishop, apparently having followed what he thought was his wife's trail, seemed to have attempted to climb out of the wadi as it narrowed, perhaps thinking that she had also done so; he had almost made his way to the top of the wadi before falling about seventy feet to the ledge.

Diane Pike took the news of her husband's death calmly. She later wrote that, after the initial encouragement of finding her husband's undershorts at a pool of water, she had a dreamlike vision at about 3:30 a.m. of his soul departing his body, and she awoke with the intuitive knowledge that her husband was dead. She remained in the Jeep as a helicopter arrived to retrieve Pike's body from its precarious position. She and her brother then returned to Jerusalem. Eventually, a medical vehicle arrived, the bishop's body was loaded into it, and the ambulance with its wrapped contents began its slow, dusty drive to Tel Aviv and the pathologist's office.

Pike had died after his fall from the effects of broken ribs, a fractured leg, shock, and dehydration, the pathologist determined. There were no other signs of violence to his body, apparently disproving the visions of several mediums that he had been murdered by Bedouins. His death was estimated to have occurred five or six days earlier, meaning that after he left their resting place following his wife on September 1, he probably fell to his death perhaps as soon as September 2. Diane Pike was certain that he had become worried about her safety and had decided to go looking for his wife rather than staying in the comparative comfort of the small cave. She identified her husband's body the evening of the day it was found, aided by her recognizing his yellow shirt and black pants. Because of its advanced decomposition and the bishop's last statement to her that he would consider himself at peace should he die in the Israeli desert, she looked for a burial plot available the next day, assisted by the U.S. consul and Anglican friends.

St. Peter's Protestant Cemetery, maintained at Jaffa by the Anglican priest at Immanuel Church there, had a small plot available for a burial. The church agreed to assist in the bishop's internment. Shortly before sunset on September 8, about thirty people, the majority of them journalists, gathered at a grave dug that afternoon near a large fig tree and within sight of the Mediterranean coastline beyond the cemetery's boundaries. Diane Pike, her brother, a handful of the bishop's friends from Jerusalem, and four Israeli policemen were present; a group of curious Arab children watched from atop a wall. The cemetery itself was small but crowded with about three dozen other graves within it, some marked simply as containing an unknown Christian. Pike's burial service was read by the Rev. John Downing, an Episcopal priest and friend of the Pikes, from Santa Barbara. He had come to Israel to help search for the bishop but arrived only in time to help bury him. "The sun shall not burn thee by day nor the moon by night," Downing read from the Book of Common Prayer's service for burial of the dead. As he read, he let fall a trickle of the cemetery's sandy soil between his fingers to form the shape of a cross on the lead coffin and the gold-colored blanket covering it. Diane Pike afterward placed an engraved copper peace symbol atop her husband's coffin alongside the bishop's pectoral cross that had been removed from his body. "Love and peace, Jim," she said quietly. She then whispered a final prayer and nodded smiling toward the grave as the coffin was lowered into it. Downing embraced both Diane and her brother.

Eulogies and obituaries of Pike were by then being undertaken in the U.K. and the United States. The news of the bishop's death had brought a temporary halt to the Episcopal Church's national convention, meeting on the campus of Notre Dame University, and his death precluded the issue of the House of Bishops' vote on whether or not he had abandoned their communion. Like it or not, his fellow prelates would have to accept the fact that Pike had died and been buried a bishop. Norman Pittenger, his friend and coauthor, was then in residence at King's College, Cambridge, and his in memoriam to Pike, printed in the London *Times* on September 13, recorded what he saw as his friend's spiritual suffering and his accomplishments:

> His tragedy is that he did not feel accepted or wanted, especially after his remarriage; he "left the Church" because he felt that his recent marriage, after his divorce, was not accepted by the authorities of the Episcopal Church even in his diocese. Because he was what he was, did what he did, and wrote what he wrote, North American Christian thinking is bolder, more open, more generous towards new kinds of thought.

The diocese that had not accepted him politically in life welcomed him in death. That same week, a service was performed for Pike at Grace Cathedral. As with his installation as bishop in 1958, his funeral was televised in the San Francisco area. Diane Pike by then had returned to California and attended the September 12 ceremony in the congregation that included Esther Pike and her children and Jane Alvies Helvern, the bishop's first wife. The bishop's mother, Pearl Chambers, also was present, and wept softly throughout the service. In what the *San Francisco Examiner* the next day described as a "spontaneous, dramatic incident," Diane Pike, standing at the end of the first row, reached out her right hand and grasped the hand of Bishop Kilmer Myers, who had forbade Pike after his third marriage from conducting ceremonies at any church in the diocese. Myers had been requested by Diane to conduct this service, and was leading a procession down the center aisle of the cathedral. As the newspaper further described the incident, the text accompanied by a photograph of an obvious startled Myers:

> The bishop turned, smiled kindly and then started to rejoin the long procession But Mrs. Pike clutched his hand.
> As the bishop took a step, she leaned over the front of the pew and looked beseechingly at him in an obvious look for friendship for all in the jammed cathedral to observe.

After a few, apparently wordless moments, Myers resumed his place at the head of the procession and the service continued. In an ecumenical choice of speakers that was appropriate to the values of the deceased, both a Jewish rabbi and an Episcopal rector, each a friend to Pike, spoke of him "courageously walking along the narrow ridge of being in quest of deeper personal experience" and of the bishop's insistence that neither "powers, nor height, nor anything in all creation will be able to separate us from God's love."

In New York City, a high requiem mass was celebrated for Pike the following Sunday at St. Clement's Episcopal Church. Duke Ellington, a longtime friend of the bishop, led the congregation in a hymn, and then played what was described as a "melancholy piece" from his latest sacred composition. The *San Francisco Chronicle*, in reporting the mass, concluded its story by noting: "When the service ended, the church secretary, wearing a red and orange mini-dress, stood in front of the altar and invited newcomers to join the congregation." The *Chronicle*'s choice of detail seemed to indicate the reluctance of many other papers to let go as a subject this bishop whose practice of worldly Christianity and joyful acceptance of the secular world so often had provided journalists with a lively quote and a story-making image.

One reporter with a scholarly perspective later wrote what was perhaps the most eloquent and balanced eulogy of the bishop. John Cogley, former religion editor at the *New York Times*, had served as the project director at the Center for the Study of Democratic Institutions during Pike's fellowship there, and wrote about his colleague in the article "Man of Faith, Child of Doubt," published in *Life* magazine three weeks after Pike's body was recovered. Cogley wrote movingly and symbolically of how, in his final hours, Pike, "who last April broke with the organized Church found himself going it alone in an unknown terrain, cut off from human contact and wholly dependent upon his own resources." Yet the bishop Cogley remembered from the center was also the public figure who "gained a reputation for glibness and raw publicity-seeking" and possessed "perhaps no more than middling intellectual gifts." However, the facts of Pike's life taken together, he argued, "produced an extraordinary human being whose impact on the world of ideas far exceeded what might have been expected of him—a churchman who was neither scholar nor saint but the twentieth-century Christian writ large." Cogley then addressed his readers directly on why he perceived the life of the bishop as deserving of extraordinary and continuing attention:

> There may be a Jim Pike hidden in every man. Most of us are part believers in our own immortality, part doubters about our own significance, part men of faith, part children of doubt. Bishop Pike became a towering figure in modern life for one reason above all others: he mirrored our weakness, our uncertainty, our desperate clinging to old beliefs and frightened acceptance of new realities. If at times he seemed almost clownish, it may have been because there is an absurdity in the ambiguity we all share. When he embarrassed us, it may have been because he dared to say in public what most of us are ashamed to think even in private—for the believer, that one might be the victim of myth; for the agnostic, that one just might be cutting oneself off from worlds that truly exist.

In November 1970, Diane Pike and her brother returned to Israel and arranged for two large stones to be taken from the Judean Desert and brought to the Jaffa cemetery, one placed on the bishop's grave and the other fixed standing upright at its head. The sides of both stones were deliberately left unfinished to symbolically represent "the rough terrain in which Jim died," his widow said in an e-mail with the author in 2003. The headstone identifies the occupant of the grave as a former bishop of the Protestant Episcopal Church of the United States of America, and the stone lying atop the grave is inscribed with the New Testament verse most frequently quoted by Pike during his lifetime.

This stone was also engraved, at his widow's request, with a verse from the first-century Gnostic document the Mandaean Book of Prayer. As she later told Stringfellow and Towne, "I thought it would be a challenge to archaeologists to figure out what the heck *that* was, and how the Mandaean Book of Prayer is related to a Protestant Episcopal bishop." Although non-Christian, the Mandaean verse is biographically appropriate to Pike as his life, and death, is twinned to Gnosticism. Indeed, like the first-century journeys of Simon Magus, the reputed father of Gnosticism who also traveled throughout the Middle East with his consort and died from a fall, Pike's attempted journey to Qumram was a Gnostic pilgrimage. "The Gnostics were, above all, individualists," Pike's friend John Allegro wrote, and he then defined that individualism in terms that could be applied directly to Pike himself: "Self-discovery and self-fulfillment were everything. They felt themselves unfettered by the conventions of ordinary men." This self-fulfillment, as both Allegro and Pike agreed, could lead either to an extreme asceticism, as in the case of the commune at Qumram, or a noticeable libertinism, with which Pike was charged on occasion by his enemies. Common to both, however, was the belief that a gnosis, or knowledge acquired through a special text or learning, "can be appropriated," as Pike enthusiastically wrote in *If This Be Heresy*, "for present fulfillment by those who *know* the realities." It was in search of this fulfillment that Pike traveled with his wife to what he literally considered a Holy Land.

The Holy Land is also a graveyard. The port city of Jaffa, now practically enclosed by the modern city of Tel Aviv, had been the traditional port for two millennia for the arrival and embarkation for Christian pilgrims, not all of whom survived to return to their native lands. A few newer graves have been added to the Anglican cemetery since Pike's burial there, but the rough stones that mark the bishop's grave are easily found. They read:

JAMES A. PIKE

Bishop
(P.E.C.U.S.A.)
BORN 1913
Oklahoma City, OKLA.
DIED 1969
Judean Wilderness
*"We have this treasure in earthen vessels that the
transcendent power belongs to God and not to us."*
—II COR: 4:7
"And life is victorious."
—MANDAEAN BOOK OF PRAYER

Notes

Works cited frequently are identified by the following abbreviations:

COL   Columbia University, Columbiana Library or Rare Books and Manuscripts Library as indicated

DCA   Archives of the Diocese of California of the Episcopal Church

DNY   Archives of the Diocese of New York of the Episcopal Church

LCA   *Living Church Annual: The Yearbook of the Episcopal Church* (Harrisburg, Penn.: Morehouse-Gorham, 1922–). Annual serial of Episcopal clergy, personnel, property, and organizations. Retitled as *The Episcopal Church Annual* in 1953 by the same publisher, and thereafter abbreviated as *ECA*.

NYT   *New York Times* newspaper

SCU   Archives of Santa Clara University

SFC   *San Francisco Chronicle* newspaper

ST   William Stringfellow and Anthony Towne, *The Death and Life of Bishop Pike* (Garden City, N.Y.: Doubleday, 1976).

SYU   Bishop James A. Pike Papers, Syracuse University Library, Special Collections Research Center

Citations for the general description of the Wadi Mashash and Pike's death in the Introduction are provided on pp. 261–63 of the endnotes for chapter IX, which describes his death in greater detail.

I   The Pious Boy from Hollywood

Page

12   **whether he was related:** SYU: Box 52, Folder "Memorabilia," n.d.

13   **She had made her way** to **diocese of Owensboro, Kentucky:** Private genealogical research on the Pike family conducted for the author in 2000 by Hattie Clements, Bardstown, KY; Benjamin J. Webb, *The Centenary of Catholicism in Kentucky* (Utica, KY: McDowell Publications, n.d.), 26–27, 156–57, 420–21; Sister Mary Romona Mattingly, *The Catholic Church on the Kentucky Frontier 1785–1812* (Washington, D.C.: Catholic University of America, 1936), 182–83, 190–93, 200–201, 220–21.

13   **control of their marriage** to **"James had known no father":** *ST*: 8, 270. Stringfellow's and Towne's biography reproduces the texts of a large number of letters and interviews by and about Pike that are not catalogued within the collection of Pike's papers at Syracuse University or within the Stringfellow collection at the Cornell University Library. They apparently remained in the possession of Stringfellow and Towne, or the Pike or Kennedy families, and were not catalogued or donated. The two-decade friendship of Stringfellow and Pike does give credence to the existence of these documents, although their content is substantiated in this biography by other primary or secondary sources whenever possible. Citations to *ST* are to the pages on which the letters or interviews are reproduced or excerpted.

14   **average yearly salary:** *Statistical Abstract of the United States 1925* (Washington, D.C.: Government Printing Office, 1925), chronological and geographic table, "Public Elementary and Secondary Schools: Number and Salary of Teachers," 100–101.

14   **"not too bad to look at"** to **"a good father":** *ST*: 72–73.

15   **6248 Afton Place** to **312 Azuma Street:** SYU: Box 2, Folder "Appli-

cation to NYS Bar," Section 2, "Exact address of every residence . . . ,"
n.d.; Basil Woon, *Incredible Land: A Jaunty Baedeker to Hollywood and the
Great Southwest* (New York: Liveright, 1933), 16–17, 33, 41, 70–71; *Los
Angeles: A Guide to the City and Its Environs Compiled by Workers of the
Writers' Program of the Works Project Administration in Southern Califor-
nia* (New York: Hastings House, 1951), 243, 239, 237; *The WPA Guide
to California: The Federal Writers' Project Guide to 1930s California* (New
York: Pantheon Books, 1984), 193, 197, 223, 380.

15 **"weird babble of tongues"** to **"heresy in embryo":** quoted in Harvey Cox, *Fire From Heaven: The Rise of Pentecostal Spirituality and the
Reshaping of Religion in the Twenty-first Century* (Reading, Mass: Addi-
son-Wesley, 1994), 59; SYU: Box 51, "Glossolalia, May, 1963."

15 **"a regular routine"** to **her second and third husbands:** *ST:* 74, 270

16 **"obedience due a father":** SYU: Box 2, Folder "Application to NYS
Bar," February 1956; Box 52, Folder "1936–1949," "Memorial to
Claude McFadden," n.d.

16 *Poinsettia* to **"Well, Mommy":** Photocopies of pp. 49 and 102 of *Poinsettia* of 1930 provided to the author in 2000 by Jerry Anker, president,
Hollywood High Alumni Association; *ST:* 74.

17 **"good men who are clever":** quoted in Gerald McKevitt, *The University of Santa Clara: A History 1851–1977* (Stanford, Calif: Stanford University Press, 1974), 213, hereafter cited as McKevitt, *History.* The
institution became known officially as Santa Clara University in 1985.
See http://www.scu.edu/news/facts/history.

17 **parody of Benito Mussolini** to *"Pax Christi":* Gerald McKevitt, letter to author, December 9, 2000; SCU, Kropp File: Kropp, letter to
James Pike, November 1, 1938; Kropp, letter to James Pike, February
15, 1966; SCU, Giambastiani File: Giambastiani, letter to editor,
National Catholic Reporter, August 31, 1968; SCU, Kropp File: Kropp,
letter to James Pike, March 13, 1936.

18 **"thoroughgoing agnostic humanist":** James A. Pike, "Speak Out
Boldly and Stay In," *National Catholic Reporter,* August 14, 1968.

18 **the only poor grade:** SYU: Box 52, "Academic Transcripts," August
21, 1943.

18 **"Speak Out Boldly":** Pike, "Speak Out Boldly."

20 **"Never once!":** SCU, Giambastiani File: Giambastiani, letter to editor, *National Catholic Reporter*, August 31, 1968.

21 **"a moral impossibility":** William James, *The Varities of Religious Experience: A Study in Human Nature* (New York: Random House, 1994), 218.

21 **"Dear friend Jimmy":** SCU, Giambastiani File: letter to editor, August 31, 1968.

21 **booed by his classmates:** McKevitt, *History*, 245.

22 **"he didn't like it":** *ST:* 74.

22 **"started out alone"** to **"camp was welcome":** SYU: Box 67, "We're Back," n.d., 50–51.

23 **"Brother James Pike"** to published the leading article: SYU: Box 52, Folder "1936–1949," "Field Member Goes to Yale," *The Paper Book: Official Publication of Delta Theta Phi* (May 1936): 79–80.

23 **"the New Deal"** to **questioned them as being "pink":** James A. Pike, ed., *Modern Canterbury Pilgrims* (New York: Morehouse-Gorham, 1956), 310, hereafter cited as Pike, *Canterbury; Encyclical Letter of His Holiness Pius XI by Divine Providence Pope* (Washington, D.C.: National Catholic Welfare Conference, 1936), 11; Raphael M. Huber, *Our Bishops Speak . . . Resolutions of Episcopal Committees and Communications of the Administrative Board of the National Catholic Welfare Conference 1919–1951* (Milwaukee, Wisc.: Bruce Publishing Company, 1952), xi, xxiii, 191, 194–95; SCU: Pike File, James Pike, letter, June 14, 1932: "P.S. I received a letter from the Catholic Council on Industrial Relations (a branch of the N.C.W.C.) from Washington, D.C. They felt we had been somewhat unfair to them in the *Owl*—the article 'Is the N.C.W.C. Pink?' . . . They sent me a package of pamphlets." Although Pike refers to the recipient as "Father," it is uncertain whether this letter written from Los Angeles was addressed to Kropp or to Giambastiani, but the latter was the faculty advisor to the student literary publication, *The Owl*.

25 **"student strikes against the war":** James Wechsler, *Revolt on the Campus* (Seattle: University of Washington Press, 1973), 180.

25 **"too smart to be at Santa Clara"** to **"rare as hens' teeth":** *ST:* 247, 262.

26 **"nostalgic appeal":** Pike, *Canterbury*, 310.

26 **"nothing seemed to fit"** to **"I wish he had":** *ST:* 75, 235.

27 **something of a dramatic side:** See the history of St. Mary's and the biography of Fr. Dodd on the church's Web site, http://acca.asn.au/AAA92/9210SM.html.

28 **"look like mother":** SYU: Box 57, Folder "Professional Records Confidential Papers on Homosexuality," 14.

28 **Pike and Alvies were married** to **"just not for James":** SYU: Box 2, Folder, "Application to NYS Bar," Section 1, "If you have ever been divorced or separated . . . ," n.d.; *ST:* 75.

11   Becoming Jim Pike, Lawyer and Priest

29 **Pike and Fisher** to **third job in 1938–39:** SYU: Box 1, Folder "1943," "Professional Experience," September 24, 1943; see also Michael L. Mickler, "James A. Pike, Bishop and Iconoclast" (Ph.D. diss., University of California at Berkeley, 1989), 11, hereafter cited as Mickler.

30 **"good piece of work":** SYU: Box 1, Folder "1940," Felix Frankfurter, letter to James Pike, December 10, 1940.

30 **"help the situation"** to **"ran out of the church":** *ST:* 246, 76. It had not been necessary for Alvies to have been confirmed as an Episcopalian prior to their marriage, as the national canons required only that the presiding priest "have ascertained that at least one of the parties has received Holy Baptism." See *Constitution and Canons for the Governance of the Protestant Episcopal Church in the United States of America* (Chicago: W. B. Conkey Company, 1949), 45, hereafter cited as *Constitution and Canons*.

31 **divorce was recorded:** SYU: Box 65, Folder "Divorce Papers 1940–1941," "Final Judgment of Divorce," October 8, 1941.

32 **"divorce on the grounds of adultery":** *ST:* 300.

32 **"I passed St. Paul's Cathedral"**: SYU: Box 48, Folder "Election as Bishop, Statement re: Divorce," n.d., 1958.

33 **Church's general convention of 1937**: Canon Law Institute, ed. Kenneth E. North, April 16, 2002, http://www.canonlaw.org/article _matrimony.htm. See also, *Constitution and Canons*, 47–48.

33 **"never was a real marriage"** to **"consider yourself in good standing"**: *ST*: 300–301.

35 **"the ol' morale"**: *ST*: 327–28.

35 **he was transferred**: SYU: Box 1, Folder "1942," Chester T. Lane, letter to Director of Naval Procurement, September 21, 1942.

36 **"clean the matter up"** to **"in between times"**: *ST*: 301, 328.

36 **birth to their first child**: The birth dates of Pike's four children are listed in DNY, the notes of William J. Moll, former director of public relations, Cathedral of St. John the Divine, Cathedral Named Persons File.

36 **"give serious intellectual consideration"**: Pike, *Canterbury*: 310.

37 *Nature, Man, and God* to **"nothing is secular to God"**: SYU: Box 47, "Professional Records Lawyer 1936–1944," "List of books studied prior to ordination," n.d. Although written for a scholarly readership, a good explication for laity of *Nature, Man, and God* and, particularly, of Temple's concept of the sacramental universe is Joseph E. Allen, "William Temple's Idea of Religious Existence; Seen as a Contribution to the Recent Philosophical Discussion of That Subject" (Ph.D. diss., Drew University, Madison, N.J., 1978), 175–76.

38 **"It is a great mistake"**: quoted in James Pike, *The Church, Politics, and Society: Dialogues on Current Problems* (New York: Morehouse-Gorham, 1955), 16–17.

38 **"more Catholic than the Church"**: Pike, *Canterbury*: 311.

39 **"I want to assure you"** to **"Axis powers stand for"**: *ST*: 265, 258.

40 **"Stop reading heretics!"**: SYU: Box 1, Folder "1943," Walter Kropp, postcard to James Pike, September 23, 1943.

40 **"I need only mention"**: SYU: Box 1, Folder "1943," James Pike, letter to Walter Kropp, October 28, 1943.

41 **"not on the Index"**: SYU: Box 1, Folder "January 1944–December 1948," James Pike, letter to Walter Kropp, January 19, 1944.

41 **William James had termed a "first-born":** William James, *The Origins of Religious Experience: A Study in Human Nature* (New York: Random House, 1944), 93.

41 **"devote my full time to the Church":** SYU: Box 47, "Professional Records Lawyer 1936–1944," "Application for admission to postulancy pursuant to Canon 1 (I) (111)," n.d.

42 **April 13, 1943 to "if you were now petitioning":** SYU: Box 52, Folder "1936–1949," news clipping, n.d.; Box 1, Folder "1942 Naval Orders," T. R. Rawlings, letter to James Pike, July 21, 1942; *ST:* 302. References in the text to the duration of Pike's marriage to Yanovsky are counted from the earlier date of their marriage in civil court, January 29, 1942, rather than the church ceremony and parish registration of their union fifteen months later in 1943.

42 **"husbands of one wife":** I Timothy 2:12, *The New Oxford Bible with the Apocrypha, RSV* (New York: Oxford University Press, 1977), 1442.

42 **apparently there is no record:** Queries by the author to the Episcopal diocese of Los Angeles in regard to the location and contents of the Bishop Bloy archives went unanswered.

43 **"the basic facts" in 1943:** DNY: Box 82, "The Basic Facts Are These," n.d.

44 **"a certificate from seminary":** SYU: Box 47, Folder "Professional Records Lawyer 1936–1944," "Postulants Standing Committee of the Diocese of Washington," n.d.

44 **"make Jim face up":** *ST:* 293.

45 **ordained at St. John's to "by the help of God":** SYU: Box 1, Folder "January 1944–December 1948," Angus Dun, letter to James Pike, December 12, 1944.

45 **"There is given hope":** William Temple, *Nature, Man, and God: Being the Gifford Lectures Delivered in the University of Glasgow in the Academic Years 1932–1933 and 1933–1934* (London: Macmillan, 1934), 486.

45 **"the law is a noble profession" to "very best universities":** *ST:* 275, 272. Pike did receive a last-minute telegram from an Oxford University administrator, after he had made arrangements to attend Union and General seminaries, advising him that he could be accepted at Oxford by 1946, provided he brought "degree certificates" attesting to his

knowledge of Greek and that he understood that the "accommodation for [his] family [is] very scarce." He apparently did not reply. SYU: Box 1, Folder "January 1944–December 1948," "Radiogram," September 1, 1945.

46 **"it does not seem likely"**: SYU: Box 1, Folder "January 1944–December 1948," H. S. Williamson, letter to James Pike, November 29, 1944.

48 **"someone raised the issue"** to **"promptly confirmed"**: DNY: Box 82, "Basic Facts," n.d.

48 **an active social life** to **"Dear Paul"** and **"Dear Jim"**: SYU: Box 61, Folder; "September 1946–August 1947," "Engagement Calendar, General Theological Seminary and Union Theological Seminary," author's examination of Pike correspondence in the Paul Tillich Archives, Andover Harvard Theological Library.

49 **"eternal breaks into the temporal"** to the **"demonic"**: quoted in *The Thought of Paul Tillich*, ed. James L. Adams et al. (San Francisco: Harper & Row: 1985), 220; and in Wilhelm and Marion Pauck, *Paul Tillich: His Life and Thought*, vol. 1 (New York: Harper & Row, 1976), 108.

50 **"Episcopal Chair of the Bible"**: SYU: Box 1, Folder "January 1944–December 1948," John E. Hines, letter to James Pike, February 24, 1947.

III   Making It: From Poughkeepsie to Columbia University

51 **an old-money neighborhood**: *New York: A Guide to the Empire State Compiled by Workers of the Writers' Program of the Work Projects Administration in the State of New York*, "Poughkeepsie," (New York: Oxford University Press, 1946), 282–83; author's visit to Christ Church grounds, October 2001.

52 **"High Church"** and **"Low Church"** to **point of contention**: William W. Manross, *The Episcopal Church in the United States, 1800–1840: A Study in Church Life* (New York: Columbia University Press, 1938), 43, 232.

53 **two brass candleholders:** *ST:* 121.

54 **gain of 155 Episcopalians:** SYU: Box 47, Folder "*Christ Church Courier,* vols. 1–3, 1947–1949," hereafter cited as *CCC,* July 1949.

54 **nursery school to Canterbury Players:** *CCC,* August 29, 1947; *CCC,* March 25, 1949; *CCC,* March 7, 1947; *CCC,* January 23, 1948.

54 **" 'People travel miles' ":** SYU: Box 52, Folder "1950–52," news clipping, "They Travel Miles," *New Hampshire Churchman,* May 1950: 4.

54 **"Repent Ye":** SYU: Folder "Sermons 1946–48," "Repent Ye," dated "Adv IV '46 Xch."

56 **"how she put up with him":** Elizabeth Daniels, interview with the author, Poughkeepsie, New York, October 2001.

56 **Men's Club clambake to "doing fine":** *CCC,* October 1, 1948; *CCC,* March 7, 1947; *CCC,* August 27, 1948; *CCC,* January 21, 1949; *CCC,* May 6, 1949; *CCC,* November 26, 1948.

57 **name had been formidable:** Kit and Frederica Konolige, *The Power of Their Glory: America's Ruling Class: The Episcopalians* (New York: Wyden Books, 1978), 21, 71; *NYT:* "Arthur Kinsolving Dead at 77; Rector of St. James for 22 Years," March 29, 1977.

58 **"Dear Mr. Pike":** SYU: Box 1, Folder "January 1944–December 1948," Arthur L. Kinsolving, letter to James Pike, February 3, 1947.

59 **"Marxist" to "avowed Communists":** *CCC,* June 24, 1949; SYU: Box 47, Folder "Vassar Controversy," typed manuscript, sermon delivered at Christ Church, "The Fate of Christianity at Vassar College," June 26, 1949.

59 **"A stand was taken":** SYU: Box 1, Folder "1949–1950," quoted in news clipping, "Dr. Pike Supports Protests by Catholics of Vassar Story, Then Hits Out at Faculty Pair," *Poughkeepsie New Yorker,* June 20, 1949.

59 **"churches should 'clean house' ":** quoted in Elizabeth Price, "The Outspoken Dean," *This Week: The Sunday Magazine* (supplement) October 18, 1953: 10, 56.

60 **"increased sharply" to "45% are ours":** *The Magnificent Enterprise: A Chronicle of Vassar College,* eds. Dorothy A. Plum and George B. Dowell (Poughkeepsie, N.Y.: Vassar College, 1961), 98, 100–101; SYU: Box 1, Folder "January 1944–December 1948," James Pike, letter to Benjamin H. Smith, December 29, 1948.

60 **"Meet the Clergy"**: SYU: Box 52, Folder "1936–1949," news clipping, "Meet the Clergy: Dr. Charles McCormick," *Poughkeepsie New
Yorker*, July 4, 1948.

61 **"Mr. McCormick does not regard"**: SYU: Box 1, Folder "January
1944–December 1948," James Pike, letter to Charles G. Profitt,
November 3, 1947.

61 **"that salesman"**: SYU: Box 1, Folder "January 1944–December
1948," quoted in James Pike, letter to Sarah Blanding, December 1,
1948.

61 **"I am only an Englishman"** to **"no consequence to me"**: SYU: Box
1, Folder "June 1949–December 1949," Bryan Green, copy of letter to
Vassar student not fully identified ("Dear Betsy"), November 7, 1949;
Bryan Green, letter to Sarah Blanding, November 21, 1949. Green
is the subject of "Anglican Evangelist," *Time*, December 13, 1948:
64–65.

62 **"My Dear Mr. Pike"** to **"an un-Christian influence"**: SYU: Box 1,
Folder "January 1944–December 1948," Sarah Blanding, letter to
James Pike, November 25, 1948; James Pike, letter to Sarah Blanding,
December 1, 1948.

63 **"not dignifying Mr. Pike"**: COL, Columbiana Library, James A. Pike:
Biographical File: Charles G. McCormack, letter to Ed McCarthy,
October 23, 1953.

63 **"I am hurt"** to **"does not hold the Christian faith"**: SYU: Box 1,
Folder "February–May 1949," James Pike, letter to Sarah Blanding,
April 5, 1949. In this letter, Pike again complains to Blanding of the
faculty's use of the "salesman" epithet.

63 **"context of Communism"**: COL: McCormack, letter to Ed
McCarthy, October 23, 1953.

64 **assistant for Pike** to **"student work at Vassar College"**: *CCC*, May
16, 1947; COL: McCormack, letter to Ed McCarthy, October 23,
1953; "Dr. Pike Supports Protests by Catholics of Vassar Story, Then
Hits Out at Faculty Pair," *Poughkeepsie New Yorker*, June 20, 1949.

64 **Episcopal chaplain to Vassar**: SYU: Box 57, Folder "Rector, Christ
Church . . . Position Statements, To the Editor," n.d. See also his biographical listing in *The Union Theological Seminary . . . Alumni Directory*

(Alumni Office 1970), 335, and the ambiguous wording in *ST*, 281: "In Poughkeepsie, for instance, while rector of Christ Church and Episcopal Chaplain to Vassar College, Pike. . . ."

64 **"assumption of the title":** COL: McCormack, letter to Ed McCarthy, October 23, 1953.

65 **"steps will be taken"** to **"Jesus said":** SYU: Box 1, Folder "June 1949–December 1949," James Pike, letter to Mrs. John D. Rockefeller, July 8, 1949; SYU: Box 1, Folder "January 1949–December 1949," James Pike, letter to Mrs. James Pilliod, June 10, 1949.

65 **closed the deal:** COL, James A Pike: Central Files: Albert C. Jacobs, letter to James Pike, April 26, 1948; Secretary of the University, letter to James Pike, January 3, 1949; Albert C. Jacobs, letter to James Pike, April 23, 1949.

66 **"seamy side"** to **over 40 percent:** *CCC:* May 16, 1947; *CCC:* November 14, 1947; *CCC,* June 10, 1949.

66 **a startling loss:** *LCA:* 1948: 292; *LCA,* 1949: 274.

67 **"thoroughly evil reflection"** to **"deplore the investigation":** SYU: Box 1, Folder "February–May 1950," Charles Shattuck, letter to Sarah Blanding, May 9, 1949; SYU: Box 1, Folder "June 1949–December 1949," Philip A. Swartz, letter to Sarah Blanding, September 12, 1949.

67 **445 Riverside Drive:** *CCC:* August 1949.

68 **"should give real consideration"** to **Eisenhower regarded Jacobs:** *NYT:* "Albert C. Jacobs Is Dead at 76," October 30, 1976; COL: James A. Pike: Biographical File.

69 **this Italian Renaissance chapel** to **"maximum flowering":** *St. Paul's Chapel,* Columbia University, February 15, 2002, available at http://www.columbia.edu./cu/ear/stpauls/about.html; author's visits to Chapel, October 2001 and April 2002; *NYT:* "Columbia Chaplain Bids Faiths Be Free," October 3, 1949; *NYT:* "Dr. Pike Is Installed," October 12, 1949.

69 **"lowest common denominator":** SYU: Box 1, Folder "June 1949–December 1949," James Pike, letter to Sarah Blanding, December 8, 1949.

69 **"More Courses in Religion":** *NYT:* "More Courses in Religion," April 4, 1950.

70 **"smooth orthodoxy":** *ST:* 285.

70 **"We have harmony all round":** SYU: Box 1, Folder "June 1949–December 1949," James Pike, letter to Sarah Blanding," December 8, 1949.

70 **"exceeded one of my accounts"** to **"today requested transfer":** COL, James A. Pike: Central Files: James Pike, letter to Grayson Kirk, June 9, 1950; James Pike, memorandum with attachments to Grayson Kirk, December 15, 1950; James Pike, letter to Assistant Provost, June 30, 1951; W. Emerson Gentzler, letter to James A. Pike, October 5, 1950.

71 **"pitfalls":** quoted in Mickler, 77, 345.

72 **"for the sake of the record":** *The Union Theological Seminary . . . Alumni Directory* (New York: Alumni Office, 1970), 335; COL, James A. Pike: Central Files: James Pike, letters to Richard Herpers, May 4, 1951, May 29, 1951.

72 **Pike threatened:** *ST:* 283.

73 **a good name:** DNY: Box 83, "Invitation to Join the Friends of the Cathedral," n.d., for Profitt et al.

IV   The Deanship at St. John the Divine

75 **two American football fields:** *Stone by Stone: The Cathedral's Story,* ed. Episcopal Diocese of New York, March 13, 2002, available at http://www.stjohndivine.org/vtour/history; SYU: Box 60, Folder, "Brochure Describing Cathedral . . . ," n.d.

75 **"mini Vatican":** Mickler, 22.

75 **"Jim was more effective":** *ST:* 298.

75 **Pike was installed:** DNY: Cathedral Named Persons Box, "The Order of Service for the Installation of the Reverend James Albert Pike . . . as Fifth Dean of the Cathedral Church of Saint John the Divine on Saturday, February Sixteenth in the Year of Our Lord One Thousand Nine Hundred and Fifty-Two at Three o'clock in the Afternoon"; *NYT:* "Dr. Pike Installed as St. John's Dean," February 17, 1952.

76 **"privately delighted"** to **"Somehow he had managed"**: *ST*: 287–89.

77 **"un-American"**: *NYT*: "Catholics in Welfare Body Bar Birth Control Agency," January 15, 1953; *NYT*: "Restudy Is Asked in Parent Unit Ban," January 18, 1953; *NYT*: "Parenthood Vote Protested by Pike," January 26, 1953.

77 **"degree in white divinity"**: *NYT*: "Dean Pike Rejects a 'White' Divinity," February 13, 1953.

78 **"owning dioceses"**: SYU: Box 49, Folder "Sewanee Controversy— Department of Christian Social Relations Report," 1953, 2.

78 **"swallowed up in the earth"** to **"like to have a Sewanee degree"**: Wayne J. Holman, *Bishop Pike Again* (self-published, 1977), 18, 2–3 "Exhibit V," n.p.

78 **resignations of eight religion faculty members:** SYU: Box 49, Folder "Sewanee Controversy—Confidential Report . . . March 1953," 4–5; Box 49, Folder "Sewanee Controversy—Letter of Faculty," n.d.

78 **"I cannot in conscience"**: SYU: Box 49, Folder "Sewanee—Refusal of Degree Press Conference," February 12, 1953; Holman, *Bishop Pike Again*, 18; see also Mickler, 109–14.

79 **" 'I Like Ike' "**: SYU: Box 2, Folder "Correspondence February," Howard Johnson, letter to James Pike, February 13, 1953.

79 **"international center for Anglican culture"**: DNY: Box 83 "Secretary to Dean Pike," n.d., 2.

80 **"we want you here"** to **"procure same at Whipple's"**: SYU: Box 4, Folder "January 1954," James Pike, letter to Howard Johnson, January 30, 1954; James Pike, letter to Howard Johnson, February 15, 1954. Johnson mentions the personal loan in SYU: Box 4, Folder "Correspondence December 1953," Howard Johnson, letter to James and Esther Pike, December 5, 1953.

80 **"at least 7,000"**: *NYT*: "Eisenhower Scores Attack on Clergy; McCarthy Aide Out," July 10, 1953.

80 **"simply not true"**: SYU: Box 81, Folder "Sermons 1954, March 21 on McCarthyism," press release on sermon, March 22, 1954.

81 **"I will only mention"**: SYU: Box 49, Folder "Sewanee Letter of Faculty," James Pike, letter to Charles R. Henry, February 24, 1953.

82   **Pike spoke in a rapid:** Author's viewing of following: *A Discussion with James A. Pike*, 1955; *Different Approaches to the Gospel*, 1955; *The Church and Socio-Economic-Political Affairs*, 1954; *A Christmas Sermon*, 1954. All videocassettes from original 16 mm film, National Council of Churches of Christ, reproduced on VHS with permission of Library of Union Theological Seminary, Virginia.

83   **"People usually think that a myth":** James A. Pike, *Doing the Truth* (Garden City, N.Y.: Doubleday, 1955), 68.

83   **"I think of it as strategy":** SYU: Box 10, Folder "Correspondence November 1957," James Pike, letter to Norman Pittenger, November 18, 1957.

83   **"reasoned commendation":** James A. Pike and John W. Pyle, *The Church, Politics, and Society* (New York: Morehouse-Gorham, 1955), 8.

83   **"highly provisional solutions":** Harvey Cox, *The Secular City: Secularization and Urbanization in Theological Perspective* (New York: Macmillan, 1965), 60–63.

84   **Video** to **Ad Lib Conversation:** DNY: Box 83, television script, *Dean Pike*, Sunday, October 9, 1953, 1:30–2:00 p.m."; DNY, Box 83, press release for *Dean Pike*, October 4, 1955.

84   **first successful program** to **DuMont Network:** Christopher O. Lynch, *Selling Catholicism: Bishop Sheen and the Power of Television* (Lexington, KY: University Press of Kentucky, 1998), 7, 23–24, 27.

85   **"dining room, or whatnot"** to **"commercial for God":** COL, Oral History Collection, Rare Books and Manuscripts Library: *Reminiscences of James A. Pike* (February 21, 1961), 2, 3, 4, 11, 13.

86   **"Baby Doll of Times Square"** to **"I don't think that I sinned":** *NYT:* "About New York: A Red-Blond Beauty with 75-Foot Legs?" October 22, 1954; *NYT:* "Cardinal Scores 'Baby Doll' Film," December 17, 1956; *NYT:* "Pike Backs Right to See 'Baby Doll,' " December 24, 1956.

87   **"blood of the Hungarians"** to **"funds from oil interests":** *NYT:* "Pike Assails U.S. on Mideast Arms," February 20, 1956; *NYT:* "Pike Chides U.S. Policy Abroad," November 19, 1956.

87   **"basically prophetic":** ST: 110.

87   **"my own Jewishness":** SYU: Box 65, Folder "Articles," James A. Pike, "A Christian Looks at Israel" *Jewish Heritage* (Fall 1958): 38; SYU: Box

48, Folder "Professional Records Itinerary of Trip to Israel 1956," February 9–February 16, 1956; *NYT:* "Dean Pike Going to Middle East; He and Wife Will Spend 12 Days in Israel and Jordan—Will See Scrolls," February 7, 1956.

88 ***"prophets* are raised up":** Pike, *Doing the Truth*, 47.

88 **"known as 'liberal Catholics' "** to **"this anti-liberal mood":** quoted in Mickler, 279.

89 **"This is not Daddy":** DNY: Cathedral Named Persons File: Catherine Pike, remark quoted in script prepared by Catherine Pike for ABC network, July 19, 1956.

90 **Pike had just received the news:** *NYT:* "Pike Elected California Bishop, But He Defers Decision on Post," February 5, 1958.

91 ***"Everyone* likes to write"** to **"complete break with the preceding":** SYU: Box 48, Folder "Election as Bishop Confidential Report the Very Reverend James A. Pike," September 30, 1957, 5; SYU: Box 48, Folder "Election as Bishop—Nominating Speech," n.d., 4–5.

91 **votes were razor-thin:** SYU: Box 48, Folder "Testimony of Election," February 4, 1958.

92 **"must have known"** to **"give my consent":** *ST:* 304, 302.

93 **"matter of permanent record":** "Canon 18. Of Regulations Respecting Holy Matrimony," *Constitution and Canons*, 47–48.

93 **"shock and concern":** SYU: Box 48, Folder "Election as Bishop Statement re; Divorce," Albert Colbourne, letter to "Presidents of Standing Committees," February 28, 1958.

93 **"My wife and I fought that"** to **"genuine marriage and four children":** *ST:* 110, 298.

94 **"Basic Facts":** SYU: Box 48, Folder "Election as Bishop Statement re: Divorce," n.d., 1958. This folder includes rough drafts with notations by both Pike and Rauch of the letter consequently sent above Rauch's name alone, and also drafts of the first-person statement, in many passages identical to Rauch's letter, issued by Pike.

94 **back at the deanery** to **answer was no:** SYU: Box 48, Folder "Election as Bishop Vote Tally Sheets," n.d.; SYU: Box 48, Folder "Refusals of Consent," Standing Committee of the Diocese of Fond du Lac, letter to Standing Committee of the Diocese of California, March 7,

1958; Standing Committee of the Diocese of South Carolina, letter to Standing Committee of the Diocese of California, March 7, 1958.

95 **vote had been close:** *NYT:* "Final Approval Given Pike as New Bishop," April 8, 1958; Box 48, Folder "Election as Bishop—Copies of Documents," Henry Knox Sherrill, letter to James Pike, April 1, 1958.

95 **"*both* brains and sense":** SYU: Box 12, Folder "Correspondence February 1–5, 1958," Norman Pittenger, letter to James Pike, February 5, 1958.

96 **"bishop *and* a prophet"** to **"people were hurt":** *ST:* 110–11.

v   An Unconventional Bishop on Nob Hill

97 **May 15, 1958** to **"not as a first, resort":** SYU: Box 48, Folder "Consecration Sermon, 'Bishops—Bound and Free'," May 15, 1958.

99 **"definitely tops":** SYU: Box 15, Folder "October 1959–November 1959," James Pike, letter to unidentified recipient, November 13, 1958.

99 **"Reverend Father"** to **Mark Hopkins Hotel:** SYU: Box 48, Folder, "Election as Bishop, Preparations for Consecration, the Consecrator, the Consecration . . . ," n.d.; Luncheon Committee, letter to "Gentlemen of the Clergy," April 16, 1958.

100 **"derived from other people":** quoted in Jerome Ellison, "Battling Bishop," *Saturday Evening Post*, October 7, 1961: 42.

100 **"fastest-growing area"** to **"lapsed Methodist":** SYU: Box 68, Folder "Writings, Articles 'One Diocesan Customary' *Witness* Draft A," 3. For a summary of the increases in population and changes in demographics, see "California, Here They Come," *Time*, December 21, 1959: 14.

101 **"This is a place":** "Montgomery Street Chapel," *Newsweek*, May 18, 1958: 100.

101 **"it is the Lord's Table":** *NYT:* "Bishop Pike Stirs Coast Diocese by Steps for Unity of Churches," April 3, 1960.

101 **"a man-made barrier"** to **"his original denomination":** James A. Pike, " 'That They May Be One': In Reply to Professor Otwell," *Christian Century*, January 13, 1960: 46.

102 **"super-Protestanism":** quoted in "The Episcopal Methodist," *Time*, December 21, 1959: 58.

102 **"in-groupness among some Episcopal"** to **"no man's orders":** Pike, " 'That They May Be One'," 47.

103 **California customary** to **"they can't breathe":** Pike's customary was reprinted in full in *The Living Church*, August 23, 1959: 10, 13; SYU: Box 68, Folder "Writings Articles 'One Diocesan Customary' *Witness* Draft A," 12, 5, 9. For letters from Episcopalians opposed to open communion and to Pike's choice of word, "Zoroasterian," see "Letters," *The Living Church*, September 6, 1959: 3, 17.

104 **"Prelatic":** quoted in Mickler, 226–77.

105 **"bigger and bolder":** SYU: Box 68, Folder "Writings Articles 'One Diocesan Customary,' *Witness*, Draft A," 3. This phrase became a favorite of Pike's.

105 **"Hegel in a chasuble":** Leslie P. Fairfield, "Modern Decline and Biblical Renewal: The Episcopal Church from 1970–2000; Anglo-Catholic Renewal," *American Anglican Council*, November 26, 2002, available at http://www.americananglican.org/Issues/Issues.cfm?ID=91.

106 **"Roman Catholic candidates"** to **"That's my business":** "The Birth Control Issue," *Time*, December 7, 1959: 22.

106 **total receipts to voluntary tithe:** *ECA*, 1959: "Table of Statistics, 8th Province," 21; James A. Shaw, "Tithing Standard Unanimously Accepted by Diocese; Churches Adopt Bishop's Request For Immediate Action," *Pacific Churchman*, March 1959.

107 **"cost of living":** SYU: Box 15, Folder "Correspondence January 1960–February 1960," James A. Pike, letter to William H. Wenneman, copy to John Coburn, February 1, 1960.

107 **exchange-student trip:** SYU: Box 15, Folder "Correspondence April–June 1960," James Pike, letter to John Coburn, June 15, 1960.

107 **"constant whisper"** to **2510 Jackson Street:** *ST:* 113; *ECA*, 1959: 175.

107 **"record spending":** "Budget Is Passed by Convention; Diocese Sees Record Spending," *Pacific Churchman*, March 1960: 2.

108 **"extraordinary places":** *ST:* 113.

108 **Piper Cub airplane:** James A. Pike, "Old Presbytery Done Small," *Christian Century,* May 6, 1959: 542.

109 **"Big Bang":** "Why the Big Bang?" *Christian Century,* January 23, 1961: 99.

109 **"Let me out!":** *ST:* 115.

110 **"highly biased account"** to **"earmarks of haste":** *Saturday Review of Literature,* May 14, 1960: 850; *School & Society,* December 17, 1960: 140.

110 **"I am with him"** to **"a sort of *Reader's Digest*":** James A. Pike, "Three-Pronged Synthesis," *Christian Century,* December 21, 1960: 140.

111 **"undermining our Christian faith"** to **"salvation through Jesus Christ":** SYU: Box 49, Folder "Professional Records, Episcopalians for the Faith," n.d.

112 **"rather far out":** William Stringfellow and Anthony Towne, *The Bishop Pike Affair: Scandals of Conscience and Heresy, Relevance and Solemnity in the Contemporary Church* (New York: Harper & Row, 1967), 11, hereafter cited as Stringfellow, *Affair.*

113 **"as a bishop and a lawyer"** to **"could not be reached":** *NYT:* "Ministers Accuse Pike of Heresies," January 29, 1961.

113 **"people who believed as he [McCarthy] believed":** DCA: "Bishop's Address 111th Diocesan Convention," January 31, 1961.

113 **"What Is Doctrinal Orthodoxy"** to **"no single bishop":** DCA: James A. Pike, pastoral letter, "What Is Doctrinal Orthodox?" February 12, 1961, later reprinted in *The Witness* March 2, 1961, 9–10; *NYT:* "DeWolfe Rebukes Pike on Virgin Birth," September 27, 1961.

114 **"Churchmen here feel":** *NYT:* "Pike Is Defended in Heresy Charge," February 13, 1961.

114 **"extremely doubtful"** to **"formulations of past centuries":** quoted in Jerome Ellison, "Battling Bishop," *Saturday Evening Post,* October 7, 1960: 39.

116 **"Pike Again Raps":** "Pike Again Raps UC on Lack of Religious Education Department," *San Francisco Examiner,* November 25, 1961.

116 **unique innovation by Pike** to **"not reaching out":** James A. Pike,

"Old Presbytery Done Small," *Christian Century*, May 6, 1959: 541–42; SYU: Box 50, Folder "Material Relating to Dismissal of Undergraduate Chaplain at Berkeley," James Pike, letter to Robert Morse, April 12, 1961.

117 **"hyperactivity":** *ST:* 321.

118 **"wild-eyed hillbillies":** quoted in "Rector and a Rumpus," *Newsweek*, July 4, 1960: 77.

118 **"personally experienced this phenomenon"** to **"I urge our clergy":** DCA: "Pastoral Letter Speaking in Tongues . . . to be read in all Churches of the Diocese at all morning services on the Third Sunday after Easter, 1963."

119 the **"third force":** Henry P. Van Dusen, "Force's Lesson For Others," *Life*, June 9, 1958: 122–24.

120 **" 'I've been speaking in tongues!' ":** *ST:* 114.

121 **"what I do believe":** James A. Pike, *A Time for Christian Candor* (New York: Harper & Row, 1964), 8, hereafter cited as Pike, *Candor*.

VI A New Theology, a New Woman, and a New Heresy Charge

122 **three hundred and fifty thousand:** *The Honest to God Debate*, ed. David L. Edwards (London: SCM Press, 1963), 7.

123 **"any other book":** Benjamin Jowett, "On the Interpretation of Scripture," in *Essays and Reviews: The 1860 Text and Its Reading*, eds. Victor Shea and William Whitla (Charlottesville, VA: University Press of Virginia, 2000), 504.

123 **"rocked the American church":** John A. T. Robinson, *Honest to God* (Philadelphia: Westminister Press: 1963), 20, hereafter cited as Robinson, *Honest*.

123 **"swinging London"** to **"Profumo can hardly be blamed":** *Time*, cover, April 15, 1966; John A. T. Robinson, *Christian Morals Today* (Philadelphia: Westminister Press, 1964), quoted in note, 8. The London phrase, "South Bank religion," is recalled in the obituary, "The Rev. Bill Skelton," *Daily Telegraph*, May 31, 2003.

124 **"Mankind has outgrown"**: *SFC:* " 'New God' Splits British Churchmen," March 25, 1963; *SFC:* "Discussion By 'Honest to God' Bishop," May 23, 1964.

124 **"twinned by him"**: *ST:* 37; In regard to the limited friendship between Pike and Robinson, consider the correspondence with author, February 21, 2003, from Clare Brown, assistant archivist, Lambeth Palace Library: "Bishop John Robinson's correspondence is not indexed letter by letter, but a quick search shows no trace of any letters from Bishop Pike."

125 **"don journalists"**: Mehta's article and usage of the term in *The New Yorker,* November 13, 1965, is reprinted in Ved Mehta, *The New Theologian* (New York: Harper & Row, 1966), 35.

126 **"for professionals and laymen"** to **"not even communion wine"**: Pike, *Candor,* 8; *ST:* 322. The Herb Caen clipping is located in SYU: Box 9, Folder "Personal."

127 **"The Trinity is not necessary"** to **"impose on new converts"**: *NYT,* "Bishop Pike Gives View on Trinity, August 31, 1964.

128 **"interesting collection of earthen vessels"** to **"primarily *existential*"**: Pike, *Candor,* 10, 12.

129 **"handsome profit"**: "Origin and Publication," *Essays and Review:* 14.

129 **"uncomfortable analogies"**: Robinson, *Honest,* 9.

129 **"the New Reformation"**: SYU: Box 50, Folder "Memorandum and Press Release About Sabbatical," July 12, 1965.

129 **"not recognized the danger"**: Pike, *Candor,* 59–60.

130 **"midst of a theological revolution"**: SYU: Box 82, Folder "This Treasure in Earthen Vessels," October 11, 1964. Pike was reported in the news account of this sermon first using the phrase "excess luggage" to describe the Trinity. See *NYT:* "Theological Dissenter: James Albert Pike," October 12, 1964; *NYT:* "4 Churchmen Ask Judge to Return," October 23, 1964.

131 **"angry, middle-aged rebel"**: *NYT:* "Pike Denounced on Trinity Attack," October 14, 1964.

131 **"transparent exploitation of racism"** to **"warned churchgoers"**: *SFC:* "Episcopalians Blast Goldwater," October 13, 1964.

132   **take "steps" against Pike:** *NYT:* "Rector Suggests Pike Heresy Trial," October 19, 1964.

133   **"This House is concerned":** *NYT:* "4 Churchmen Ask Judge to Return," October 23, 1964.

134   **completion of Grace Cathedral:** *Grace Cathedral, San Francisco* (London: Pitkin Pictorials Ltd: 1967), 4, 6, 17;

135   **"and their generation":** Robinson, *Honest*, 6.

135   **"To my son, Jim"** to **drafts of Romilar:** Pike, *Candor*, 4; James A. Pike and Diane Kennedy, *The Other Side* (Garden City, N.Y.: Doubleday, 1968), 12, hereafter cited as Pike, *Other*. The description of the younger Pike's residence is from the news report of his death, "Baffling Suicide: Bishop Pike's Son," *New York Herald Tribune*, February 6, 1966.

135   **he would sleep elsewhere** to **"out of a suitcase":** *ST:* 58–59

136   **"presentation is facile"** to **"vast oversimplifications":** *Times Literary Supplement:* "Christian Change," May 27, 1965: 435; *NYT:* " 'Plausible' Is the Key Word," January 3, 1965.

137   **"what he is up to"** to **"charmed magic":** James M. Gessell, "Book Reviews," *St. Luke's Journal of Theology* 11 (April 1968): 108.

138   **"assail men like Pike"** to **"applied promiscuously":** David J. Narot, "Toward a New Theology?" *Yale Alumni Magazine* 29 (December 1965): 22, 24, 28.

139   **"far back as he could remember"** to **living openly with Maren Bergrud:** *ST:* 59, 321.

139   **Dr. Martin Luther King Jr.** to **"wave upon wave":** "On Being 'With It' with Jim Pike," *The Living Church*, May 3, 1970: 9–10; "Pike Urges a Wave of Marchers," *San Francisco Examiner*, March 11, 1965.

140   **his wife told him:** "With It," 9–10.

140   **"Mrs. Bishop":** *ST:* 321.

141   **"much easier to be in favor of Negroes":** SYU: Box 50, Folder "House of Bishops, Wheeling West Virginia, Transcription of CBC (Candian Broadcast Corporation), October 1966." For the death of Reeb, see *NYT:* "Clergyman Dies of Selma Beating," March 12, 1965.

141 **murder of Emmett Till** to **"did not speak":** James A. Pike, letter to *Life*, October 11, 1956; "LA Chief Calls Pike 'Ignorant,' " *San Francisco Examiner*, January 19, 1965.

142 **"absolute discretion"** to **majority of two to one:** quoted in Mickler, 117; *SFC:* "Defeat of Proposition 14 Sought," January 6, 1964; Philip Wogaman, "California Churches in the Aftermath of Defeat," *Christian Century*, February 3, 1965: 139–40.

142 **first public appearance:** *NYT:* "Dr. King Suggests Nation Boycott Alabama Goods," March 29, 1965; *Dr. Martin Luther King, Jr. Visits Grace Cathedral*, ed. Episcopal Diocese of California. October 11, 2002, available at http://www.gracecathedral.org/enrichment/crypt/cry _20021002.shtml.

144 **wait for the fight:** "Episcopalians: Attorney for the Defense," *Time*, September 17, 1965: 106.

145 **"direct slap at our church":** *SFC:* "Pike's Independence Day Sermon Assails Luci Banes Johnson's Baptism," July 4, 1965.

146 **"Auto Row"** to **"cut him off":** SYU: Box 83, Folder "Miscellaneous Writings," "Formal Statement," April 13, 1964; *ST:* 335.

147 **"year of austerity"** to **"hope of better times":** DCA: "Bishop's Address," *Journal of the 112th Convention* (Diocese of California: 1962), 89–90; "Bishop's Address," *Journal of the 113th Convention* (Diocese of California: 1963), 94; *Proceedings of the Convention: One Hundred and Fourteenth Convention* (Diocese of California: 1964), 100, 107–108; *Proceedings of the Convention: One Hundred and Fifteenth Convention* (Diocese of California: 1965), 81; "Convention Approves 1962 'Austerity' Program," *Pacific Churchman*, March 1962: 1; "The Bitter Aftertaste," *Pacific Churchman*, May 1967: 4.

148 **request of fourteen priests** to **chairman of the House of Bishops:** *SFC:* "Church Dispute: Pike Charged with Heresy," August 18, 1965; "Pike: Heretic or Iconoclast?" *Christian Century*, September 1, 1965: 1051–52; SYU: Box 19, Folder "Convention August 18th–31st," John E. Hines, letter to James Pike, August 31, 1965. For a reproduction of the Arizona bishop's petition and the presentment by Bishop Louttit, see appendix, Stringfellow, *Affair*, 198–201.

149 **"testing of the vessels"** to **"Dear Hank"**: "Pike Off the Hook," *Time*, September 20, 1965: 56.

150 **" 'Reaffirm My Loyalty' "** to **"mild public nuisance"**: "Bishop Pike: 'I Reaffirm My Loyalty to the Church,' " *San Francisco Examiner*, September 10, 1965; *SFC*: "Bishop Pike Considered," January 17, 1966.

150 **"half sabbatical"** to **"their family schedule"**: DCA, untitled press release, August 17, 1965.

VII   The Years of Deception and Nightmare, 1966–1968

152 **bishop's "secretary"** to **manipulated dates**: *ST*: 68–69, 90.

153 **cigarettes containing marijuana** to **9 Carlton Court**: Pike, *Other*, 16, 19.

153 **"America's Bishop of Woolwich"** to **Edward G. Robinson**: SYU: Box 58, Folder "Biography: May–December," press clippings, n.d.

154 **Pike "intuitively"**: quoted in Mickler, 322.

155 **chronic smoker of hashish**: *ST*: 91–93.

155 **"to my critics"**: James A. Pike, *What Is This Treasure* (New York: Harper & Row, 1966), 11. An interesting comparison of Pike and Tillich is John J. Carey, "Life on the Boundary," *Duke Divinity School Review* (Autumn 1977): 149–64.

156 **airport in Salisbury** to **Brunton had sent a letter**: SYU: Box 58, Folder "Biography May–December," "Bishop Pike Back in Israel from Rhodesia," *Jerusalem Post*, n.d.; "Pike Kicked Out of Rhodesia," *San Francisco Examiner*, December 29, 1965; Pike, *Other*: 55–56.

157 **nation of Malawi**: *NYT*: "Bishop Scores Rhodesia," January 18, 1966.

157 **"interpreted as a move"**: "Bishop Pike Returning to Protect Rule," *San Francisco Examiner*, February 1, 1966.

158 **a different flight**: Pike, *Other*: 65–66.

158 **an "angry" Pike**: *SFC*: "An Angry Reply: Bishop Pike's Dramatic Return," February 4, 1966.

159 **frantic drama unseen**: Pike, *Other*: 67–71.

159 **Hadson Hotel** to **unresolved homosexual longings**: "Bishop Pike's Son Apparent Suicide," *World Telegram* (New York), February 5, 1966;

"Suicide of Bishop Pike's Son: Rambling 'Goodbye' Notes," *Journal American* (New York), February 5, 1966; *SFC*: "Bishop Pike's Son a Suicide," February 5, 1966; *ST*: 90, 227, 235.

161 **John Krumm:** *NYT*: "Suicide Identified as Son of Bishop," February 6, 1966.

161 **"one less pike":** *ST*: 136.

163 **"righteous conflict"** to **freewheeling interview:** *SFC*: "Pike Backs U.S. Role in Vietnam," *NYT*: "Pike Asks Search for New Meaning," February 13, 1966.

163 **Once in Cambridge** to **"world of dark magic":** Pike, *Other*, 80–81; John Marco Allegro, "The Untold Story of the Dead Sea Scrolls," *Harper's*, August 1966: 54.

164 **"altered state of consciousness"** to **two men observed:** *ST*: 92; Pike, *Other*, 83–84.

166 **met with Twigg** to **"whole new attitude":** Pike, *Other*, 103, 116; *ST*: 96.

167 **"Space Age God"** to **Pike promised to write:** Christopher S. Wren, "An American Bishop's Search for a Space-Age God," *Look*, February 22, 1966: 25–29; Stringfellow, *Affair*, 45–48.

168 **"fewer beliefs and more belief":** *NYT*: "Pike Says Christianity Needs Fewer Beliefs and More Belief," April 7, 1966.

168 **Alcoholics Anonymous** to **"eighty thousand homosexuals":** *NYT*: "Pike Challenges Alcoholism View," April 16, 1966.

169 **"Back on the job":** *ST*: 137.

169 **filed for divorce** to **books and a used car:** *SFC*: "Bishop Pike Is Sued for Divorce," June 22, 1967; *NYT*: "Wife Will Divorce Pike After 23 Years of Marriage," July 22, 1967; SYU; Box 9, Folder "Personal Records," n.d.

171 **"where I wanted to be":** *NYT*: "Bishop Pike to Drop Duties, Join Center on Democracy," May 12, 1966; *NYT*: "U.S. Think Tanks: In Santa Barbara Dialogue Is the Thing," January 13, 1967.

171 **Coast Village Road** to **Bergrud rented:** the Santa Barbara address and apartment numbers are contained in SYU: Box 9, Folder "Personal"; Pike, *Other*: 158–59.

171 **séances with Daisley:** *ST*: 152.

172 **Dick in 1966** to **"my good friends"**: Lawrence Sutin, *Divine Invasion: A Life of Philip K. Dick* (New York: Harmony Books, 1989), 143, 149; Pike, *Other*, viii. Dick somewhat based the main character of his 1982 novel, *The Transmigration of Timothy Archer*, on his memories of Pike, and in his 1970 novel, *A Maze of Death*, thanked Pike for having "brought forth a wealth of theological information, none of which I was previously acquainted with." See *A Maze of Death* (Garden City, N.Y.: Doubleday, 1970), "Author's Foreword," n.p.

172 **farewell dinner** to **"conservative bishop"**: SYU: Box 9, Folder "Personal"; *ST*: 140.

173 **"overflow crowd"** to **"make an honest man"**: *NYT*: "Bishop Pike Assails Homosexuality Law," October 11, 1966; SYU: Box 50, Folder "House of Bishops, Wheeling West Virginia, Transcripts of CBC (Canadian Broadcast Corporation) interview with Louttit, October 1966," 14.

174 **"investigate and be damned"** to **"more important things"**: *NYT*: "Group of Bishops Support Pike; Urge an Investigation of Accuser," October 24, 1966; SYU: Box 50, Folder "House of Bishops, Wheeling, West Virginia, Journal of the General Assembly, Special Meeting of the House of Bishops," "Statement Regarding Bishop Pike," 1966; *NYT*: "Bishops Assail Pike but Oppose a Trial for Heresy," October 26, 1966.

176 **"some marriage problems"**: "Heretic or Prophet?" *Time*, November 11, 1966: 63.

176 **"serious financial problems"**: SYU: Box 9, Folder "Personal Records," Ben Margolis, letter to James Pike, August 18, 1967; Ben Margolis, memo to James Pike, n.d.

177 **such an event anachronistic**: *NYT*: "Pike Agrees to a Delay of His Heresy Hearing; Committee Named by Hines to Advise Him on Issue; Bayne to Head 11-Man Unit Which Includes Laymen," January 13, 1967; *NYT*: "Church Divided on Heresy Issue: Episcopal Wing Opposes a Report Assailing Concept," August 21, 1967; *NYT*: "Bishop Pike Renews Demand for a Heresy Trial; Acts After Colleagues 'Affirm' Rather than Adopt Report Critical of Heresy View," September 26, 1967.

178 **hotel room on fire** to **Bergrud had stopped breathing:** *ST:* 62–65. Stringfellow and Towne's book is the sole printed source for Pike's actions the night of Bergrud's suicide. Although the two biographers included no citations or other bibliographic information within their book, their account presumably is based upon their subsequent conversations and their personal acquaintanceship with the bishop. Diane Kennedy Pike confirmed in an e-mail to this author in 2003 that she considered their account of Bergrud's death to be consistent with her knowledge of the facts at the time.

179 **"Secretary of Pike Dies"** to **reception was to be held:** *SFC:* "Secretary of Pike Dies—Maren Bergrud," June 15, 1967; "Bergrud Rites," *Santa Barbara News-Press,* June 16, 1967; *SFC:* "Mystery of Pike Aide's Suicide Note," June 16, 1967; *SFC:* "Bishop Pike Holds Rites for Aide," June 16, 1967; *SFC:* "Bishop's Daughter," June 22, 1967.

180 **divorce was declared final:** *SFC:* "Bishop Pike's Divorce Final," August 29, 1968.

181 **"superficial stuff":** *SFC:* "Anglican Primate Arrives in S.F.," September 18, 1967.

181 **"flower power"** to **Pike agreed to withdraw:** Anthony Towne, "Séance in Seattle: Ruminations in a Ruin," *Christian Century,* November 8, 1967: 1442–44.

182 **bizarre act** to **"Eerie Events":** *NYT:* "Religion: The Bishop's Séance," October 1, 1967; *NYT:* "Professional Medium," September 28, 1967; *NYT:* "Bishop Pike Tells of Eerie Events," September 28, 1967; *NYT:* "WNEW-TV to Show the Pike Séance," October 4, 1967.

183 **"not be in the best interest":** *NYT:* "Church Here Calls Off Lenten Sermons by Pike; St. Thomas Rector Cancels Invitation Over Bishop's Talk of Spiritualism," November 10, 1967.

184 *Joe Pyne Show:* SYU: Box 34, Folder "October 11–19, 1967," James Pike, letter to Stanley Sher, October 18, 1967.

185 **"responded satisfactorily":** *ST:* 82; *NYT:* "Daughter of Bishop Pike Treated for Sedative Use," February 16, 1968.

185 **no wild beasts:** *Ammianus Marcellinus,* trans. John C. Rolfe, vol. 2 (Cambridge, Mass.: Harvard University Press, 1935), 203.

VIII   A God-Shaped Blank: Pike as Spiritualist,
Heretic, and Iconoclast

186   **"trouble with the whole question"** to **"psi factor"**: Temple quoted
in Rene Kollar, *Searching for Raymond: Anglicanism, Spiritualism, and
Bereavement Between the Two World Wars* (Lanham, Md.: Lexington
Books, 2000), 86; James A. Pike, *If This Be Heresy* (New York: Harper &
Row, 1967), 127, hereafter cited as Pike, *Heresy*.

187   **"keep in touch"**: quoted in Kollar, *Searching for Raymond*, 119.

187   **death of his son** to **young Arthur Ford**: Ruth Brandon, *The Spiritual-
ists: The Passion for the Occult in the Nineteenth and Twentieth Centuries*
(New York: Alfred A. Knopf, 1983), 210; in the interview, "Professional
Medium," in *NYT,* September 28, 1967, Ford brags of having known
what he calls "the big boys" of psychic research in the 1920s, including
Lodge.

188   **one duplicity practiced:** *NYT:* "Cheating in Pike's Séance Is Alleged,"
March 11, 1973. Ford's lifelong psychical control, "Fletcher," suppos-
edly his childhood friend in Florida, appears to have been appropriated
without any mention of credit from Lodge's book on his son. One of
Raymond Lodge's closest military friends was the Britisher Lt. Eric
Fletcher, and the historical Fletcher's letter of condolence is reprinted
in *Raymond.* See Oliver L. Lodge, *Raymond, or Life and Death* (New
York: George H. Doran, 1916), 75.

189   **"abbreviated LSD!"**: Pike, *Heresy*, note, 129.

190   **"Perhaps ESP"** to **"facts + faith"**: *SFC:* review, *"The Other Side,"*
December 3, 1968; *NYT:* "New Bishop Pike Book Calls Facts Basis for
Belief," September 13, 1967.

191   **drink more wine:** Lawrence Sutin, *Divine Invasions: A Life of Philip K.
Dick* (New York: Harmony Books, 1989), 221.

191   **"no sensitive or empathetic"** to **"a bit absurd"**: SYU: Box 10, Folder
"Personal Records," Connie Pike, letter to James Pike, n.d.

192   **"committee God"**: Pike quoted in "Pike in the Bishop's Pond," *The
Guardian,* n.d., 1961, in SYU: Box 58, Folder "Bio: May–December
1961."

192 **" 'free' sexual ethic"** to **"questionable notion":** James A. Pike, *Teenagers and Sex* (Englewood Cliffs, N.J.: Prentice-Hall, 1965), 27; Fletcher quoted in Mickler, 253.

193 **not even heard of Death of God** to **"I don't dig it":** Christopher S. Wren, "An American Bishop's Search for a Space-Age God," *Look,* February 22, 1966: 29; *SFC:* " 'Nonsense' Says Pike to God Is Dead Idea," March 24, 1966; "Pike Derides 'Death of God' Theology," *Washington Post,* April 2, 1966.

194 ***Playboy* magazine** to **"no God-shaped blank":** SYU: "Miscellaneous Writings," "To the Editor, Playboy," n.d.; Thomas Altizer and William Hamilton, "Radical Theology and the Death of God," November 6, 2002, available at http://www.religion-online.org/cgi-bin/re/searchd .dll/shpwchapter?chapter_id-587.

195 **"if there's no God":** "Heretic or Prophet?" *Time,* November 11, 1966: 57.

195 **"righteous conflict"** to **risk fines or imprisonment:** "Vietnam War Is Upheld," *Pacific Churchman,* March 1966; *NYT:* "Pike Says Ho Chi Minh Would Win in Election," February 14, 1967; *NYT:* "320 Vow to Help Draft Resisters, September 27, 1967; *NYT:* "18 Clerics Back Draft Resisters," October 26, 1967.

196 **"murder of tens of thousands"** to **"Law and Order Is Dead":** *NYT:* "U.S. Policy Scorned at Geneva Parley," May 30, 1967; *NYT:* "Marya Mannes in Geneva, Berates U.S. on War," May 31, 1967; *NYT:* "Pacem in Terris Conference Ends on an Anti-American Note," June 1, 1967; *NYT:* "Pike Likens Jesus to Dr. King, Vietcong, and Others in Revolt," April 9, 1968.

196 **"faked an eye test":** quoted in Mickler, 147.

197 **"celebrity counsel"** to **"what pill I can give":** William Kunstler, *My Life as a Radical Lawyer* (Secaucus, N.J.: Carol Publishers, 1994), 188–89; *ST:* 39–44; *NYT:* "9 War Foes Begin Baltimore Trial; 1,500 Supporters Heckled as They Stage a March," October 8, 1968.

199 **Malcolm Boyd:** Malcolm Boyd, *As I Live and Breathe: Stages of an Autobiography* (New York: Random House, 1969), 115.

200 **"Until recently"** to **"it was touch and go":** Pike, *Heresy,* 46, 45, 47.

ix Leaving the Church, a Fascination with the Dead Sea Scrolls, and Death

205 **"Jim—the ease"**: *ST:* 65.

206 **"off the track"**: SYU: Box 34, Folder "October 11–19, 1967," James Pike, letter to Robert Marshall, October 18, 1967.

206 **"bought into Allegro"**: *ST:* 109.

206 **"woman half his age"** to **"had to do with sex"**: *NYT:* "Pike to Defy Superior," December 15, 1968; Diane Pike, *My Journey into Self: Phase One* (San Diego: LP Publications: 1979), 123, hereafter cited as Diane Pike, *Journey.*

208 **cigarette ashes** to **"their love"**: Diane Pike, *Journey,* 107, 130–31, 126.

209 **"Smith wedding"**: *ST:* 389.

210 **"couple cannot be married"**: Daniel B. Stevick, *Canon Law: A Handbook* (New York: Seabury Press: 1965), 151, 154–57.

210 **judgment by telegram** to **"Kim Myers will get hell"**: *ST:* 388–89; SYU: Box 10, Folder "Personal," Connie Pike, letter to James Pike, n.d.

212 **"Diane, you are the one"** to **"no canonical authority"**: *SFC:* "A Self-Designed Pike Wedding," December 18, 1968; *SFC:* "Bishop Pike's Defiant Wedding," December 20, 1968; *SFC:* "Pike's Unusual Wedding—Church OKs Marriage," December 21, 1968; This article was written by Lester Kinsolving, an ally of Pike's in previous ecclesiastical and theological disputes. Kinsolving asserts in the first paragraph that "the wedding had been sanctified quietly by the church ten days ago." *SFC:* "Furor in Church Over Bishop Pike's Wedding," December 24, 1968; *NYT:* "Coast Bishop Curbs Pike Over Marriage," December 24, 1968.

212 **"conflict of interest"**: *SFC:* "Church Ousts Pike Lawyer," January 24, 1969.

213 **"gone to great lengths"**: James A. Pike, "Why I'm Leaving the Church," *Look,* April 29, 1969: 57–58, hereafter cited as Pike, "Why."

213 **large copy of canon law**: Mickler, 43.

214 **"depart in peace"**: Diane Pike, *Journey:* 120.

214 **"only hurt so long"**: *ST:* 393.

214 **"sick—even dying"** to **"wish the pilgrim well"**: *NYT:* "Pike Plans to Leave the Episcopal Church as 'Dying Institution,' " April 15, 1969.

216 **The Next Step:** *NYT:* " 'Next Step' Provides Clerical Dropout with Advice," November 17, 1968.

216 **loss of his job:** *NYT:* "Study Center Bids Five Fellows Quit," June 14, 1969.

216 **"varied psychic phenomena"** to **"clearing the way"**: Pike, "Why," 58.

218 **florid necktie** to **"see the wilderness"**: See the photograph of the Pikes accompanying *NYT:* "Pike Reported Missing in Judea; Wife Says Car Broke Down in Wilderness," September 3, 1969. The personal symbolism of the "peace" emblem on his clothing or his accoutrements is explained by his wife in "Bishop Pike Laid to Rest in Jaffa Cemetery," *Jerusalem Post,* September 9, 1969.

219 **"time is no longer significant"**: Pike, *Other,* 54.

219 **two bottles of Coca-Cola** to **"If I die here"**: Diane Pike, *Search: The Personal Story of a Wilderness Journey* (Garden City, N.Y.: Doubleday, 1970), 2–4, 6–7, 9, 21, 24, 29–31, hereafter cited as Diane Pike, *Search.*

223 **"get help for Jim"**: quoted in *NYT:* "Israelis Press Search for Pike but Hope for Survival Fading," September 4, 1969.

223 **Pike reported as lost:** "Pike Feared Lost in Desert Near Judea," *Times* (London), September 3, 1969; "Diana [*sic*] Pike's Ordeal in the Judean Desert," *Jerusalem Post,* September 4, 1969.

224 **"breaking into sobs"** to **"vision of my husband"**: "Bishop Pike Still Missing," *Jerusalem Post,* September 4, 1969.

224 **"TWIGG/PIKE: Help me"**: Ena Twigg et al., *Ena Twigg: Medium* (New York: Hawthorne Books, 1972), 163.

225 **"don't think he can hold out"** to **"their skepticism"**: *NYT:* "Official Hunt for Pike Called Off; Israeli Trackers Will Try Again," September 5, 1969; *SFC:* "Pike Search—Directions from Beyond," September 6, 1969; *NYT:* "Searchers for Dr. Pike Will Use Guidance Provided by Mediums," September 6, 1969; *NYT:* "Israeli Searchers Unable to Find Dr. Pike; Shorts in Desert provide a Clue," September 7, 1969. For the

Israeli military's withdrawal from the search, see "Israelis Puzzled Over Pike," *San Francisco Examiner*, September 5, 1969.

226 **A pair of his sunglasses** to **looked for a burial plot**: Diane Pike, *Search*, 135, 136, 140, 143, 155–56. See also "Pike's Body Found on Desert Craig," *Jerusalem Post*, September 8, 1969; *NYT*: "Dr. Pike's Body Is Found on Ledge Near Dead Sea," September 8, 1969.

227 **"sun shall not burn thee"**: Book of Common Prayer quoted in "Pike Buried in Jaffa Plot Overlooking Sea," *Los Angeles Times*, September 9, 1969; *NYT*: "Dr. Pike Is Buried with a 'Peace' Cross Near the Sea in Jaffa," September 9, 1969; "Bishop Pike Laid to Rest in Jaffa Cemetery," *Jerusalem Post*, September 9, 1969.

228 **"feel accepted or wanted"**: Norman Pittenger, "Bishop Pike's Effect on Christian Thinking," *Times* (London), September 13, 1969.

228 **"spontaneous, dramatic incident"**: "A Friendly Hand," and "Pike's Widow Gives Hand of Friendship to Bishop," *San Francisco Examiner*, September 12, 1969.

229 **"courageously walking"** to **"mini-dress"**: *SFC*: "An Unorthodox Mass for Bishop Pike in New York," September 15, 1969.

230 **"There may be a Jim Pike"**: John Cogley, "Man of Faith, Child of Doubt," *Look*, September 19, 1969: 63–64.

230 **"what the heck *that* was"**: *ST*: 419.

231 **"above all, individualists"**: John M. Allegro, *The Dead Sea Scrolls and the Christian Myth* (Buffalo, N.Y.: Prometheus Books, 1984), 137; Pike, *Heresy*, 45.

Index

Photographic Credits

Grateful acknowledgment is made to the following for permission to reprint photographs appearing on the insert pages indicated below:

Episcopal Diocese of California: 4, 5 (top and lower left), 6 (lower right)
Episcopal Diocese of New York: 1, 2, 3, 5 (lower right), 6
San Francisco Chronicle: 7, 8

A NOTE ABOUT THE AUTHOR

David Robertson is the author of two prior biographies, of the slave rebel Denmark Vesey and of former U.S. secretary of state James F. Byrnes, and is the author of a historical novel about John Wilkes Booth. His poetry has appeared in the *Sewanee Review* and other journals, and he has provided political and literary commentary to ABC News, National Public Radio, and the *Washington Post*. He has published in the *William & Mary Quarterly* and lectured to American Studies programs nationally. Currently, he is researching the life of the Native American war chief William Weatherford on the southern frontier in the early nineteenth century. He was educated in Alabama and lives in Ohio.